SLEEPING WITH SOLDIERS

IN SEARCH OF

SLEEPING WITH SOLDIERS

THE MACHO MAN

ROSEMARY DANIELL

HOLT, RINEHART AND WINSTON
NEW YORK

First published in January 1985 by Holt, Rinehart and Winston,
383 Madison Avenue, New York, New York 10017.
Published simultaneously in Canada by Holt, Rinehart
and Winston of Canada, Limited.

Library of Congress Cataloging in Publication Data
Daniell, Rosemary.
Sleeping with soldiers.
1. Daniell, Rosemary—Relations with men.   2. Authors,
American—20th century—Biography.   I. Title.
PS3554.A56Z477   1984   818'.5409 [B]   84-6701
ISBN 0-03-062431-2

First Edition

Designer: Susan Mitchell
Printed in the United States of America
1 3 5 7 9 10 8 6 4 2

Permission to quote from "Outlaw Woman," and "Woman
I've Never Had" by Hank Williams, Jr., has been granted
by J. R. Smith. All rights reserved.

The line of poetry on page 62 is excerpted from
The Collected Works of Billy the Kid by
Michael Ondaatje. Copyright © 1970 by Michael
Ondaatje. Reprinted by permission of the publisher
W. W. Norton & Co., Inc.

ISBN 0-03-062431-2

*For my father, Donald, who lived and died without
my understanding, and for Tim, through whom I learned
at last to love him.*

With special thanks to Jennifer Josephy

THE BANDAGED SOLDIER

He said that he hurt himself on a wall or that he fell.
But perhaps there was another reason
for the bandaged shoulder.

With a somewhat forceful movement:
to bring down from a shelf some
photographs that he wants to see at close range,
the bandage was loosened and a little blood ran.

I bandaged the shoulder again, and in tieing it
I was somewhat slow; because it did not hurt,
and I liked to look at the blood.
That blood was part of my love.

After he left I found a rag drenched in blood
on a chair in front, from the bandages,
which I brought to my lips,
a rag that was headed for the garbage;
and which I held there for a long time—
the blood of love on my lips.

—C. P. Cavafy, *The Complete
Poems of Cavafy*, translated
by Rae Dalven

*"I wanna be an airborne Ranger
live a life of sex and danger—
blood, guts, sex and danger—
Oo-Ah! Oo-AH!*
     —U.S. Army
      marching song

PART ONE

THE
PENDULUM
PHENOMENON

At six a.m., I drive my lover to the Savannah army base where he is to board an early flight for a month as a paratrooper in the Idaho scrub deserts. On the airfield, guiding me through a plane that looks like a huge, olive-drab insect, he describes the jump procedures and the six-hour trip during which the troops will sit on the few uncomfortable canvas seats that line each side of the interior, or on the floor among the heavy equipment.

As he introduces me to other hard, olive-drab-clad men, he holds me possessively close; when he speaks, his bronze hair glints, his steel-blue eyes harden, before the rising sun. Feeling the rumble of words deep in his chest, the pressure of his muscle against my shoulder blade, I imagine the parachute tattooed across his biceps, the firm feel of his arms around me that morning in bed.

At last—the kit bag in his permanently callused hand, his body bulging almost obscenely against the rough cloth of his camouflage clothes—he bends me to him in a kiss, then walks decisively toward the plane. And my belly grabs with what's known in the South as "a little gut wrench." Despite my self-disgust, I feel an intense arousal, a sense of biological femininity that belies my professed aversion to everything military, my status as an independent woman.

The next morning, after an overnight train trip, I arrive at my twenty-two-year-old daughter Darcy's West Village apartment in New York. "It's very different here for a Southern woman who's used to being woed [sic] from every angle," she had written me when she had first come up to the city two years before. Now I find her distracted, upset, caught in the maelstrom of three overly passionate suitors; though she has been playing them against one another in the best Southern tradition, they are threatening each other, and pressuring her.

Night after night over drinks at One Fifth Avenue, meals at Village restaurants, I try—her suddenly staid mother—to talk my beautiful girl-child out of her present company. Yet as I speak, I realize my hypocrisy. Though I had set—or hoped I had set—an example of personal growth and integrity, of intellectual exploration and honesty, I had also—beginning long before I had left her "straight" architect-father—set an example of another kind: that of sex as adventure, a means to exploring the world, which often meant sex with macho—even dangerous—men.

It had always seemed to me that the hardest thing about being a mother was that whatever one experienced—or experimented with—as an individual, affected, in turn, those one loves most: one's children. I had long been a woman struggling—selfishly, some would say—to break free of the prison of the bourgeois, the ladylike, indeed, the cloistered room I had been brought up as a proper Southern young woman to inhabit. And now I wonder how I can fault my daughter for taking similar risks.

Sensing my ambivalence, Darcy raises her heart-shaped—and heartbreaking—face above the plate of sashimi in the little restaurant to which I have momentarily been able to seduce her from the melodrama that is her life. "But mother," she protests as, conjuring up new arguments, I hesitate: "I *want* to take my chances—I don't *want* to lead a boring life!"

"I don't want to lead a boring life"—wasn't Darcy just carrying on the family tradition? Hadn't that been *my* motivation, as well as the motivation of the men with whom I had been involved? There are some people, psychologists say, who desire more than ordinary adventure, risk, sensation, and that this desire is not necessarily pathological, but rather a desire to assert mastery, to do instead of think; to act upon the world, rather than be acted upon. Though I spend much of my time in a small study in front of a typewriter—surrounded by books, a kitten on my lap—I identify most with the kind of man who takes risks, tries to beat the system, lives by his wits and/or biceps; who—ironically, since *I* was seeking to escape the role I had been brought up as woman to fulfill—measures himself by his gender, his sexuality.

During the five years since my last divorce, I had dated men who built buildings, deep-sea dived, sailed boats, drilled for oil, drove trucks or raced cars, herded cattle, flew fighter helicopters, jumped out of airplanes, rode in rodeos, welded steel, and smuggled drugs.

I had also spent time with men who performed eye surgery, gave psychotherapy, made films, took photographs, managed businesses, practiced law, reported the evening news, taught in universities; and several who, like me, wrote: all suitable lovers and friends—or what my mother and grandmother would have called "good husband material."

But despite the pleasures of the company of the second group, it was the first who had held my deepest interest. Though I had avoided for my whole life a real addiction to cigarettes, drugs, or booze, I had been unable to resist the magnetic pull of a certain kind of man, a certain kind of relationship. And recently, at forty-five, I had begun living with Zane, a younger man providently named by his parents after the Western adventure writer—a sky diver/truck driver/paratrooper whose telephone doodles described drop zones and gun assemblies; who—as though he might flee at any moment—kept books on foreign mercenaries on his bed table, an application for the French Foreign Legion among his papers.

For despite the pink flowers in a glass bowl, rose-splashed afghan on the bed, lace curtains blowing at the window that symbolized my homebound writing life, the renegade was my hero, as well as the hero of other would-be macho men; it was our mutual daring—our willingness to risk, to act—that was the source of our attraction. Together, we were Indiana Jones and his lady, adventuring in search of the Ark of the Lost Covenant—in our case, the ultimate excitement.

THE PENDULUM PHENOMENON

At twenty-three, I sat on the steps of our backyard patio with my husband, watching our children sway on a Sears Roebuck swing set. Released by the rhythmic motion of the swings, the sound of the frogs and cicadas, the heat of a Georgia July afternoon, my brain drifted into an alpha state. As though a secret door had been opened—like a movie screen rolling down for a sneak preview—I was suddenly suffused with radiant visions of myself in some future, exotic place, doing unknown things with unknown people.

But by the time of my third divorce at forty, I had never lived alone; nor—except for those brief fantasies of escape, entertained as a young housewife with three babies in diapers, a split-level house to clean, and a husband more interested in his zoysia lawn than in me—had I ever imagined doing so. With a proximity to rival Elizabeth Taylor's, I had dovetailed my marriages; as firmly as Liz—and every Southern woman I had known—I believed woman's natural habitat to be the conjugal corral, no matter how uncomfortably fenced in that enclosure might feel.

I had often been the kind of woman whom other women envied for my ability to attract men, the sheer plethora of my suitors. My sister, Anne, told me she had hated attending Tucker High School after me because I had the reputation of having more dates than any girl who had ever gone to that small-town Georgia center of lower education. During those years, I had had—among a cast of dozens—two main boyfriends. At sixteen, I had naturally chosen— given my unacknowledged bent toward the macho man—the no-good good ole boy over the studious professional-to-be; and with a determination only an act of God could have stopped, dropped out of school to marry him. But since junior high school, I had kept "extra" boyfriends on the back burner as insurance against being left, or worse—*manless*. At twenty, a divorcée with a two-year-old son, I married the other one, by then a stable, if boring, young architect, and promptly had two daughters. When I was thirty-three, my second husband moved out; and the next day, the handsome Northeastern Jewish prince nine years my junior, whom I had met at a writers' conference and chosen as my third, moved in.

But while I was good at getting husbands, I wasn't good at keeping them. Assertiveness training had not yet come into fashion; indeed, as a Southern woman I had been brought up to believe the opposite: that my feminine charms depended upon my swallowing any resentments or frustration, particularly in regard to the men in my life; "If you can't say sumpthin' sweet, don't say anythang at all," my mother, grandmothers, and aunts told me time after time as I grew up, describing the philosophy by which they—and all the other Southern women I knew—apparently lived. It was a philosophy that would ultimately end in Mother's death, but as I didn't yet understand that, I lived by it as well. Indeed, the Jewish prince said he had first been attracted to me by the way I had waited on him in the university cafeteria, bringing him second glasses of milk, servings of fried chicken. It was subservience that undoubtedly reminded him of his Jewish mama; and there was no reason to think it was a sham. Or that while I traveled with the momentum of a hurricane from one husband to the next, I would liberally pepper my way with extramarital lovers, the one—and most pleasurable—

means I had come up with to deal with the as yet unexplored rage existing beneath my consciousness.

I was as deluded as Liz, too, in romanticizing my own carnivorousness, my hunger for action. Imagining every man I lusted after to be my true love, my destiny, I felt that once lust had reached consciousness, any attempts to stem its fulfillment would be as futile as trying to hold back a tidal wave. To think was to act; even though I was supposedly an adult, and the mother of maturing children, I had not yet learned the difference between fantasy and action.

Despite early evidence to the contrary, I believed myself, throughout those years, to be fragile, dependent, vulnerable to the point of hysteria: a retiring, aspiring writer, perversely uninterested in the bridge games, coffee klatches, and garden-club meetings that went on in the subdivision around me; almost too shy to answer the telephone. Never mind the outspoken nature of my prose, my out-of-town affairs with wild poets, painters, and steel-guitar players; my Southern-belle image had taken root in my imagination, if not in reality. Besides, as a well-brought-up Southern woman, I knew that what happens when one is in "New Yawk"—away from home—or under the influence of Black Jack doesn't count. Nor did the fact that, as part of my work for the Poetry in the Schools programs in Georgia, South Carolina, and Wyoming—undertaken to fulfill *family* responsibilities rather than for fun, of course—I drove alone through the pine woods and red clay hills of the deep South, and the mesas and buttes of the wild West, and spent weeks as the only woman in motels full of miners and soldiers, or in a room with a bath down the hall in the Chelsea Hotel in New York. But still, after each gig, I hurried home, paranoid, to my "real" life as wife and mother.

I had grown up watching my perpetually girlish and manipulative mother tearfully dominate, if not control, my passive-aggressive alcoholic father; giving in to my own mania for control, I masterminded my husbands' and children's lives, imposing menus, tacking up lists of chores, harassing the troops like a female drill sergeant. Because we had a maid for the after-school hours while I was away, I left detailed instructions for preliminary dinner preparations; one of her worst chores must have been boiling and peeling the huge beef tongues of which Ben, my third husband, and I were fond, leaving me only the gourmet touches of slicing and saucing.

Between meals, the children were allowed only dried apricots or prunes, carrot and bell-pepper sticks. ("Once—just *once*—you let us buy one of those boxes of yucky cookies that were really just vanilla wafers with marshmallows stuck between them," Darcy laughed years later.) At dinner they were to listen to French language records, and not allowed up from the table until they repeated the phrase, "May I be excused please, my dear parents?" To avoid their growing up in the same frozen Bible Belt channel I had, I took them to the Unitarian Church wearing tennis shoes and to, say, a Chinese restaurant on Easter Sunday. My son, David, deliberately disrupted the acting classes that I insisted—out of my passion for culture—he attend; and after a while, all three rebelled at the art openings to which I dragged them.

Years later, my older daughters, Laura and Darcy, told me how much they hated the "family meetings"—undertaken out of my fashionable sixties zest for humanistic psychology—that always ended up in screaming matches over allowances and who had helped most in the kitchen. If Mother—in real life as crazy as the star and the character—had been Vivien Leigh playing Blanche DuBois, I was the same actress playing a determined and domineering Scarlett. And, like Scarlett, I was fast becoming—in my maternal family, at least—the maverick, the wild card. I had been married three times—to my provincial relatives, almost as bad as never having married at all; had given up my stable life as a suburban housewife to a respectable Atlanta architect for the fluctuating security of life as a writer; and to support myself, had often taken strange jobs that took me from whatever weird hearth I had. "All anybody talked about, aside from George's exploits in Peru, were the wild things you're doing," Anne told me, lumping me with a male cousin who was the other renegade in the family, after an annual reunion that I had been unable to attend because of my current employment; "They were a lot more impressed by *that* than the fact that you have a book coming out next spring!"

Dear Rosemary,
My name is Louisa Plowden Williams.
I read your beautiful article in the Journal *Sunday. As I was reading the part about your mother being the "Sweetheart of Sigma Nu," I had this funny feeling like I was reading a part of my own past and when you told your daddy's name my heart was*

beating real fast. Because Don was my first real sweetheart, be-
fore your mother. . . .

Out of an envelope embossed Gold Kist Inc. fell four photos.
There was an attractive brown-haired woman with slightly bucked
teeth, striped middy blouse; not so nearly so voluptuous as
Mother, yet pretty: Miss Louisa Plowden, of 678 Moreland Avenue, Atlanta, Ga., read the caption. But it was the other picture
that magnetized me: three slick, fading images featuring Daddy,
one foot up on the running board of his Model T; Daddy, squatting
in the sunlight, squinting against a Georgia backdrop of dirt road,
piny woods; Daddy, arm in arm with Miss Plowden—more buck-
toothed here—and three fraternity brothers who, like Daddy,
wore sleeveless V-necked sweaters embossed with the Sigma Nu
emblem over white shirts with the sleeves rolled up toward their
youthful biceps. Daddy's hair is sleek, slicked back, the gaze on his
dark slender face pensive; in one photo, the faintest hopeful smile
plays at the corner of his sensuous mouth. Looking at them, something catches inside my chest: Daddy is tremulously, excruciatingly
handsome—a voluptuous beauty, a real heartthrob.

Throughout my childhood, I imagined my father—swarthily
handsome thanks to his tint of Cherokee blood—as the rapier-
wielding pirate in my favorite adventure stories, or the Mongol
sheikh of my erotic dreams, rising above me on a muscular white
stallion. Yet my fantasy of him, it turned out, was not just a daughter's fabrication. After the publication of the autobiographical *Fatal
Flowers*, several older women wrote me in detail of their infatuation with him, stories that emphasized a charisma, an appeal, that
lasted long after his drinking had taken its toll. Daddy was, by
turns, boisterous, romantic, earthy, elegant—a born charmer who
had played the saxophone in his own band at the University of
Georgia, and captured the hand of "the prettiest girl in Atlanta," as
Anne and I had been told time after time.

He was also, I now realize, in the process during most of my
young life of numbing his personal tragedy: his failure as a real
man in the real world; as tire salesman, husband and father, and
would-be participant in the Second World War. In her letter
to me, Louisa Plowden described how Daddy had pleaded with
her, after his divorce by Mother, to leave her husband and marry
him; she concluded by thinking that if she had "I might have had

some years of happiness myself with a man I had always loved in my heart. . . ." Rereading it, I realized Daddy had not only failed as a man in a man's world, but had failed in achieving the romantic happiness so important to his generation as well.

That Daddy wrote verse, sang funny songs, had pained rather than pleased me as a child; I had always assigned the beginnings of my interest in writing to Mother and, like her, wanted, craved, a strong, patriarchal, safe father, not some irresponsible, drunken— if amusing—bard. Yet even his sense of absurdity, the ludicrous, had been a dark gallows humor, the hallmark of a man in pain —a pain he medicated in the traditional Southern way, that is, through liberal doses of Old Grand-Dad and Virginia Gentleman, plus various forms of outrageous behavior to which Mother responded equally traditionally, in her role as martyred belle, the wife done wrong.

As her partisan, I echoed her air of superiority, the disgust that showed itself even through her tears, her pleadings. Men were obviously children in need of constant nurturing and direction— morally inferior beings over whom we must maintain continual vigilance and control. Following her in her disapproval of him, I never fully allowed myself to experience a love she would have considered contraband, or the pain of what I considered his rejection of *me*. "I was a door till my father slammed me," wrote a first grader in one of my poetry classes. By the same age, I thought I had permanently rejected Daddy, and his kind—Daddy, the sexy charmer and drunk; Daddy, the elegant yet failed con man; Daddy, who was, though I didn't know it then, the precursor of all the macho-men-to-come in my life.

But as Carl Jung wrote, "everything dropped must be picked up." After Daddy's death when I was forty, Anne and I talked about our memories of him. My sister recalled private moments, jokes, the feelings of being his "favorite"; the sense that her slim, olive, not-yet-breasted body was patterned on his, and recalled riding about with him in his tire-company truck, or sitting beside him on a riverbank as he adjusted her bamboo fishing pole, put the worm on her hook—of having him tease, when she painted her toenails, that "your toes are bleeding!"

But rake memory as I would, I couldn't come up with one moment of personal warmth between us. My impressions of Daddy were either vague sexual images, barely recalled through a dirty fog; or else quick snaps—impersonal, objective, harsh—of his voluptuous, sullen face, his sleek black hair; of watching him shave, or tell jokes to a group of men. Overlapping these pictures were those of his pouring a glass of water over my head as I talked on the phone to a friend; and his drunkenly driving my girl friends and me—as I writhed, humiliated—to cheerleading practice. And worse, of drunken night drives, my terror, and Anne and Mother's screams; of Mother locking him naked in the bedroom, where he raged "whore!" and "slut!" from behind the door as my tenth-grade date rang the bell to pick me up; or nearer the time I left home at sixteen via marriage, of Daddy holding a butcher knife over my head, Mother struggling to force his arm away from me.

As a teenager—disgusted by my recent memories of Daddy's abuse or caresses; the chaos of life with a man with "problems"—I followed Mother's rules for spouse selection. She and my maternal grandmother's dictum, early etched deeply into my and Anne's brains, was that "you are who you marry." In *My Mother/My Self*, Nancy Friday claims that we marry the men our mothers find safe, rather than the ones we find sexual. To ward off the sexual devils inside her, Anne was a member of Youth for Christ, carrying her Bible everywhere with her during high school; and as quickly as possible after her graduation from a three-year nursing school, she married a handsome yet stable man. Because of my own sexual guilt—too depleted by my efforts to put Satan behind me to even think of anything like secretarial school, much less college—I had already dropped out of the eleventh grade to wed, an act that automatically conferred on me matronhood, and thus grace. Then, retaining my new status—and determining not to repeat Mother's mistakes—I ridded myself of my wild young first husband as soon as he fully evidenced the very wildness to which I had undoubtedly first—and viscerally—been attracted.

Thereafter, I looked for my husbands among the Ashley Wilkeses of the world, my lovers from among the Rhett Butlers. When Zane repeated the chant—"This is my weapon/This is my gun/One is for killing/One is for fun"—sung by Army basic trainees, I was shocked. I didn't yet realize that I held to a credo as shocking as the madonna-whore complex, that is, that some men are for marrying, others for romance and/or fucking; or that the amputated version of the same credo, held by more "respectable" —or less liberated or rebellious—ladies, states only that some men are for marrying, period. I failed to recognize that though my life had been peppered with Rhett Butler–James Dickey–even-Billy Carter types, I had chosen my spouses from Mother's "good husband material" category. I had swung, a predictable pendulum, from sexy, macho lovers to suitably tamed mates.

It seemed as though I should have learned from my experience with my third husband, Ben. As he hunched naked over his desk, scribbling unpublishable poetry or frowning over nihilistic philosophies, I thrilled to the length of the lashes shading his green eyes, the exotic curls gracing the nape of his Jewish-princely neck, the comeliness of his circumcised cock. But after reading *The Denial of Death* by Ernest Becker—the same volume Woody Allen handed Diane Keaton in *Annie Hall*, a film he had never seen—he told me, paraphrasing Woody almost exactly, that he had realized there was no use fucking, or being married, or—since we were all going to die anyway—doing *any*thing but cooking perfect meals from Julia Child and walking down to the package store for just the right wine, waiting out one's days, preferably alone. As he emphasized his intention to do just that by tearing a work shirt in half, and throwing a chair across the room, I was anguished, suddenly seeing in him a potential for the violence I craved—all the while thinking it was his "sensitivity" I would miss.

Even after our divorce, living alone and on the loose for the first time in my life, my delusional system let me continue to think that my consistent taste in lovers was not a part of my real life. The year of my and Ben's final separation was also the year in which Mother committed suicide, Daddy died of a fast-growing cancer, and my youngest child left home. To soothe my existential pangs—salve the loss of my parents, and the mate I still grieved—I tamped down my Bible Belt upbringing, my sexual shame, with alcohol and drugs, and indulged in relationships with partners who were definitely more sexual than suitable, sometimes, without realizing it, confusing the two groups. "You're just lookin' for somebody to take your ex-husband's place!" accused an earthily handsome political writer, sensing that I was getting sweet on him. He had just lost his job with a major newspaper after punching out the managing editor. We were sitting in an Atlanta after-hours bar at five a.m., surrounded by dwarfs, drag queens, drug dealers, and ladies of the night, and were looking around for someone to take home with us. He was the last thing I needed on a permanent basis.

Still, when the manic activity, the speeded-up screwing around that had accompanied my angst slowed, I went on consorting with men who, except under the influence of an altered consciousness, I would have previously considered out-of-bounds.

Following my divorce from Ben, I lived part of each year in my home city, Atlanta, and the other part in the seaport town of Savannah. Atlanta is serious business—a boomtown of narcissistic neon, ever-expanding suburbs, and freeways to equal Houston or L.A., a metropolis that can accurately be labeled *glossy*. My second husband, an architect, had had his hand in designing many of the glass phalluses, the sports arenas, the broad shopping malls of a city that was rapidly losing its *Gone with the Wind* mystique.

Savannah, by contrast, is a sleazily decaying, yet lovely, pastel dream of tight cobbled streets, elegantly austere eighteenth-century and frilly Victorian nineteenth-century houses, overhanging Spanish moss, masses of azaleas and oleander. It is said that the first thing one is asked in Atlanta is "What do you do?"; in Charleston, "Who were your ancestors?"; and in Savannah, "What would you like to drink?" When a New Yorker asked a Savannah society woman what she did, she looked at him, puzzled. "Why, ah *live*— ah *live* in Sa-vannah!" she replied with proper hauteur.

Indeed, it is a town in which everything—aristocracy, historic architecture, booze, drugs, even flowers—is excessive. My manicurist is a transsexual, my dentist wears a pistol in his boot, my internist mentions threesomes in Chicago over the examining table, and my plumber was, until recently, salvaging ships off Key West, when he was struck by the "Keys Disease"—a malaise in which one starts out in the morning to buy a loaf of bread and doesn't return home until after midnight. He was now in Savannah, he told me while disassembling the toilet tank, to help a local couple build a replica of Ernest Hemingway's house, and to save money for his coming trip down the Amazon in his 1930s yacht.

Then there are the legendary scenes of sex-and-violence, extreme enough to rival any dreamed up by Tennessee Williams:

Poet Conrad Aiken heard his father shoot his mother, and then himself, in the bedroom of one of the beautiful town houses when the poet was eleven. During the twenties, a son of a wealthy Savannah family was said to be dating the singer–girl friend of a local bootlegger; one night, someone rang the doorbell of the family mansion and, when the door was opened, threw the young man's severed testicles through the doorway—a story allegedly kept out of the local newspapers, yet passed down decade after decade. Savannah is the first place in which I had had among my everyday contacts—from repairmen to social acquaintances—a number of people actually involved in murder trials. ("Now don't say anything about that thing that happened in this building," a hostess whispered, referring to a particularly gruesome murder involving cocaine, solicitation, a blow to the head with a conch shell, a stabbing, a toothbrush shoved up the victim's anus, and an attempt to burn the body in a bathtub. "Her son was charged with it, you know.") Bars and cocktail parties—where women serve things with names like Jezebel (a spicy conserve poured over cream cheese, spread on crackers) and, of course, mint juleps—became frequent settings for psychodrama.

"Savannah's a seaport town—ships and sailors," a Savannah Police Department spokesman said on the front page of the *Savannah News-Press*, trying to explain a crime rate often among the highest in the nation; "It's no longer a question of how to control it—it's probably beyond control." If the unconscious is the seat of sex and aggression, Savannah is that part of the psyche made manifest.

Before long, the two cities—Savannah and Atlanta—had become metaphors for the two parts of myself. And for a woman in search of the macho man, Savannah was the natural habitat; even the mayor—a charismatic, four-times-elected, blue-eyed Greek-American patriarch—is macho; a black state representative was arrested for possession of cocaine with little loss of popularity; foreign sailors and drug smugglers walk the streets; and Army Rangers fill the waterfront bars.

It is the kind of town in which one might be walking down the street, hear the telephone in a nearby booth ring, and—as happened to my gay friend, Robert John—answer it to hear a stranger suggest meeting for sex; indeed, a place that might be symbolized by the black boy of about nine, walking on the sidewalk beneath my window one balmy morning, lustily singing at the top of his lungs:

Why don't you jes'
pull up yo' dress—
All I wanna do is
ug-AH! ug-AH!

Yet even as I enjoyed my new bohemianism, I renewed my search—as relentlessly as Liz again—for the right mate. Indeed, I even hoped that, as a published writer, I would "meet a better class of man," as Erica Jong claimed to have done after the publication of *Fear of Flying.* The split that let me separate my life into parts as disparate as my right and left brain let me also continue to believe that, romantically, my destiny still lay with one of my more sensitive, middle-class male peers; in other words, the academics, artists, professionals, and media men who fueled Atlanta with the very force of their ambition.

My first prospect was a cuddly, kissy-faced movie critic who liked having me on his arm as long as I radiated just the right degree of preppy sexuality, but who primarily orgasmed—I learned after a dozen frustrating nights together—from the excitement of Beautiful People parties. Then there was the satanically handsome plastic surgeon who drowned the pain of paying $40,000 a year child support in a quart of Dewar's each night—who, despite my black lace garter belts, black seamed stockings, my agreement that, yes, maybe a dagger tattooed on my inner thigh *might* be nice, even my compliance in picking up topless or bottomless dancers for ménages à trois—still couldn't get it up. Next arrived—it couldn't probably be said he had *come*—the good-looking blond university department chairman who invited me to spend a weekend, but who wore starched pajamas to our shared bed, then jumped up at dawn to jog and play tennis, leaving me alone to search his apartment for nonexistent pornography. It was then that I learned—contrary to Gloria Steinem's statement that a woman who allows a copy of *Playboy* in her home is the equivalent of a Jew with *Mein Kampf* on his coffee table—never to trust the impulses of a single man with nary a girlie magazine on hand: my host finally made a halfhearted pass fifteen minutes before it was time for me to leave Monday morning.

For a while I even considered marriage to a paunchy, duck-footed, pipe-smoking computer expert who was so thoroughly into "I'm okay, you're okay" that he saw no reason for self-improvement, despite the fact that he read no books or magazines other than est pamphlets and lived in a house decorated throughout in what could only be called shit brown. The source of his high self-esteem was the fact that he had been est'ed. He generously told me we could marry as soon as I cleaned up my act, became less sexually demanding—and agreed to be est'ed myself. But when he came back from five weeks' work in Morocco to regale me with the wondrous passivity of Moroccan women ("They don't even *care* whether they have orgasms," he beamed admiringly; "Why, all *they* care about is pleasing the man they're with. In fact, if they *did* have one, they would probably be embarrassed, try to conceal it"), I lost control, pummeling him out the door of my Savannah apartment, screaming that he was a pathetic wimp. As he retreated, he put his fat arms above his head, a look of real fear in his eyes.

Sometimes—as though to test out their adventurousness, their potential for "wildness," as in the ultimate good-ole-girl compliment, "*He* is *wild!*"—I invited my Atlanta or New York prospects to visit me in Savannah. It was a test that should have made the importance to me of certain qualities more obvious than it did. Indeed, one of my favorite unconscious ploys to rid myself of a lover I had already unknowingly crossed off as a possible mate was to get him on my new turf and act as outrageous as possible—drinking too much, dragging him around to my favorite sleazy joints, flirting with other men, or—as I did with the frustrating plastic surgeon and a pretentious New York filmmaker—having him visit at the same time as one of my lesbian friends, then sleeping with her rather than him. Sometimes, I even tried to involve them in ménages à trois with my new gay men friends. I had formed a notion that a heterosexual man's willingness to have sex with another man was the ultimate proof of his liberation—a quality I had decided was essential in my next spouse. All I wanted was a man who was at once stable and tractable enough to be what Mother would have called "good husband material" and a wild, risk-taking adventurer!

What I didn't yet realize was that in looking for my true love among my more civilized acquaintances, I was looking in the wrong bullpen: that true wildness is the domain of the macho men of this world. As my latest fiasco, the fat computer engineer, hastily revved up the motor of his Honda automobile—if nothing else, he was *practical*—and sped off, I lay across my four-poster bed, the rest of my failures rattling through my brain like some perverse rosary. The Cordon Bleu chef who preferred holding hands while watching old movies starring Bette Davis or Joan Crawford to the crassness of actually "doing it." "Sorry about that," he had said briskly, adjusting his ascot in the mirror as I complained the morning after our third sexless night together. The newly divorced junior attorney who—à la Jill Clayburgh in *An Unmarried Woman*—had panicked when I suggested bed: "I couldn't *possibly* sleep with someone I'm not engaged to," he had gasped as girlishly as Mother had always hoped I would. The filmmaker who had answered the door of his Manhattan apartment dressed only in a silk scarf, but had declined sex with the excuse of a perpetually active case of herpes. The skinny, redheaded creative writing professor and vegetarian who had been celibate for eight months and intended to stay that way. The psychotherapist who wanted me to be the Significant Other, but nothing more, in his open relationship with his therapist wife . . .

If my former lovers sound like caricatures, it is because they *were*: our relationships had been abortive, sketchy: "You fear involvement and harbor the fantasy of finding a father to look after you," the therapist told me, throwing in some free psychology with our lovemaking. What *was* wrong with me, I wondered. Did I actually hate men? Or did I like them *too* much? Was I really too interested in sex, as the movie critic, the engineer, and the Cordon Bleu chef had accused? Was I so thoroughly convinced that I didn't deserve these superior specimens of manhood that I communicated my inferiority complex, my lack of self-esteem, mutely yet clearly? Or was I too independent, assertive, as a journalist-lover had suggested?

I still hadn't made the connection between my unresolved relationship with my charismatic father and my problems with less engrossing men, or my attraction to the other kind. Nor had I noticed that the "inappropriate" men I continued to see and sleep with while I searched for Mr. Right never complained about my sexuality, assertiveness, or intelligence. To them, any aggressiveness I might muster was about as distracting as a fly to an elephant—as in "You're so cute when you're mad." Thus, the more macho the man, the more traditionally feminine—passive and virtuous—I felt. In addition, my masochism was more readily satisfied by his craziness; with other men, there was an absence of pain—but also of passion.

I ignored the fact that I soaked up the energy for my renewed quest during nights and weekends in bed with a macho man and viewed our sex as sport-fucking, emotional skydiving—a way of staying free, avoiding intimacy, while I kept my emotional virginity intact, on hold, for the great new love—one of my own kind—I was sure I would still find. When I read in *A Little Original Sin*, Millicent Dillon's biography of Jane Bowles's obsession with the native Moroccan woman Cherifa, I viewed it as a part of her search for Other, the primitive. In the same way, I saw my tug toward the macho man as something akin to my attraction to people with scars: superficial, symbolic, rather than genuinely characteristic. Indeed, since men who ride in rodeos, jump from planes, drive motorcycles, are more likely to have scars than most, it was frequently a predilection I could indulge simultaneously.

But like a mule with blinders on, I ignored the signs of my real identification with such lovers. I didn't want to believe that while a woman living in a mobile home, hair in fat pink rollers, a baby on each hip, might thrill to a lawyer in a three-piece pin-striped suit, I still had a taste for the bad guys. After all, what would it say about *me* if I confessed that the men I was most drawn to were also the ones who got drunk or into fistfights, shot pool and sometimes people? I couldn't yet admit to myself that despite having developed tastes for caviar and smoked salmon, breakfasted at the Carlyle and summered at the Cape, my synapses still clicked to the same old image: that even disguised in a silk designer dress and Maude Frizon high heels, I still responded to the local hunks at Maebob's Pool Hall and Lunch Room bellying up to the bar to order their daily ration of pit barbecue, blackeyed peas, and Pabst's.

I blacked out memories of swimming at the rock quarry with the wild boys and the fact that my favorite childhood fantasy had been of going into the jungle to tame wild animals. Just as I would later conjure up a hurt, a need for the kind of tenderness only I, as a woman, could give, behind the most brutish macho façade, as a child I imagined lions and tigers could be soothed—transformed into the most loving pets—if only one talked to them softly, stroked them gently. I forgot that my favorite album cut was Hank Williams, Jr., lauding the macha female in "Outlaw Woman"; that I thrilled involuntarily to movies like *Conan the Barbarian* or *The Godfather*; and, despite my literary inclinations, sank enthralled into Robert Ludlum thrillers and Earl Thompson adventure novels. While I loved going into the jungle, I still imagined I was afraid of the snakes.

Phil Donahue, America's very arbiter of liberated mental health, stated on his show on father-daughter incest that "Women who prefer unstable—exciting—relationships [instead of steady, secure love] usually had absent or unpredictable fathers." And I was still in search of traditional—if liberated—mental health.

Mild-mannered guru Donahue is not, I now know, the kind of man to whom I am attracted; such cool rationality could never be the piece to fit my primal puzzle. But he was right when he said, on the same program, that "passivity is the female disease." No matter how I enjoyed them—no matter how strong my sense that having to answer for one's comings and goings in the world is tantamount to psychological castration—I considered my adventurous impulses an aberration. Never mind that sometimes on the road, driving from, say, Savannah to Jacksonville, fantasies would float between my eyes and the dashboard—fantasies of just keeping on down Highway A1A, no destination in mind, on the road-or-lam again like the male heroes of all my favorite country-western songs. Lulled by the ribbon of road, I could imagine leaving responsibilities behind as carelessly as the most no-good good ole boy. Vague images of being on my own, sleeping in strange motels with strange men, would float, unmoored, about my brain. They were fantasies I could later at least partly fulfill, finding them to be almost as pleasurable as I had dreamed. But my maternal grandmother Lee, the perfectly passive and stoic Southern woman in every regard, had spent her life waiting on others; her greatest thrill probably was in baking up a fresh Bundt cake; while the drunken carousing that Mr. Carroll—my Scotch-Irish grandfather and her second husband—and each of his three sons in turn had indulged in, sounded like *fun*. Why did women always have to be "good"? It was a question that, unanchored, I could ask myself. But as I approached my destination—a writing class or reading—I would brush my thoughts away, gear myself to responsibility. I may have thrilled to Boxcar Bertha's autobiography, Robyn Davidson's story in *Tracks*, of trekking across 1,700 miles of Australian outback with three camels, but I wouldn't really want to do it, would I?

I knew of one woman in Savannah who had allowed herself to become unmoored, who had followed her bohemian instincts to their fullest, and ultimately come to the bad end—the destitution, the homelessness—I had been taught was inevitable to women who didn't follow the rules. Betty the Bag Lady, known in the city for sleeping in the parks and prostituting herself to make her living, had been a proper young woman from an old Savannah family during the forties; after four years at a sedate Georgia finishing school, Breneau Academy, she had come home, married a young Air Force officer stationed nearby, and had two children. But when he divorced her and left the city, she left her toddlers in the suburbs in her parents' care, and remained downtown with new friends, ultimately evolving a life-style that resembled more that of a homeless alley cat than a well-brought-up Savannah matron. "All she knew how to do was please people," her long-estranged son told me sadly after her death. When he finally came back to the city, she was dying of cancer; he rented an apartment that he shared with her for the brief remainder of her life, "but I had to drag her there like a wild animal, she was so used to being on the streets," he said, still cringing painfully at the memory. At her funeral, she was eulogized as a city character, a part of local color.

Following our own head was a risk that writer Alice Walker and I had once discussed. As women *and* artists, we felt particularly vulnerable, unprotected. Alice had edited the Zora Neale Hurston reader, a collection of the works of the forgotten black woman writer from Florida who had been buried in a pauper's grave. Perhaps women shouldn't take too many risks, at least not all those allowed to men. And wise women stayed chastely at home, didn't they? "I didn't *mean* to become a matriarch," the perfect home-town hostess—perfect mother to the five generations under her roof—said wearily to me, the visiting writer, over coffee one morning. "But . . ." I knew what the rest of her sentence would be: if the cowgirls wanted to be cowboys, if even the Indians wanted to be Indians, where would the family be? It was a question I had heard from women wherever I traveled, but recalling the frustrations of my marriages, the restraints of family life, I chafed at her unspoken comment. Yet I, too, feared my adventurous impulses, the fate of ending up like Betty the Bag Lady, who, for all I knew, might have just been another frustrated creative artist, a woman who refused—as I had so often longed to do—to fit into society's foreordained slot for her.

At the same time, I was just as distressed by manifestations of passivity in men. When I worked for two days in a private mental hospital, conducting poetry workshops with the patients, I found the drugged male patients sadder, more disturbing, than the females—women were *supposed* to be weak, teary, passive, weren't they?—while the men, sitting like totems, tripped my anxiety. It was the same queasy feeling I had had watching a male stripper in a bar, sensuously taking on the woman's seductive role, curving his body to softness; or seeing a lover jokingly tuck his penis between his thighs, turning suddenly womanish. Yet I misread my apprehension as only confirmation of my desire to castrate men, rather than as fear of my own possible psychic castration, or a reminder of my own powerlessness.

My disturbance dissipated after several years in Savannah, where drag queens were among my new pals. There, I grew so used to men behaving in ways traditionally considered feminine that when I saw a size-twelve high-heeled shoe discarded near the curb of the cobbled sidewalk where I walked, I absently thought to myself, That's a man's high heel. When an especially macho writer told me he had a surprise for me—and emerged from my bathroom dressed for our date in hot pants, panty hose, high heels, and a blond wig, I spoiled his fun by showing little surprise. I enjoyed *La Cage aux Folles*, the comic French film about sex roles; but by the time *Victor/Victoria*—with the usually prim-roled Julie Andrews playing a woman in drag as a man in drag as a woman—was released, I had begun to find transvestism unremarkable—and to agree with rock poet Patti Smith's comment that "to be any gender is a drag!"

In any case, I never experienced anxiety about sex roles with the macho man. With a man who was a Real Man, I was certain of his masculinity and, thus, my femininity. Yet with other men, I had a long-standing history of failure. "You think you can't get ahead with them," my therapist told me, "just like some people think they can never get ahead financially."

During my frustrating affairs with less lusty men, I had longingly recalled the mutely handsome high school jock who had so forcefully divested me of my virginity at fifteen; I had always misread the title of Flannery O'Connor's story as "A Hard Man Is Good to Find," and I was tired of talking—always talking—to men about their post-divorce traumas, mid-life crises, and the positive powers of primal scream therapy. Now I was economically independent, if perpetually broke, my children had left home, and I could choose out of my gut, rather than my brain. If anything, my failures had freed me to get back to basics, to indulge my love for Daddy—to openly seek out the macho man.

When the job on the oil rig presented itself—a shimmering biceptual heaven, a shining oasis in an erotic desert—I felt as though I had tapped sexual gold. In reality, I was about to find out more about the macho man than even I had ever wanted to know!

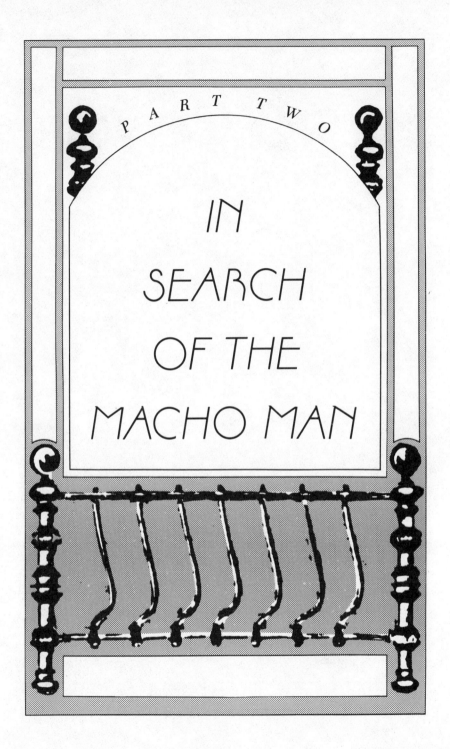

PART TWO

IN
SEARCH
OF THE
MACHO MAN

It started one Saturday morning in June 1979.

Watching an ocean liner move as slowly as sorghum syrup down the Savannah River, my friend Madge and I sat sipping Bloody Marys. Madge, a visual artist, seemed to be one of those women spawned by the women's movement: though sometimes subject to a healthy lust, she had none of the driving urge of women of my generation toward marriage or motherhood; she could take men or leave them, yet wasn't a lesbian, either. Though she had told me that she had been a quiet, near-dateless girl during college in the Midwest, she had recently gone to a Hilton Head fat farm to lose twenty pounds, had gotten a frizzy perm in her long strawberry-blond hair, and had learned to flirt, causing local construction workers and married playboys to deluge her with invitations.

But now she had a more serious problem. Like me, she was broke, and looking for a job. "I heard of one you might like, too," she teased. "It's on an oil rig a hundred miles out. They want women aboard to help 'civilize' the men." Despite the difference in our ages—my forty-three to her thirty—Madge and I shared a taste for cream-filled Dunkin' Donuts, azalea-pink nail polish, and a certain kind of girl talk. We both laughed self-consciously, visions of male sugar plums dancing in our heads.

I had just come back to Savannah from an artists' retreat on a wild, unpopulated island off the coast of Georgia, where I had lived in a pink stucco mansion with a dozen other writers and artists for a month. There I had made the final corrections on *Fatal Flowers* and, over cocktails and dinners served by old retainers at a long, elegant table, had indulged in clever, often bitchy, conversations with the same kind of men who so vexed me on the mainland.

On my first Friday night back in Savannah I had attended a dinner party with one of them—a celibate vegetarian creative writing teacher—who was passing through on his way back to California. During a meal served in an enclosed garden, we drank the mint juleps in frosted silver cups served by our white-linen-suited host, and sipped Southern Comfort, and surreptitiously clawed at our mosquito bites as our hostess read a chapter from *The Wind in the Willows*. Yet despite the sensuality of the evening, the professor had still refused, when he had let me off at my door, to end his island celibacy, leaving me agitated in a way more extreme than that caused by the welts left by my insect bites. Now I was home in my furnished apartment and, as usual, worried about money. Laura was in graduate school, and my 1973 Fiat was on the blink, but I planned to suppress my anxieties and start writing a novel, hoping I could sell the first chapters before total insolvency set in.

Early Monday, Madge banged at my door, waking me out of sexy dreams. "Put on your jeans, don't wear any makeup, and look like you can work hard!" she commanded. In twenty minutes we sat in the trailer-office of an offshore oil company, listening to a tough-looking man with a cigar hanging from the side of his mouth talk about how we would "Keep 'em frum drinkin', fightin', 'n' runnin' 'round nekkid." Aside from that little goal, we would only be required to work the same round-the-clock shifts as the men, scrubbing and cleaning twelve hours a day, eighty-four hours a week, two weeks on and two weeks off. "Do you think it'll be like Club Med?" Madge whispered to me as the mouth with the cigar went on, "Now some of the boys've been out there a while, but I know you li'l ladies'll know how to handle yoreselves."

"Just be sure you don't have syphilis," said the med tech drawing blood from inside Madge's elbow. She looked at me indignantly, but we knew there was no going back. During the next thirty-six hours—the time until our helicopter would leave—we phoned each other in fits of paranoia. "You'll get gang-banged and thrown overboard!" a male friend exclaimed. "You're crazy, woman!" Madge's soon-to-be-ex-boyfriend shook his head disgustedly. I called my sister and two daughters in case I never saw them again, then went to McCrory's basement to buy blue rubber maid shoes for $3.59.

To keep from inciting rape, we agreed to wear old clothes and no makeup. Early Wednesday, wearing the ugly blue maid shoes, I waited at my door with bags weighted by illicit quarts of Black Jack and Mount Gay Rum ("No drugs, drankin', or foolin' around," the mouth with the cigar had said). Then Madge drove up wearing Pango Pink Revlon and the turquoise blouse that sharpened her strawberry coloring. "Wait a minute!" I yelled, "I'm going back inside." By the time we arrived at the airport, my favorite plum eye shadow was smeared across my lids, the ties of my sexiest espadrilles rose about my calves. When I coyly asked a younger man with amazing biceps to carry my bags out to the yellow helicopter awaiting us across the airfield, Madge, lugging her own, fumed. But she brightened when we arrived beside the craft and several muscular men vied to help us with the puzzling straps of our orange life jackets, then to lift us inside as though we were 120 pounds of Hawaiian Gold. As the copter rose over the Savannah coastline, we grinned at each other like kids let loose in a donut store, and stuck the stereo headphones over our heads. While the sound system poured Jimmy Buffett singing "Why don't we get drunk and screw . . ." into our ears, I looked down at blue, blue lagoons, then at the man with the amazing biceps. Sitting snugly knee-to-knee with me, he stared back so frankly that I looked out the window and blushed.

After almost an hour of redneck lust, we hovered over a tiny speck in the ocean, which became a pancake standing on skinny legs, then the deck of a ship with what looked like the tail of a Texas scorpion rising at its stern. Later I would learn that the *Venus* was one of three self-propelled oil rigs in the world; a ship with a complete oil rig projecting off its rear deck, it was raised, when not in motion, almost a hundred feet above the sea's surface by four retractable steel jack legs.

"I think this might be interesting," I whispered to Madge as we were gallantly disentangled from our life jackets, and handed down to a deck barely larger than the helicopter. A crowd of cloned Marlboro Men, dressed in what I would come to think of as Animal Anti-Chic—randomly torn Levis and T-shirts or ugly Sears Roebuck jumpsuits—stared at us silently and hungrily, parting like a viscous sea as we were led through them. In my oversized pink sunglasses, flimsy peach blouse, and *very* snug jeans—my long auburn hair blowing in the sea breeze—I felt like Brigitte Bardot in *And God Created Woman*.

Madge didn't seem to notice the thousands of pounds of male flesh surrounding us. "Yes, but do you think we'll get to sunbathe today?" she replied. I suspected by the stern look of the man escorting us that we wouldn't. Hey, I wanted to protest as he hustled us into an elevator—you didn't give us a chance to meet the press or respond to our fans!

As we stepped out on a lower deck, I looked around curiously. I had never been aboard a ship, and the interior was more compact than I had imagined. "This is where the men come in off the rig and take off their work boots," the man explained, indicating a gruesome cemetery of grimy boots piled beside a door and a wall that looked as though it had been attacked by a baby smearing black grease instead of feces. "You'll keep this bulkhead"—one of the many ship terms I'd be learning during the next few days—"scrubbed clean *at all times*."

Leading us down the narrow companionway past frightening signs about what to do in case of fire, blowouts, or poisonous gas, he described the deck where we stood as the accommodations for the Tool Pusher, or rig boss; the Tour Pusher, or night boss; the Company Man—another heavy, I could tell by his tone; plus assorted drillers, derrick men, crane operators, and welders. "And that"—barely concealing his disgust, he lifted a pinky toward a filthy stairwell—"is C deck, where the *animals*—the roustabouts and roughnecks—live." Oh, no, not here, too, I thought as I watched his raised pinky, the effete sniff out of context in his weathered face.

Before my unpleasant flash could register, our leader swished around a corner, where he indicated the "rec room"—a dim space in which loomed a tiny pool table, an out-of-focus TV, and several bodies straight from a Brueghel painting; and—again, that respectful tone—"The Tool Pusher's office"; inside, I heard someone speaking loud redneckese over a shortwave radio. A few feet farther on, a half-opened door revealed a tiny cabin crammed with four bunks, strewn laundry, and shredded girlie magazines. As we turned another corner, we passed a steam-filled laundry room and, as though we were playing follow-the-leader, stepped over piles of T-shirts and Levis (I soon learned riggers don't indulge in anything as sissy as underwear) from which the scent of stale sweat emanated like an aura. During our odyssey, I was conscious of the eyes of men, more macho men than I had ever seen in one place in my life, staring at us from every doorway, staircase, and corridor.

In the galley, we were introduced to a chef who grinned toothlessly beneath a grimy chef's hat, then offered us mugs of coffee from fists at the ends of forearms that looked like color-illustrated hams ("What *is* this?" Madge asked me, "*Satyricon?*"). Over coffee, our captor—who now confessed his name was Ed—described our duties: we would work from eight in the morning until eight at night, with thirty minutes for lunch. Besides keeping the bulkhead pristine, we were to make eighty bunks, sweep, dust, mop, and straighten each cabin (beginning, *first thing*, with the cabins of the Tool Pusher, Tour Pusher, Company Man, and Ship's Captain, above on A deck), and clean the baths between the better cabins. Next we would clean the latrines, and sweep, mop, and wax the companionways on each deck, then clean the rec room and Tool Pusher's office. Each evening, we were to help serve food from the steam trays, and scrub the pots and pans after supper, then swab down the tables and sweep and mop the galley. In our *spare* time, we were to consult the chalkboard in the galley for wake-up times, and wake the men in their cabins for their shifts; the big shots, Ed said coyly, *liked* a cup of coffee in bed, and it was *good* to find out *how* they liked it. Oh, yes, and polish the brass that adorned the doorstep of every cabin and latrine—there was *nothing* as distasteful as mossy brass, didn't we agree?

Glancing at Madge, I saw that she, too, appeared delicately faint. Ignoring our feminine pallor, Ed looked us up and down, and announced that Madge would be in charge of C deck; I, B deck— "since *you*," he accused with a comment I had never before heard, "look too skinny." That day, since we had gotten a late start, we would do the work together; and since Wednesday was sheet-change day, and this was Wednesday—well. Suggesting that our getups might not be appropriate for what was to come, he showed us to our cabin, "one with a bath," he said resentfully. As soon as the door closed, Madge plunked down into the one chair, I plopped on the bottom bunk. "Well, so much for fun and games," I said. "And so much for sunbathing," Madge said after a long silence. I lugged my suitcase into horizontal and dug out the ugly blue maid shoes.

The rest of the day became a blur of scrubbing grease from the bulkhead and breaking each of my carefully Revloned nails tugging dirty sheets off top bunks. As Madge and I wearily sloshed around in latrines filthier than any I had seen on a trip to Guatemala, swabbing at grimy tiles, a row of slimy basins, men in various states of undress stood around us, offering protection from the others— "Wolves protecting sheep from wolves," Madge said sarcastically— and saying things like "Ah'd marry yo' dawg to git to you, honey," or "You go with me, baby, ah'll take keer a you lak a dawg takes keer a 'is bone." But the sweat pouring down my forehead kept me from seeing them at all.

That night, lying in my bunk, the ceiling six hot inches above my face, every muscle in my body throbbing—I thought of Patty Hearst in her closet, blacks hijacked from Africa, and fantasized escape. "I wouldn't do that, honey," a voice behind me had said that afternoon as—dumping the "dinner," or midday meal, leftovers into the sea—I had looked longingly down at the ocean. "The water's full'a barr'cudas 'n' shark 'round hyah." Soon, I was dreaming about muscular, bearded babies, born with tattooed forearms.

Every day for the next two weeks, surrounded by biceps etched with vultures, sharks, hearts inscribed "Mother," I collected crusty towels and filthy sheets from beneath spilled ashtrays and the ubiquitous centerfolds from magazines like *Birds*, *Oui*, and *High Society*. In their choice of visuals, the men were divided, the earthiest and crudest of them preferring the shots showing the most pink; the more sentimental choosing the veiled and romanticized, if still hairy, nudes. "She looks jes' lak a peach with the pit took out, don't she?" Otis the Welder asked admiringly of his choice. "But thet one," he went on engagingly, critiquing his bunkmate's beaver shot, "she looks jes' lak a muddy road a mule done pulled a plow through, don't she?" Otis, whom we would soon nickname the "Marquis de Quim" because of his appreciation of womanflesh, was six-foot-four and claimed to have gone "barefoot down on the Mississippi homeplace till ah wuz fifteen. . . . 'N' the main thang ah learned down on the farm wuz thet yuh always lick it first!"

Never before had I felt so acutely what Southern comedian Brother Dave Gardner called "the power of the puss"; travelers from another planet visiting the cabins of the rig would have imagined earth men to have worshiped the lower half of the female anatomy. Just after my third divorce, I had projected onto my solitary bedroom wall imaginary images of inflated and glistening purple phalluses. But now even I began to wonder why slipping the penis into that slick pink sheath was of such monumental concern. Was it *that* different from a man's own right hand?

Waking naked men for their shifts, I found that their fingers turned to tentacles during their first lucid moments and constantly fended hands, if not eyes, off my ass. "Do you realize," Madge said wearily from the top bunk, "that every time you do *any*thing here—and especially when you're bending over to make a top bunk—some man's eyes are glued to your ass?"

I didn't care anymore. My main goal was to live through the shift. Within days, my mind had turned to the kind of mush recommended by Indian mystics. I tried to make notes for the oil-rig article I planned to write, but couldn't recall how to dot an *i*.

Ironically, it was a situation for which my Southern upbringing had particularly prepared me. As though all the years between had never happened, I had soon reverted, with something like relief, to the docile, honey-dripping, man-pleasing ways at which I had been so adept as a fifteen-year-old cheerleader. As a woman who had been boy-crazy since fifth grade, I once again perceived the rig—sans the mopping—as a situation ripe with possibility. A dozen times a day, Madge and I battled for space before the one tiny broken mirror in our cabin, reapplying mascara and lip gloss. Telling each other they were cooler, we now wore flowered cotton skirts and low-necked blouses, bare feet, and painted toenails. In the late sixties, married to a Northeastern liberal, I had obediently let the hair grow beneath my arms; now, to please blue-collar tastes, I silkened my underarms with a scented pink cream. The only thing I lacked in life was a flower to stick in my sweat-tendriled hair.

"She always wears skirts 'n' bends ovah a lot," said a roustabout, succinctly describing his ideal woman—and, above all, working on the rig meant bending over a lot! My curves had always been too rounded for *Vogue*, but fortunately for Madge and me, the riggers were mostly ass-men. I loved the groans, the moans, I got by simply leaning over a broom or toilet brush. "You jes' *made* my day, gal," drooled Otis the Welder, the juice from a fat peach dripping down his burly chin as I bent braless over my mop in the galley. When an Atlanta television crew came out to do a special news report, I was filmed bending over a top bunk. "How do you like being one of four women among seventy-five men?" the reporter asked, referring, besides Madge and me, to the two gay women who had also become part of the crew. Since rig rules decreed that any man who bothered us would be fired (or "sent back to the house"), we were at an advantage. Madge confessed that what she liked best was walking down the companionway pretending she was

Miss America, pointing her toes just so, swiveling her blond head from side to side as she inspected each room, while I bragged that "I've never pinched so many asses in my life!"

Two days later, I tried *not* to giggle too much as during a trial ride in the enclosed buoyed lifeboat that hung over the ship's side two riggers competed to explain seriously to Madge and me that "This hyah's the three-ring cock, yuh jes' put the male in the female 'n' pull this hyah lever down to steer 'er." When we were escorted—calloused hands gripping our comparatively fragile elbows—up the ladder to tour the oil rig (by a man who walked *beneath* us, of course), we beamed at one another from under borrowed hard hats. While the other men watched jealously, Bill the Tool Pusher tucked his Red Man into a cheek and explained the graphs and dials that indicated the depth of the drill pipe beneath the ocean's bottom, then put his arms around our shoulders to have his picture taken.

"Isn't that the sexiest thing you ever saw?" Madge gasped to me as the greased drill pipe, guided by sweaty, straining men, throbbed into what was—naturally—called the Hole. "That must be what makes our bunks vibrate that delicious way!" I said, visualizing the rig as a potential hedonist's heaven, complete with prime ribs at lunch and Magic Fingers mattresses.

That night, Madge and I spent our last conscious minutes in our quivering bunks planning new ways to please our fans. "The poor things—they really *need* us!" she slurred. We had been hitting the Black Jack; combined with our exhaustion, it made us euphoric as we plotted cut flowers for the galley, pastel sheets for the bunks, perfumed sachets on their pillows, and artistic prints to replace the ugly GYN shots with which our pitiful charges felt driven to decorate their even uglier cabins. "This *is* an oil rig, girls," Bill the Tool Pusher said gently the next day, after listening to our arguments about the men's need for aesthetic enrichment—maybe even after-hours classes in, say, figure drawing or poetry writing.

I knew my reversion to domesticity was serious when our new white cotton mops arrived on the supply boat that visited the rig from Savannah each day. I was as excited as I had been about my first book contract! And why had I ever wanted to *think* about anything—much less, write my thoughts down—when just *being* was enough, I wondered vaguely, giving in to the pleasure of sloshing my new mop in Pine-Sol.

Back in Savannah at the end of our first shift, I realized our lobotomies were complete. At the airport, the floor shifting beneath our sea legs, Madge and I went into the ladies' room and stared down at the tiles: "I *must* mop this floor!" we cried simultaneously, like twin Marabel Morgans. Back at my apartment, a whisk broom lay near my parked Fiat; I fought a near-irresistible urge to sweep the street. A few days later, Madge and I stood in Revco, choosing new nail polish; and, feeling a sudden magnetic tug, I turned to see behind me the stack of fresh yellow sponge mops.

Drowning in a sea of blue-collar workers, I found back on dry land, was apparently the desire of every woman I met. After the newspaper and television publicity, the oil company was deluged with applications from women who wanted to do laundry and scrub floors for macho men. Wherever Madge and I went, we were the center of cocktail conversation, and the one thing everyone wanted to know, when they were not too polite to ask, was whether and how much we got laid. ("How many men a day did you service?" David Susskind sneered a year later when I appeared on his show.) "I heard you fucked eighteen men the first two weeks," a woman whispered to me at a Savannah garden party. "When I heard that," she went on, to my amazement, "I tried to figure out how you would do it—it came down to one-point-three men a day." I wore a little pink sundress, a flower in my hair, and hoped I looked ladylike. "Oh, *no*," I demurred in my best butter-wouldn't-melt-in-my-mouth voice, spouting the company line on the gentlemanliness of our protectors, our heavenly life on the *Venus*: "You've got it *all* wrong. . . ."

THE REAL STORY

During the first shift, I hung out with Madge in our cabin after-hours, drinking Black Jack from bottles that I hid beneath the life jacket under my bunk, then threw in the sea through the hatch at night, where they floated to the surface in the pink plastic bag in which I'd put them, causing the "gov'ment" men (or inspectors) to complain that someone was littering the sea.

But soon, living in what could only be called close quarters with sprawling, drawling, brawling men—ex-Army Rangers, rodeo riders, cowboys, and barroom buddies—I began to believe I really *was* that dance-hall girl in the saloon I had fantasized being so long before and began to get in touch, for the first time, with the Power of Sheer Lust. Surrounded by men with whom I still believed it impossible for me to have a "relationship," I felt as though I were chawing Spanish Fly as vigorously as they were chawing Red Man. Sweat, I had to confess, could definitely be an aphrodisiac; I had to admit as well that eating black-eyed peas beside a man in filthy Levis, arms smeared with black grease, turned me on as much as sharing caviar with a man in an Yves St. Laurent suit ever had.

Yes, these were Real Men who put first things—like sex, country music, sex, pickup trucks, sex, good bourbon, sex, cockfighting—first, I told myself, noting how *they* noted everything about me, every moment of every day. "Yah-HOO!" yelled three riggers at once amid a burst of spontaneous applause as I emerged from the walk-in freezer off the galley kitchen with a frosty Coke—and hard nipples. Before I knew it, my never-strong inhibitions had been further weakened: I was getting laid in such idyllic spots as the dirty forward mooring space, the perilously swaying lifeboats, or a bottom bunk with someone else in the top.

In theory—given my feminine version of the double standard, my inability to see the riggers as real people—I believed it was as much my right to fuck oil riggers and truck drivers as it was my white-collar male peers' to bed waitresses and secretaries. In reality, I still prided myself on choosing lovers for such "finer" qualities as sensitivity, intelligence, aesthetic refinement, and that catch-all seventies virtue, *awareness*—which was probably why I had ended up, pre-rig, with so many hormone-deficient boyfriends. But on the *Venus* I was discovering that my ethereal motives were just so much bullshit; indeed, in the first object of my lust, *none* of the above applied.

A curly-haired blond hulk with a chipped front tooth and muscles like tan logs bulging through his torn black T-shirt, Bobby pushed himself back in his seat across from me at the galley table and chewed on a steak bone. "Thank Gawd ah'm gittin' off this thang!" he said across—or was it to?—the bottles of A-1, Hunt's ketchup, and Louisiana Hot Sauce. "Been on hyah three weeks now," he added, carving the steak shreds from between his molars.

"What do you plan to do first?" I asked in my best social-worker voice. It was a tone I had found drove the men mad—undoubtedly reminding them of mama—and at the same time, kept them at bay.

"Whut do yuh thank?! Ah'm goin' into Savannah to git me some!"

"Do you know anyone there?" I responded brightly, recalling the way he had looked at my tits when I had come out of the freezer.

"Nope!"

"Well, how do you know you'll be able to—uh—'git some'?"

He looked at me as though I were infinitely stupid: "Ah'll jes' *git some*—that's all!"

Here was a man who was sexually confident, yet definitely in need, I thought as he casually changed—or seemed to change— the subject: "I'm gonna be fishin' up off the deck later on. Why doncha come on up 'n' set a while?"

After Madge and I swabbed down the galley, I showered and changed into a flowered skirt and blouse and hot-pink bikini panties. When I arrived on deck, the wind blew my skirt crotch-level; holding it down à la Marilyn, I walked across the heliport toward Bobby, who had looked up from his rod and reel. Still staring at my thighs, he offered me his chair and straddled the gear stashed at the rail. As the moon rose, and waves washed the wet decks of the supply boat below, he thrilled me with tales of his sad life as a Ranger, paratrooper, and sniper in Nam; as a bronco-bustin' rodeo-ridin' cowboy in south "Flarda"; of his marriage to a bad wo-man and the loss of his child. "Ah lost it all to the love of a lady," he said mournfully. His words tugged at my heartstrings like the lyrics to a Willie Nelson song, rousing my tenderer instincts, at the same time fusing a direct line to my belly. He *was* sensitive, I told my-self; the thighs bulging like tree trunks from his khaki cutoffs had nothing—at least not *everything*—to do with it.

When he opened a nearby hatch, and climbed down the ladder, I descended after him, holding his outstretched hand and pre-tending not to notice as he looked up my skirt at my panties. ("We mustn't let them see your 'smalls,'" Ed had said, explaining why Madge and I should wash our lingerie in the sink in our cabin, instead of including them in the general laundry. "The *animals* might go beserk, and steal them to put over their heads at night. . . .") Before I knew it, we were back on another deck at the ship's stern, Bobby's hard-on pinning me and my skirt against a wall, kissing in a blinding light that—since I didn't yet understand the layout of the rig—meant we were in full view of the men on the raised drill floor behind the ship's accommodations. From that direction, I suddenly heard "Ya-HOO!"'s and a burst of applause: Bobby grinned and took a bow, but before I could become embarrassed, pulled me against the wind up the staircase toward the wildly swinging lifeboat, where he struggled futilely to open the door. Tugging me back downstairs to laughter and jeers—"Whut's the matter, Bobby? Can't yuh git 'er down?"—he shot a bird toward the rig, then pulled me toward the radio man's cabin, where the radio man, smoking a joint, smirked and left the room.

What would sex with Bobby be like, I wondered, recovering myself? Would he be the macho man of my dreams, more effective in every way than my male peers? I didn't have time to think about it. "Ah saw yuh gittin' off that copter with thet purty red hair 'n' ah knew ah had to have yuh," he slobbered into my neck, tearing my blouse, skirt, and bikinis off in one motion. "'N' ah jes' *love* suckin' pussy, girl," he added, pushing me into the bottom bunk with one hand, unzipping his cutoffs with the other. Crouching in the narrow space beside me, he forced my thighs backward for what seemed like a minute of lapping by an overenthusiastic German shepherd, then five minutes of fucking that felt as though I were alternately being pounded by skin-covered rocks or smushed by a ten-ton tractor. "Well, how'd yuh lak it, girl?" he asked proudly. "It was—breathtaking," I replied honestly. "Wall, guess we better be gittin' on back," he said, lifting my hair to inspect the bruise I could feel developing at the side of my throat. When I got up to dress, I noted with chagrin the menstrual-blood-and-come flowering the radio man's sheets.

Something had happened, and I knew it wasn't orgasm. So it must be that other thing. My physical frustration had immediately transformed itself into romantic poignancy. "I think I'm in love," I told Madge back in our cabin. She sat naked in our one chair, her painted toenails poised on the edge of my bunk; we were stuffing chunks of cake with white icing into our mouths and washing them down with straight Black Jack. "What? With that hunk?" she snorted. "Besides, I thought you didn't want to get involved." A native Minnesotan, she had a clear Northwestern vision denied me as a Southern woman. "Hey," she went on, "he must be something in the sack—I mean, bunk—to make you say that after giving you that gross hickey!" "Well, he's sweet," I defended, ignoring her comment that maybe—just maybe—his spectacular build might have something to do with it.

Bobby reminded me of Ferdinand the Bull, or the second-grade boyfriend I had had in the fifth—both were easy to please. I doubted that he would ever—like some of the screwed-up urban men I knew—choose jogging or transcendental meditation over fucking, or insist on black stockings and garter belt sans panties for dates for which he arrived three hours late, already too drunk to get it up. No, I suspected that as long as I had two breasts and two legs—and was willing to open them at his command—he would be as euphoric as Ferdinand in a pasture with ten cows.

For the next five days until his shift ended, I kept him happy by going down on him, his massive back against his cabin door (yes, he *did* like sucking—me, of him); and letting him fuck me during minutes stolen from my endless mopping (once leaving a tampon in a C-deck wastebasket to be emptied by an incredulous Madge), or flop sweatily on top of me in the middle of the night, despite Madge's irritated comments from the top bunk. "I have to put my hands over my ears, it's like he's killing you—and damn it, I can't even get up—he tries to pull my sheet off, and me into bed, too!" she griped—until the time *I* had to try to sleep and/or keep from laughing while *her* lover described inches above me all the things he planned to do to her with leather and chains.

Reverting to my Southern mother's teachings about the fragility of the male ego, I tried not to use words like "extraneous" and "credibility," never mind that Bobby didn't know what "incompatible" meant ("mah wife said it meant we didn't git along too good"). When Bobby came in off his shift, grinning and sweating in his torn jeans, to swagger past me and grab my ass, I understood for the first time what men see in the kind of two-digit-I.Q. females that the rest of us women scorn as "only sex objects."

And he wasn't really *that* dumb, I told myself, probably using the same kind of reasoning men use; it was just a different *kind* of intelligence. And he definitely wasn't humorless: when Bill the Tool Pusher decreed—after observing the effects of our bending on the men—that Madge and I were to be bra-clad, Bobby protested by stretching my bra around his broad chest beneath his T-shirt, then wearing it into the galley, where he leaped onto a table and did an impromptu strip to the roars of the men.

Despite our disparate life-styles, I began to picture me clinging to his biceps in the pages of *People* magazine. Just as I had once imagined taming a jungle lion, making him my pet, I fantasized that Bobby could be trained in the arts of graceful living, equality of the sexes, even open relationships. "Ah'm not gonna hold yuh to not doin' it with anybody else," he said as he bent me backward in a spine-rending kiss before boarding the helicopter at the end of his shift.

With the naïveté of a post-sixties liberal, I believed him, too oblivious to realize that even, *especially*, if he was an animal, he wanted the undisputed possession and certainty that every other man I had ever known had wanted. Thus, it didn't seem too important when I let J.T. the Tour Pusher—the craggy, sixtyish night boss—tug me into his bunk when I went into his cabin to wake him with a cup of black coffee. I admired his still-powerful nude torso, his macho tales of oil-field fights and South American whorehouses. Then, too, I had been mopping all day, and wanted to lie down.

"I kin make thangs easy out here fur yuh, gal," he said persuasively, adding the bit of pull necessary to make me melt onto the mattress beside him. "Why, with *yore* face 'n' figure, you'll never have to do without!" When it turned out that he liked foreplay—at least, he-to-me—even less than Bobby, I told myself it was a generation gap—a notion reinforced when he told me that his sweet li'l wife of thirty years "never *touched* me down there with 'er mouth." But I wasn't a wife, was I? In J.T.'s view, it was okay for me to harbor sluttish obsessions. On the other hand, my status as oil-field trash made it unnecessary for *him* to please *me*. The whole thing was over in less-than-satisfying minutes.

And what difference did it make if I let Jimmy, Jr., glue an oil-company sticker to my ass as I mopped or teased Otis as we sat in the galley? I enjoyed his story about the time he bought baby goats for his children, stopped at an Alabama roadhouse, emerging drunk five hours later to find a Chevy full of goat shit; and the one about working in a water show in Biloxi after he got out of the Navy: "I did tricks with porpoises, yuh see"—he forked up a bite of what I call cottage cheese and spinach, but what he labeled "curds 'n' greens." "Wall, I got to rubbin' one of them dolphins' pussy after hours. Then, when we went on to do the show, she wouldn't do the tricks no mo', jes' kept flippin' over wantin' me to rub 'er pussy. Why, when 'er baby wuz born, ev'rybody said that fish looked jes' lak me!" At this point, Otis caught me looking down the unsnapped side of the Sears overalls under which he wore nothing. "Lawd, Lawd, I wish you wimmen'd never come out here," he moaned soulfully. Cutting a peach carefully in half with his pocketknife, he removed the pit and slowly squeezed the pink center in and out, in and out.

"One year, I wuz in so many fights thet I changed jobs nineteen times. Then I wuz made driller, I wuz only nineteen—the wildest 'un in South Texas, 'n' the gal I marrid wuz the purtiest. Fur the longest, I didn't even try to kiss 'er. Fin'lly one night I said, 'I'm gonna kiss yuh, gal, 'n' if you try to stop me, I'm gonna slap yuh.' So she let me kiss 'er 'n' other thangs, too. . . .

"When I wuz datin' mah wife, I didn't really love 'er. The first year we wuz marrid, I would leave the house 'n' go away fur days atta time without tellin' 'er. I kept on goin' out with oil field trash— I liked to drive 'em wild, gittin' 'em hot, makin' 'em come with mah hand, then laughin' in their faces, knowin' I wuzn't goin' to go out on mah wife. I never let *her* look at me or touch me down there. I still don't lak a nekkid wo-man—I wont 'er to wear a li'l baby doll pajama or sumpthin'. The purtiest thang I *ever* seen is a mare with 'er colt, or a cow with 'er calf—though I wouldn't lak the birthin'— *thet* would make me sick. I guest I hated wimmen in a way. . . .

"The first one I fucked wuz mah seventh grade teacher—her boyfriend wuz the coach 'n' he caught us behind the curtains in the school auditorium. Then there wuz a gang of girls in town when I wuz fifteen called the Scarlet Angels—to join up, they had to fuck twenty-six boys at onc't. One of 'em ast me to help 'er git the boys, 'n' I did, 'n' set up a li'l cot for 'er out in the woods. We all went out there 'n' fucked 'er, then beat 'er up. Most of them girls turned out whores. . . .

"There wuz this one girl, one of the boys wuz really in love with 'er. I made a bet I could git 'er to fuck— the rest of 'em would be waitin' out where I said we'd park to watch through the windahs a the pickup. Well, the boy who loved 'er said, 'go on, do it!'—lak thet, a dare. Well, I did it—got 'er to fuck, with him 'n' the rest watchin' without her knowin', 'n' the next day at school, he looked like he might cry. We wuz boxin' in the gym—I wuz Golden Gloves—'n' he said he wonnid to box me. I said, 'uh uh, don't do this,' but he did, 'n' I broke 'is jaw, almost beat 'im to death—the other boys had to pull me off 'im. Later on, when a boy wuz mean to *my* boy at school, I went over to 'is house 'n' called him 'n' his daddy out, 'n' drew a circle in the dirt, 'n' told thet boy to stand inside it, 'n' stay there while I beat 'is daddy up. . . .

"After mah baby boy wuz burnt up out on the rig—we wuz jes' lak *thet*"—he crossed his callused fingers—"I tore up the truck he'd got kilt in, burned it, too. Mah hair turned white overnight, 'n' mah wife's did, too. I never did keer whether I lived or died—twict, I fell off the derrick, I forgot mah seatbelt, had a concussion onc't 'n' went into a coma. Now when I git off the rig, mah wife meets me at the airport, we go somewhere to eat 'n' she tells me about all the relatives I don't give a damn about 'n' when we git to the house, I don't even go in, jes' go out to git mah fishin' pole, or look at the garden. . . .

"But at the funeral, *his* baby—mah grandbaby—crawled up into mah lap, he never done thet before, as though he meant to take mah boy's place. I believe in thangs lak thet. . . .

"Also, thet there's an afterlife. Are you sure you 'n' me didn't know each other in another life?"

As he talked, Bill the Tool Pusher spit tobacco juice over the rail into the sea. We were sitting on the deck on a couch he had ordered two roustabouts, like slaves in old Rome, to bring up for us when I said I wanted to look at the ocean after supper. Bill had begun coming up to me two dozen times a day to make some out-of-context comment about my qualities as a cleaning woman; it had taken me a while to realize that, rusty from thirty years on oil rigs, nearly as many of monogamous marriage, he was flirting.

Bill's jeans were tight over his ass, his work shirt stretched across labor-broadened shoulders, his eyes were a hard clear blue, projecting a gaze respected by every man on the rig. Now they followed me with a look of infatuation, but it was not just sex he wanted: Bill followed his own rules, and one of his rules forbade fucking on the rig. "How would yuh feel about bein' put on a pedestal, taken keer of, somebody's baby?" he had asked me a few days before over midday "dinner" in the galley; I had explained how I lacked respect for women who allowed themselves to be financially supported for a lazy lifetime. The next day, he had shifted his tack: "Ah sho' would lak to set you up in a li'l apartment somewhere, let

yuh write whatever yuh want, see whut yuh come up with. . . ."
The part of me that still yearned to be taken care of had involuntarily leaped alive, at the same time that my brain had toted up
the price.

Now, as he said he was thinking of moving to a rig in Peru and
taking me with him, I was puzzled; why didn't he just make a pass,
since everyone on the rig already assumed he was sleeping with
me? "Nope. It's all 'er nuthin'," he said firmly. I felt flattered but
uncomfortable, my Bible Belt upbringing, and what would only be
called respect, rising like a trained snake from a basket. As a Southern woman brought up to indulge Daddy, and revere God the
Father, I found his patriarchal approach incestuously sexy. I wondered aloud how he would feel if he knew how I really lived, but
apparently he was ready to forgive, even love, a Mary Magdalene.
"I don't keer whut you done before," he said with a grave simplicity. "Thet's between you 'n' yore God. Lots of wimmen are lak
ten-cent novels," he went on, "but you—you're lak a book a man
could read furever."

On the last night of my shift—the July-off-Georgia temperature
102°, the air conditioning broken again—Bill commanded two
roustabouts to carry mattresses up to the pilot house where the two
of us might sleep more comfortably. Around ten, through with his
rig chores, he joined me. "I cain't sleep up here 'side you," he
shook his head sadly; "I jes' re-lized—the men would thank I wuz
sleepin' *with* you 'n' lose respect." I giggled; hadn't they already
watched the animals tote the mattresses up for us? He laid his big
hand on my thigh, uncovered where my legs crossed beneath my
cotton shirt. "No man has ever wonnid you in yore life as much as I
do. But I cain't stay up here with you tonight."

Where does that leave my desire to get laid, I wondered crossly
as I rode the elevator back down to B deck; while I still admired
Bill's strength of character, it was beginning to seem extreme.
Walking past Otis's cabin, I saw him toweling his home-grown extra-large torso. "What you doin'?" I asked. Within minutes, we
were in the bottom bunk, my painted toenails sticking through the
inadequate curtains, sliding around like crazy beneath the picture
of the girl who looked like a peach "with the pit took out." "Remember thet thang ah said ah learned down on the farm?" Otis
whispered moistly into my ear. True to his word, he adored all the

nuances Bobby, J.T.—and probably, I guessed, Bill—neglected; despite going barefoot in Mississippi until fifteen, he was at least cognizant of the existence of the clit.

When I got back to my cabin, Madge was lying in her bunk, dipping soda crackers into a can of Hershey's chocolate syrup ripped off from the galley. "You look like the cat that swallowed the canary—or something," she smirked. "Who was it this time?"

"Did you know Otis is possibly the best lay on this rig?" I asked.

"But what about Bobby? *He's* the one you're *in love* with? And J.T.? And Bill?"

I mentioned J.T.'s madonna-whore split, Bill's preference for mares and colts, and the fact that Otis was being transferred before long to a rig at the South Pole, then inquired seriously, "What do you *really* think about these guys, anyway?"

"Well," she said, a stream of chocolate dribbling down her chin, "they're just like any others, I guess."

"But don't you think that—despite their lack of, uh, subtlety—they're high-energy, passionate, adventurous—just like the pioneers who settled the West?"

"Nope," she yawned, dabbing at her chin with a Kleenex. "They're just like all the rest!"

Back in Savannah for two weeks, I joined Madge in trips to Dunkin' Donuts and riverfront bars and in showing over and over—till our "outside" friends began to gag—the slides she had taken of the drill-rig floor, the lifeboats, the galley, and us naked in our cabin, or sitting in the laps of our muscular-and-tattooed new pals. The plastic surgeon with the taste for garter belts particularly disapproved of my fondness for the riggers: "I guess *their* pricks are always sticking straight up," he said sarcastically. "Don't you women know it's bad manners—like guys sitting around talking about tits-and-ass—to obsess about these rednecks all the time?" Madge's old boyfriend protested petulantly.

In a few days, Bobby phoned from South Tampa, alternating several phrases like "Ah love yuh" and "Did yuh do it with anybody else?" and "You're muh wo-man 'n' ah'm comin' up thyah." Before I knew it, he was throwing his Bowie knife at the roses in my wallpaper, enthusing about what a good gun rack my French armoire would make, and lying around naked in my four-poster bed.

I was running to the liquor store for more Chivas—riggers are big spenders—or standing over a hot stove in July, boiling up crabs or gumbo; and—since the sign of a genuine good ole boy is that he wears his cowboy boots even in summer—pulling off his sweaty boots.

"Hey, girl," he said, lying back on my ruffled chaise longue, flipping through the galleys of my book, "this hyah's got a lot of words the av'rage person wouldn't understand." Bobby, off the rig, was something else. For one thing, he was drunker. For another, he had an uncanny—well, *animal*—intelligence. When he went fishing one afternoon, he came back within an hour. "Ah *knew* there wuz a man here," he growled, grabbing my ass possessively, then smiling half-threateningly at the nervous man friend who had just stopped by.

With none of his energy absorbed by twelve-hour shifts on the rig, Bobby was as overpowering as an Act of God. Indeed, Hurricane David had come through Savannah during the first part of his visit, but instead of protecting me as I had hoped, Bobby had rushed out to the beach alone to cast his reel into the surf as the tide crashed in—"Hurr'canes make real good fishin'"—then had come back to crawl drunkenly, sandily between my sheets. As I anxiously searched for candles, and sat in the dark looking out the window at the oak trees bending over, the branches crashing around my car, he had slept the sleep of the near dead.

Each day since his arrival, however, he had faithfully phoned his sweet li'l mama down in "Flarda": "Come on, girl," he now commanded, "we're goin' down thyah!" Fifteen minutes later he stood impatiently beside my car as—stepping over broken limbs and debris—I lugged out a cooler of Heineken's and an inflatable beach float; then, holding my nose, threw out the plastic bucket of bait-shrimp he had left rotting in the backseat two days before. As we squealed out of town, he took off his dark aviator glasses, and, adding them to the wreckage about town, wordlessly threw them out the car window. "Why'd you do *that*?" I asked. "Broke," he answered monosyllabically. Later, after I had had a boyfriend who threw a television set through a motel window, another who had thrown a rival down my apartment stairs, I would have known better than to ask. Nor would I have been surprised when, that night, Bobby grinned and tugged me toward the bed in the cheap motel halfway to Tampa where he lay drinking Maddog 20-20. How could he possibly want sex, I wondered—he'd stopped every hundred miles for a blow job.

The next day, we stopped at a souvenir stand where I bought—as Southern kitsch—a laminated wooden box depicting, in full color, the Last Supper on its lid. "Thet's bea-*u*tiful!" he moaned appreciatively as I pulled it from the sack.

When we pulled into a Hess station outside Tampa, a pretty but worn-looking Clairol-blonde attendant in a miniskirted green-and-white uniform came out. "Thet's Jo-lene," he grinned. "She married. But she'll be jealous when she sees yuh." I was quickly learning from his variegated comments that my lover was the stud of South Florida. "Naow don't be sayin' 'black this' 'n' 'black thet' when we git there," he warned as we drove into the outskirts of town. "Daddy's in the Ku Klux Klan."

Big Bobby, Bobby's daddy, looked like the daddy of all South Florida rednecks. "Daddy got arrested for D.W.I. last month," Bobby confided admiringly. "When they took 'im in, he 'bout *tore* thet jail up!" Bobby's mama's mouth was prim as she dished out the field peas at the dinette in their mobile home: we weren't married, and instead of a good local girl, I was oil-field trash. The boys were drinking Pabst, and I wanted one, too, but I knew that since I was female, that wouldn't do. Determined to be submissive, I drank sweetened iced tea and looked at baby pictures of Bobby for two hours while he and Big Bobby went off to shoot their guns and inspect the cows and the red wiggler worm bed.

Coming into South Florida, Bobby had pointed out rivers and creeks with Seminole names, and I had been impressed with his knowledge of Indian lore. Now, as he drove to a nearby riverbank, we passed an ugly concrete block building—"the shrimp processin' plant"—and he told me the sad story of working there twelve hours a day, six days a week, for minimum wage, wringing my heart-strings as he had when we first met.

On the cool, dim river, he guided our rented canoe effort-lessly, soundlessly around and beneath roots, rocks, hanging vines, through the sure presence of snakes and primordial ooze, an eery silence and an ambiance of mysterious life just below the surface. As he passed me the bottle of Maddog 20-20, I examined his light features for traces of the dark Seminole grandmother he had mentioned. I was in the thrall of nature, the primeval again, admiring the way he guided our vessel, cutting through the water as though he was born to it; till, imagining myself an Indian princess with her brave, I stepped delicately from the boat toward the dock, falling instead into the water between. As I struggled, drenched, bedraggled onto the pier, Bobby laughed until he was indeed red-faced.

On the way back to his parents' mobile-home-made-into-a-house (by virtue of a carport added onto one side, a makeshift "addition" on the other), we stopped at the farm where Bobby's "baby brother" and his wife lived so he could look at the cows again. As he and his brother talked out by the cow shed, I walked among the scroungy bluetick hounds, the red wiggler beds, a snorting hog encapsulated in a cage barely larger than its huge body, feeling like Miles Franklin in *My Brilliant Career*, the Australian novel and film in which a sensitive and creative young woman clings to her dreams in the raw environment of a farm on the outback.

But my musings were disrupted by a fight between the brothers: I looked up to see Bobby in his cutoff Levis and rubber flipflops, grinning malevolently as he jumped up and down on top of the red wiggler beds, and his brother running toward the ramshackle barn, then returning with a pitchfork aimed right at Bobby, who now grabbed me by the forearm, shoved me into my car, jumped in himself, and drove off, burning rubber. In the midst of a classic comic chase scene, it was hard to feel any longer like a romantic heroine.

The next day, Bobby's li'l mama took the Greyhound to visit her sister in Eufala, and Bobby and I went out to look at Ford pickups. I waited while the paperwork was done on a green Ranger. "The 'surance wuz fourteen-hundred dollahs 'cause I done wrecked all them Trans Ams," Bobby said proudly as we drove away. When he stopped at a supermarket, he instructed me to go inside and buy Pabst and chicken gizzard while "Ah'll jes' set out here 'n' look at the pussy." That night I fried the gizzards and made cream gravy, but this time I matched Bobby and Big Bobby beer for beer.

Back in Savannah, we put the slats back in my four-poster bed, then I packed Bobby's bag for the rig. "Ah'm gonna have us pendants made with rebel flags on 'em," he exclaimed, swigging Chivas on the side of the bed, "'n' we're gonna wear 'em the *rest* of our lives!" When I allowed as how I doubted I would wear such a thing, he asked, "Wall, how 'bout an ankle bracelet?" Grabbing my wrist, he tugged off my favorite silver band and fitted it—just barely—around his own. "'N' keep *this*"—he shoved me back on the tangled sheets, pushed up my nightgown, and clipped a pubic curl with his pocketknife—"in mah billfold to sniff on."

As I drove to the airport, I stopped several times so Bobby could throw up. He grinned as though his nausea had nothing to do with his massive consumption of Chivas: "Ah always git this way when I have to leave somebody I love." Why was I so exhausted as I drove away from the airport, Bobby, his duffel bag, rod and reel silhouetted against the morning sky? It was as though a plug had been pulled and my will had been sucked down a drain. And I had only a week to recuperate before my second shift on the *Venus*.

When I arrived with an azalea in my hair, Bobby pushed me against the jack-house wall and kissed me out of view of the others, but he wore a scowl. "The word's out Bill'll fire me if he finds out. Ev'rybody says he's after yuh—'n' a *lot* of other thangs, too!" he growled, enumerating a list of reputed fuckees that amazed even me.

In addition to scrubbing and mopping twelve hours a day, I now had—since I was "in love"—to reassure him by going down on him five times a day instead of three. Bill insisted I eat every meal with him in the galley and spend my evenings with him on the deck. And with the force of a semi hurtling down the straightaway between Macon and Savannah, J.T. and Otis forged ahead in their belief that since they had had it once, my body was theirs forever. "Yuh know, some folks git into trouble by the thangs they do," warned Jimmy, Jr., whose advances I had spurned despite his claim to having played backup with Willie Nelson. "Ev'ry wo-man's got sumphin' ev'ry man wonts—'n' if she plays 'er cards right, she kin git anythang she wonts." But all I got as the boss's girl was the right to take a nap each afternoon when, likely as not, I would find Bobby, all 225 pounds of him, sacked out in my bunk awaiting the matinee he now considered his due. "J.T. told me you did some thangs," Bill told me over his nightly mashed potatoes and gravy. "I told 'im to shet his filthy mouth!" I was finding out that the sexual freedom I took for granted as a single woman could become cause for chaos in the closed world of the rig. As Jimmy, Jr., said, "You wimmen may wont it thet way, you may thank it kin be thet way, but it just ain't thet way!"

"One 'a you gals is gonna be attacked," Calvin the Craneman

said to me casually as I threw the leftovers from the galley into the water below. I had been recalling sitting in Alfredo's Trattoria in Greenwich Village with New York friends, Alfredo Viazzi himself bringing a bottle of fine Ruffino to our table. . . . But now I watched the sharks and barracudas swerve to the surface for a moment, recalling the way the two sharks faced one another on Calvin's shoulder blades when he went shirtless, then looked at his knuckles as he lit a Camel. For the first time, I noticed the LOVE and HATE crudely etched on either hand. "What do you mean?" I asked. "Ah jes' thank one a you girls will git attacked," he repeated firmly. That night, he asked Madge to walk with him on the deck. In fifteen minutes, she was back, slamming our cabin door breathlessly. "That man *attacked* me," she gasped crossly.

The riggers had minds unmuddied by the torments of conscience of middle-class men in flux. When Bill sent a new woman "back to the house" for sleeping with the Company Man, while the man stayed on, he couldn't understand my anger. "Whut's it to you? She's not yore special friend or anythang—'n' the way she wuz swangin' them thangs around in thet T-shirt, the ends looked lak ten-penny nails!" As I tried to explain sexism and situation ethics, he looked as puzzled as though I had been speaking Chinese. After all, a woman's place was back in the mobile home or the whorehouse waiting, wasn't it? He looked at me suspiciously, a thought dawning for the first time: "You gals ain't spies for Getty Oil, are yuh?"

He was beginning to remind me of an incipient good ole boy in my writing class in a north Georgia high school. In a poem entitled "The Man Who Did What He Said," the student had described a meter reader who complained of a barking dog, and when the dog's owner failed to respond, simply took out his pocketknife and cut off the dog's head. I was learning that despite the tremulous look that crossed his face at the sound of the word "Texas" or John Denver singing "Country Roads," Bill's sensitivity didn't extend to blacks, Jews, women, or anyone who didn't toe the line.

"Have you noticed that while most of the guys use the words 'nigger' or 'queer' in the first sentence of almost anything they say, they still accept Ed because he's one of them?" I mused to Madge in our cabin.

She lay naked on the bottom bunk, reading a copy of *Offshore Life*, her favorite reading since she had decided she wanted to become a roustabout. "I don't understand why you care about all that stuff," she mumbled, "or about Linda getting fired either. You know," she went on, "I heard J.T. say that he thought you were getting a *bad attitude*." It was a phrase used around the rig about anyone who didn't fit in smoothly.

"Why the hell did he say that?" I asked crossly.

"It says here that according to a Global Marine company spokesman, 'the offshore drilling industry remains one of the few where people are injured or killed on a regular basis,'" she read enthusiastically.

"Aside from not being able to get me back in the sack—why *did* he say it?" I persisted.

"Oh, probably those big words you use. And the way you talk about books, politics, even the E.R.A., for God's sake! Nobody—but *no*body—cares about things like that out here!" Excitedly popping an Oreo into her mouth, she held up a full-color shot of a rig going up in black smoke. "Wow, look at *that* mother!"

"It's the work that forms their views," said the ex-med student soon-to-be-ex-roughneck, as he commiserated over coffee in the galley.

On the oil rig, I had realized that it was not just the sexual simplicity—the ease of role-playing, the black-and-white of "men are men, women are women"—that drew me. ("Of course it's macho!" exclaimed the ex-med student, "you can't *manipulate* oil out of the ocean!") It was also identification. The anger that was the riggers' common denominator echoed my own frustration as a woman in society. Though I had become a writer and a liberal, and they were mostly Johnny Six-Packs who strove to fit, and expected their women to fit, their hard, working-class view of things, I, too, felt at home listening to country-western bands playing songs such as "Take This Job and Shove It." I also had experienced their societal impotence and had sometimes indulged in their favorite means—hard drinking and sexual compulsion—to relieve it.

On the rig, I had received more positive reinforcement for my femininity in one day than the average woman in New York gets in a year. There, too, several myths had permanently hit the dust for me—the one that says macho men just act that way because they're uncertain of their masculinity; and the other that claims certain—

or common—interests, politics, and social class as the most reliable indicator of intelligence, and the basis for sexual and emotional attraction. Despite my overlay of literacy and liberalism, not to mention my basic training as a feminist, I had inexorably succumbed to the desire—lately out of fashion—to be possessed by a strong man.

Yet while the job offshore was a lark for me, it was serious business for the riggers, a way for a high school dropout or an ex-felon to make a good living, to advance, with the few assets of well-developed biceps, animal grace, common sense, and guts. It was a situation in which the maintenance of a macho image was imperative: older tool pushers could be pushed out by young men who had learned in a few years at drilling school what it took the former a lifetime to master; roustabouts jousted to become roughnecks, derrick men to make assistant driller, and the "company men" rose from the ranks—or geology school—to boss everyone.

But now my constant anger was interfering with my occasional bursts of empathy. That morning, folding a T-shirt that read, "Hondas were created to keep niggers off Harleys," I wondered what else would enrage me that day. I was beginning to feel I was living amidst a chorus of randy Randy Newmans constantly singing "Good Old Boys"; yet instead of enjoying their attentions, I felt like slapping them off like mosquitoes. I was turning into a shrew with seventy-five husbands, a blue-collar wife who yelled at the men whenever they walked over my freshly mopped floors. Now I wore the ugly blue maid shoes all the time. "Don't you have any work to do?" I lashed out at Bill when he interrupted my scrubbing for the twentieth time that day. "If you wanted us out here for companionship, you should've hired geisha girls!"

What, I wondered, had happened to the woman who worked with her brain instead of brawn, and slept with whom she pleased? I was tired of making forty bunks a day: I already knew the sheets would be grease-gray and come-crusted, no matter how recently we had changed them, that the small bound notebooks on each man's desk contained not romantic personal entries, but numbers and scrawled drawings of the drill rig, and that the only books on board aside from "girlie books" were Louis L'Amour Westerns and nautical adventure stories.

"You cudda learned jes' as much about oil rigs by readin' a *book*," Bobby accused me suspiciously. When he told me at the end of my second shift that he wanted me to quit "'cause ah cain't stand 'em lookin' at yuh 'n' knowin' whut they're thankin'," I agreed with relief. For each of my two shifts of fourteen straight days, 168 hours, I had earned $1,033 less taxes. Back on dry land, I drove straight to my apartment, stuffed the ugly blue maid shoes in the trash, and phoned in my resignation, then lay down for a few days to sort out my brains.

Twice during his next shift, Bobby called over the shortwave radio to say maudlin things that I knew could be heard over the entire rig; at his shift's end, he phoned again from Tampa. "Come on down hyah, girl—ah want yuh," he ordered. He was drunk, but by now I understood that that was normal for someone just released from the prison of the rig. "Ah'll meet yuh at the entrunce to the state park"—I recalled an ominous wooded spot we had passed— "Ah love you so much, girl," he went on, tugging at my heartstrings in that Willie Nelson way again. Never mind that it was a six-hour drive, that I would arrive at one a.m. Being a Good Woman to a Good Man had become, over the past weeks, my challenge; this was my chance to prove that, free of the distractions of the oil rig, I could stand by my man in the best Tammy Wynette fashion and at the same time tame a genuine wild animal.

A half-dozen hours later—somewhere around Ocala—I dialed the number he had given me. "This 'ere's 'is cousin," said a girl. "Who 'er you?" "Didn't he tell you I was coming?" I asked. "Naw. He 'n' D.R. went over to the roadhouse. They'd been drankin'. . . ."

It was 2:00 a.m. when I drove past the desolate state park. Feeling like the perfect target for a passing pickup, I drove up to an isolated 7-11. Why does *every*thing to do with Bobby always turn out to be a black comedy, I thought disloyally, walking through the electronic glass doors of the store just as a massive electrical storm broke loose, lightning streaking the sky, sheets of warm water falling right behind me. "Aw, shit!" said the girl behind the counter, who was the only other person in the place. "Ev'ry time thet happens, those 'lectric doors git stuck 'n' won't open till it stops, 'n' ah cain't go home. . . ." True to her comment, I found that we were indeed to be companions until the storm's end. In the meantime, I phoned Bobby's Mama and Daddy's mobile home, and Bobby answered the phone. "Where you at, girl?" he laughed as though he had never dreamed I might actually come.

When I finally pulled up to his parents' trailer out of the still-driving rainstorm, he came out into the carport and enveloped me in a bear hug. "Ah love you so much, gal," he growled into my wet hair. But inside, he collapsed on the couch, and ordered me—since *I* had traveled so far to serve him—to "take mah boots off, baby—ah'm tired." Then, as li'l Mama sat narrow-lipped in her chenille bathrobe with the peacock on the back, he and Big Bobby elbowed each other and guffawed as I described the difficulties of the trip.

In bed in the spare room, Bobby regaled me with the things he planned to do to my body and, despite my fatigue, did a few of them. The next morning, he turned to me on the pillow. "Did yuh do it with anybody else?" he asked, his eyes narrowing. "Bobby, you were gone a *month* . . . ," I started to protest, indulging in my oblivious liberal honesty. "If ah wuz mah daddy," he snarled, "ah'd knock you clear 'cross this room!"

On that note, I quickly dressed and went into the combination living-dining room, where Bobby's Mama, sitting at the formica dinette, offered me a cup of coffee. "You know, Li'l Bobby wuz so upset las' week," she began. "He wuz drunk 'n' cryin' 'bout Rayline, thet wife 'a his. He won't *never* love nobody but Rayline, yuh know." Next came a long tale of the cruel marriage between Li'l Bobby and Rayline, and the kidnapping of her only grandchild. "Why, she even wonid 'im to pay *chile* support. Thet boy's so broke up, he'll *never* git over it. 'N' you know?"—she looked at me pointedly—"*she* wuz older 'n' him, too!" As though compelled by some force, I looked up toward the sideboard to see one of my favorite photos of my daughter Darcy, looking, in her glamour pose, with her fashion model's stance, a *Vogue*ish thirty rather than twenty—the very picture Bobby had threatened to snitch from my apartment to put over his bunk instead of a centerfold. "He says thet's your *daughter*," Li'l Mama said accusingly.

Contemplating these things, I looked down at the table, where I saw a half-opened letter, written in a spiral design on round stationery. "Dear Bobby," I read in words written alternatively in blue, red, and green Pentel, "I went to the beach today. My boobs got burned. The baby was kicking a lot. . . . I wish you'd admit it was yours and take me with you. . . ." By the time Bobby lumbered out of the bedroom, stretching like a bear coming out of six months' hibernation, the phone calls from the girls had started. "Tell 'em ah'm not home, Ma," he said, grinning as though pleased with his own cleverness.

I had read that apprehension was an aphrodisiac, but now I decided it was time for this idyll to end. Without looking at a truck driver or construction worker, or stopping at a truck stop to indulge my fantasy of working as a waitress in one, I drove straight back to Savannah. That night, as I lay in bed trying to recuperate, Bobby called me again from Tampa, drunk: "Ah've been thankin' 'n' thankin' 'n' ah jes' cain't stand it thet yuh did it with J.T."

"But Bobby, you *said*—"

"Another thang," he slurred, "all them books 'n' thangs at yore house. I know whut yuh really thank—thet ah'm a dummy or a chauvinist or sumpthin'. . . ."

"Bobby, I *never* said that."

"Why, you don't even know *how* to be a good Southern wo-man," he went on drunkenly. "A good Southern wo-man would've slapped mah face when ah said all them thangs about doin' it with dawgs, or other people. And a good Southern wo-man sure as *hail* never would've took me to a fag bar where ah ended up in a three-some with a queer. . . ."

"But Bobby, *you* were the one who asked him to go home with us."

"Must be 'cause you're from Etlanta, 'n' there's so many Yankees up there," he concluded angrily, clicking down the receiver.

I didn't care. My rose-printed wallpaper, French armoire, and I were safe. I was sure I had O.D.'d on macho men, and the romance of the working-class life.

APRÈS RIG REFLECTIONS, OR IS THERE LIFE AFTER MACHO MAN?

At first, the muscles of my more civilized men friends felt like Silly Putty beneath the sleeves of their Cardin jackets. I alternately shuddered at the memory, and missed the intensity of life on the rig.

In a few months, Madge called from Galveston, where the *Venus* had moved. "Bobby told Bill that you slept with J.T. and Bill had to be kept from killing J.T. . . ." It sounded like the words to a song I hadn't heard lately. "Bobby's getting married to a twenty-one-year-old virgin; they're moving into a new mobile home. And oh, yes, Bill's leaving his wife and taking the new girl to Peru with him.

"Another thing," she went on. "We women feel like we're living in a nunnery these days. We've found out that with these guys, we *have* to stay on that pedestal." She chuckled. "But they sure do remember those *wild* days when *you* were there!"

When the book tour for *Fatal Flowers* rolled around six months later, I was sure I was cured of my rhinestone-cowgirl predilections. In Houston, it seemed safe to put on my pink cowboy hat and ask the limo driver to take Madge and me out to Gilley's, billed as the biggest cowboy bar in the country. "I put your book jacket on the bulletin board," Madge told me as we rode through Texas City and the scent of oil refineries, "but Bobby stuck the virgin's picture on top of it." While Madge, still surfeited on muscle tissue, sat at a table and drank Lone Star, I watched the Texans fall off the mechanical bulls, then danced with shitkickers who held me tight around the neck and pulled me across the concrete floor in a fast two-step.

In Atlanta, a few weeks later, I went out to dinner with an urban attorney whose articulateness seemed like a relief—until I found out he was more interested in talking than going to bed. A few days later, I met friends in the bar at the Dixie Hunt Hotel in Gainesville, Georgia, then went with them to a down-home redneck roadhouse with a tiny dance floor, a live country-western band, and probably more cowboy hats per square yard than anywhere beside Gilley's. As I slow-danced with a bearded hunk, he pulled me tight in a bear's embrace. "You're so purty," he crooned. "Ah'm a ranger up in White County. Lookin' fur me a wife. Kin you cook?"

PART THREE

THE
MACHO MAN
DEFINED

Needless to say, the macho men I encountered on the oil rig were not the first in my life, nor would they be the last. For years, with the same intensity with which Jane Goodall observed chimps, I had—albeit unconsciously—studied them. "I would like to come back as a man," wrote a nine-year-old girl in my poetry class. "It would be like two bodies in one. Once I was the behelded and now I would be the beholder." Without my knowing it, that had been my mission as well.

As part of my unacknowledged pendulum phenomenon, I had "abused myself," as we say in the South, with an array of such men, starting with the incipient good ole boys at Tucker High School and its rural environs, through my brutish young soldier–first husband, to—after my discovery of my artistic interests—macho musicians, poets, and painters who had at least an avocation, if not a vocation as no-good good ole boys; indeed, in whom the very "femininity" of their chosen occupations led to overcompensation in the areas of pistol totin', hard-drinkin', 'n' womanizin'.

"You understand *men* better than women," complained a conservative and somewhat disgruntled male psychologist, after hearing me read from *Fatal Flowers*, my book on growing up Southern and female. Helmut Newton, in his book of photographs of *White Women*, portrayed—through images of pornographic wealth, sexual objectification—a narrow view of femininity, womanhood. It may have been that my view of men was as narrow; my relation to them as shallow, unresolved; yet after my oil-rig experience, I realized how long, and with what dedication, I had unconsciously been "beholding" men, particularly macho men.

I already knew, for instance, that while the riggers—like factory workers, shrimpers, real or hard-hat cowboys, and other working-class laborers—represent one clearly defined type, there are numbers of others. The macho man may come in the form of a professional jock, adventurer, or—like my new amour—warrior; he may work as a policeman, fireman, taxi driver, or bartender. He might be a renegade member of the middle class, like my cousin

George; a flamboyant entrepreneur, or even a macho professional —lawyer or politician. He can be an artist or writer, clothing himself in either a real or a contrived—à la Norman Mailer or James Dickey—tough-guy image. He is almost always the drug smuggler, gunrunner, hit man, street hustler. He may be in prison, gay, or, perhaps the ultimate macho, a black man (who, because of my lack of experience of him, I was inadequate to define).

While he comes in urban and rural varieties, I was aware, too, of his natural habitats—the streets of Brooklyn and the Bronx; the surfing beaches and the mountains, but not the cities of California; the ranches and land rigs, but not the ski slopes, of Colorado, Wyoming, Montana, the Dakotas; the deep Southeast and -west, particularly Louisiana and Texas; Brownsville, Galveston, New Orleans, all sleazy port cities; near each fishing lake and in every remote mountain area; in Alaska, or the French Foreign Legion, and—if he's a serious smuggler—Colombia, South America.

He is the natural habitué of rodeos and VFW halls, army towns and truck stops, gun ranges and service stations with beer coolers in them, and bars with names like Jaw's Tavern or Humpin' Hannah's. His bona fide accoutrements include the ubiquitous keys, nail clippers, and pocketknives; hunting dogs, "gee-tars" and banjos; guns, parachutes, canoes, boat motors, and planes; four-wheel-drive vehicles equipped with CB radio, oversized tires, an American flag on the fender, a "How 'Bout Them Hostages?" bumper sticker; old issues of *Soldier of Fortune* or *Guns and Ammo* magazines (though, one would hope, not a copy of *How to Kill*, volume 5, sold in their pages), plus the girlie "books" that contain—in accordance with his earthy tastes—the most graphic GYN shots; and in certain circles, twenty-four-karat-gold coke straws, or a bracelet spelling out his name in diamonds.

The macho man rarely drinks daiquiris, takes cooking lessons, hangs out at libraries or poetry readings (why writers like James Dickey have such a problem with image), or decorates interiors with *any*thing beyond moose skulls, bearskins, Rebel flags, wall hangings composed of guns and/or bows and arrows, and oversized coffee tables topped by oversized ashtrays and fuzzy dice. He does guzzle Lone Star or Black Jack straight up, skewer the boar at a barbecue, or shovel the bivalves at an oyster roast; he also makes Miracle Whip–and–processed-cheese sandwiches on white bread, and goes out to the store for more beer or Lucky Strikes.

And though he races cars, jumps out of airplanes, rides in rodeos, and wields blow torches, he never jogs, rides a bicycle, throws a Frisbee, or plays golf or tennis; and *never* does he don a shirt with a small animal on it. He also eschews Docksiders, crewneck sweaters, and Ralph Lauren or L.L. Bean imitations ("He ain't no real cowboy!" snarled my oil-rigger lover when I showed him his lookalike, fashionably dressed in the style of *Urban Cowboy*, on the cover of *Gentlemen's Quarterly*). He does don olive drab and camouflage fatigues, wrinkled Hawaiian shirts open to the navel; T-shirts with pictures printed on them; real work shirts and Sears Roebuck plaid flannels; Levis, cutoffs, jumpsuits, and down or leather jackets. His footwear includes flipflops, brogans, work boots, and "gen-u-wine" cowboy boots; among his accessories are Peterbilt belt buckles and hats of all kinds—Red Rose Feed, Claxton Rattlesnake Roundup, or army fatigue caps, and, of course, hard and cowboy hats. He usually sports crinkles à la Clint Eastwood around his eyes, may still roll his Camels' pack in his T-shirt sleeve, and often comes decorated with from one to four tattoos— from the most rudimentary image to complementary, full-color productions such as the two sharks facing one another on the shoulder blades of a shirtless seaman–oil rigger. Indeed, just about the only time macho costume is questionable is when one wonders whether an Army Ranger who dons a dress for his male lover is still macho!

Yes, as a woman who had done lifelong homework, I knew a macho man when I saw one. I knew that Clint Eastwood and the Cowboy in the White House were macho, that Burt Reynolds and Willie Nelson are not particularly. I could go to a party and instantly assess whether there were any macho men present. "How 'bout *me*?" four old boyfriends—sailboating, hedonistic playboys all—clamored at a recent gathering when I said I might be writing about women and macho men. I didn't even have to think about it: "Not you—you're too refined," was my immediate—and insulting—response. I knew the real macho man never asks, or argues about whether he *is* one. In fact, he may actively object to the image, as did novelist and woodsman Jim Harrison in a letter to *The New York Times Book Review* on September 19, 1982, regarding an advertisement for one of his books.

The political issues of the macho man are gun control, organized labor, and, above all, stemming the Red Tide; with the exception of the maverick, he identifies with patriarchal authority—the drill sergeant, the tool pusher, the Cowboy in the White House. But he often disagrees with other macho men as to what is appropriate or moral, and holds his own prejudices within the group, as in the case of a gunrunner who considers dope smugglers to be lowlife, and the soldier who hates "gun nuts," cowboys, and rednecks. "Do you know why cowboys wear tennis shoes?" asks a good-ole-boy joke: "So folks won't think they're truck drivers!" It's like the one that describes a redneck queer as a boy from Alabama who laks girls better'n football. Both draw a line.

For, almost always, the macho man has a clearly defined set of values. "The three thangs most important to a man," stated Rogene, a Southern cowboy whose monicker is a slurring of "Roger Eugene," "are whiskey; cows, 'cause cows mean money, 'n' if you're not too good lookin', you cain't git wimmen without money; and wimmen." Having put women in their place, he went on to advise that a man should "never hurt a cow or insult a man who kin make yuh money."

He is usually consistent, particularly in his pride, his refusal to be integrated into the system. My father was only macho in that he refused, throughout his failed life, to ride a bus or work as anything but a tire salesman. And he often clings to his provincialism. David Bottoms, author of *Shooting Rats at the Bibb County Dump*, a work with what must be the quintessential macho book title, told me before he had ever been there that he knew what New York was like: "The sidewalks on either side of the street are movin' ramps crammed four abreast with Jews, Chinese, Italians, and Puerto Ricans, all drinkin' daiquiris—'n' once you git on, you cain't git off!"

Unfortunately, facilitated by his early Insensitivity Training, the macho man often permits himself a slew of common prejudices, easily dividing the world into himself and his kind, and Others—a position that enables him to hate niggers, wops, polacks, chinks, and queers (unless he is one), and when necessary to kill gooks and Commies. In addition, this "it's a lick" attitude allows him to risk his own life and feelings, which he hasn't learned to value much either. Indeed, the macho man might come closer than any other in living out Yeats's dictum that the only subjects worth serious consideration are sex and death.

For macho, as I sometimes painfully learned, means more than dressing up like John Travolta in *Urban Cowboy*, or hanging out with the boys at the Eleven-Mile Highway State Line Bar and Service Station. "But zay bod-ees, zay ees so be-oou-ti-fool, zay minds, zay ees so square—not like zee New York faggots!" enthused my French friend Christiane after she followed me onto the oil rig. Three months later, Christiane the Animal Lover cried out to me over the phone that "Zay ees an-i-mools!" describing how, when migrating egrets and finches—"birds like jewels, from the islands"—lost at sea, weak and in need of water, feathers falling off, staggered about the rig, the men kicked them aside in irritation, stepped on them like cockroaches, and ignored their screeches as they were fried alive in the pipes on the deck. The black-and-white views that at first seem such a relief after life's ambiguities turn out to have a hard, bottom-line reality—a line that, at times, moves beyond mere image into reality.

And though the macho man jokes, as he does about almost everything else, about that brutality ("Let's go beat his ass!" a usually literate male friend exclaimed when I told him that a Florida State criminologist had written a paper claiming the South to be no more violent than any other part of the country), it is a line that, too often, can shift to include even someone he once "loved"—as in the case of the jealous drug dealer who threatened to have acid thrown into the face of the woman who—despite his tearful entreaties—had rejected him. His attitude is exemplified in Willie Nelson's album *Redheaded Stranger*, in which the protagonist shoots the woman he loves, as well as her lover, when he finds she has been unfaithful, then—in a frenzy of self-pity at his loss—kills the woman who steals her horse. According to Albert Goldman's *Elvis*, the sensuous singer's women were emotionally seduced, excessively romanticized, then reduced to pseudo mothers—a pattern common in the macho man. Despite—perhaps *because* of— the macho man's need of his woman, his easy sentimentalization of their relationship, she is not exempt from his callousness—as evidenced by the popularity of caps inscribed with mottoes like "Bitch, Bitch, Bitch," and bars where "nice" women, e.g., wives and mothers, rarely enter.

And any defection from her role is quickly punished. A long-distance truck driver staggered drunkenly into his house to a screeching, nightgown-clad wife; tossed her over his shoulder, took her outside, threw her into the back of his refrigerated truck, and slammed the door; then went back inside and fell asleep on the couch: if he had not suddenly wakened an hour later, wondering where she was, she might have died. Joe, a Greek patriarch with the popular macho habit of hanging out at a bar each evening till his drunkenness overcomes him, reported going home one nine p.m. to find that sacrilege had taken place: dinner had been eaten, the leftovers thrown out, the dishes done, without him. "Make me a sandwich," he commanded his long-suffering, housebound wife; when she rebelliously replied that there was nothing in the refrigerator, he went into the kitchen, spilled the eggs, milk, and mayonnaise onto the floor, yelling, "You're right—there's nothing in there!" Indeed, for many a macho man, nagging wives are a matter of course, "the way women are"; instead of changing his ways, he simply develops devices for dealing with incipient hysteria. Marty, a four-times-wed Key West shrimper, came up with a means known among his barroom buddies as "Marty's Method": instead of sneaking into the house after a binge, he enters noisily, pulling off his clothes as he climbs the stairs and loudly calls, "Anybody wanna fuck?"—at which his understandably turned-off spouse represses her rage and pretends sleep.

But while comments such as "Commere, you heifer, you!" or "I'm gonna take you home 'n' fuck yore brains out!"—usually accompanied by aggressive physical gestures—may give a woman a sense of imperative missing in her other, less lusty relationships, remarks like "Why, I wouldn't hurt you for the world!" convey the possibility of their opposite. Asked by the proprietor of a small Western hotel if he wants "the bridal," the cowboy bridegroom in a poem by Michael Ondaatje says, "I'll hold onto her ears until I get used to it."

"Nobody ever puts anyone on a pedestal except to knock them off," Savannah therapist Charles Tuggle said. And the macho man never *asks* whether he can indulge in "skull-fucking" (semi-forced oral sex), engage in anal intercourse, or begin sex without contraception—an act that that "prisoner of sex," Norman Mailer, with his anti-female-and-contraceptive views, would undoubtedly applaud. For along with his early Insensitivity Training, the macho man also receives seminars in sentimentality about himself and what is his, even unto his sperm, if not the women into whom he sticks them—making him an ardent, if unlikely, Pro-lifer. "If you killed mah baby, why, ah guess ah'd jes' have to kill *you*," my oil-rig boyfriend, Bobby, whispered self-righteously to me in bed, just moments after, almost in the same breath with, his protests of love and lust.

When Anne visited me in the north Georgia mountains where I was teaching poetry in the local high school, angel-faced twins, banjo pickers in the band at a local honky-tonk, said they would like to dedicate their newest song to her. As a hillbilly in muddy boots at my end of the table tried to persuade me "to go out to the pickup fur a minute," she chatted pleasantly with the lead musician, asking whether the twins were as sweet as they looked. "'Bout as sweet as rattlesnakes!" he guffawed, elbowing the hillbilly, whose name had turned out to be Lamar. Still, we both gasped when he announced the name of the number as "Whips and Chains," then went on to join in lyrics that jovially evoked new images of sadomasochism in every verse.

Even the supposedly more sensitive macho artist manifests many of the macho man's worst characteristics. The Famous Southern Poet gave inebriated readings and made crass remarks to faculty wives. Florida novelist Harry Crews drunkenly propositioned young women students from the podium at Agnes Scott College, a sedate Presbyterian women's school ("All you girls who're under twenty-one, and willing, meet me out back after the reading"), then later that evening, ate the butterfly bandage off the forehead of a woman reporter who had recently been in an automobile accident. A male associate in the Poetry in the Schools program yelled, "Hey, baby!" or worse, crudely imagistic suggestions at women we passed as we sped to our teaching assignments. And a sentimental steel-guitar player, reduced to a reptilian state by the kind of good whiskey that—according to country-western singer Hank Williams, Jr.—is not supposed to let you lose your place, began our friendship with social rape.

Yet the steel-guitar player enjoyed discussing the origins of bluegrass as much as playing it and drinking. But it was as though his sensitivity, his aesthetic interests—what he might regard as the "feminine" parts of himself—were deficits to be contradicted. "Your muscles feel like a truck driver's instead of a professor's," I said, thinking to compliment the visiting English-department head with whom I close-danced on the dais of a riverfront bar. "I'm not a professor—I'm a poet!" he protested, enjoying the blue-collar image, yet calling on the categorization that says macho and poet match, macho and scholar don't. In order to make his point, he stayed up till four that morning, getting blind drunk on Black Jack, dancing on the tabletop at a local pub, despite the fact that he was scheduled to speak at a Savannah college at nine the next morning. For just as I—in order to stay, despite my literary activities, a good ole girl in good standing—must spend a certain amount of time on hair, nails, clothes, the macho artist must remain—in order to maintain his image of himself—instantly able to fall back into the rawer role.

"It's more fun to be one of the bad guys," Kin Shriner, star of the soap "General Hospital," said on "Donahue." "It's boring to be a good guy. And besides, the bad guys have their own music." Though Shriner was speaking of his show's sound track, it's true: the "bad guys" do have their own music. Such country-western musicians as Hank Williams, Jr., who likes to have "Women I've Never Had" (according to one song title), his self-destructive father, Hank Williams, Sr., and the equally self-damned Jerry Lee Lewis, as well as David Allen Coe and Waylon Jennings, who had each spent time in prison, might be said to be the macho man's philosophical gurus.

Indeed, "good ole boy" is just another way of saying sociopath. In his worst moments, the macho man really *is* the insensitive brute he often appears to be. And just as I once imagined—because of my puritanical Bible Belt background—that I was one of the few women who experienced the "sin" of sexual desire, I also thought for a long time that only crazy women like me—or Elvis's girl friends—would put up with the extremities of such scoundrels.

I didn't yet realize—despite my unconscious research—how many different types of macho men there were, or how much that cruel word, *class*, had to do with many of their choices.

All I knew was that in my more confident moments, the man with whom I most identified was the maverick who apparently had escaped the dictates of conformity—who, against great odds, controlled his own life, embodied the activity and assertion that I, as a Southern woman, had been brought up to deny myself. Freely and fearlessly, it seemed, he took the risks, acted out the aggressive impulses I had learned early to repress, or else judge myself crazy—"The only man more masculine than you are," my sportsy woman therapist would explain later.

He was macho to my macha, my embedded twin, the part of me

that—rather than staying put, or doing what I'm told—*flies*: simply, the man I would have been.

THE OUTLAW AS HERO, HERO AS OUTLAW. OR THE MACHO MAN'S MACHO MAN.

It was not until I was divorced for the third time, and living alone for the first, that I intimately encountered the macho man in his pure form, the man who—without literary associations, or an artist's license for his craziness—makes no excuse for his role, indeed glories in it, who, deliberately eschewing the right wines, classical music, and *The New York Times Book Review* as the domain of "pussies," is thoroughly what he is, seemingly at one with his image, his code. Then, during the five years between my third divorce and the time I met Zane, I involved myself with a number of them.

When I first met the Pirate in a River Street bar, he approached me with an original line. "What's a girl like *you* doing in a place like *this?*" he asked, his long-lashed blue eyes taking in my then-fashionable gaucho boots, my twill skirt, my jacket with the designer label on the pocket. He wore a billed seaman's cap, had boyishly regular features, a curly blond beard, and was only slightly taller than I. When I agreed to sit down at a table, listen to the music, and have a drink, he said he was from Charleston, a deep-sea diver with his own company, and was thirty-one. He asked how old I was, and when I replied, "forty-one," said, "I'm really thirty-nine—I just thought you wouldn't go out with me unless I lied." Later, drunker, we took in the topless, but not the Spider Lady's, act at the Emerald Lounge, then went on to close-dance at Dr. Feelgood's, where he pulled my red panties off in a dark corner while I giggled in ambivalent reluctance. As we finally fell into my four-poster bed, I thought to ask his name. "Just call me the Pirate," he growled, grabbing me by my long hair, pulling my head backward. For the rest of the night, he whispered fantasies of swashbuckling seamen, ravished maidens, into my ears, pounding my flesh from every angle.

The next morning, I woke to see his clothes draped over the wicker chair across the room. His designer jeans still held the curve of his ass; the cloth of his shirt looked soft, expensive. The shoes he had left on the raspberry-colored carpet beside my bed were the very style I had begged my ex-husband Ben (who had preferred the heavy brogans that Laura and Darcy teased were a sign of his uncertainty about his masculinity) to buy because I found them so sexy: wedged chamois loafers and these were very worn, as though they were among the Pirate's favorites.

Despite our mutual tastes in footwear and erotic fantasy, I considered him, like my other macho boyfriends, a diversion, a one-night stand. "A sign like that makes me want to *tear* things up!" he said, looking at the Do Not Disturb notice on my studio door, and I laughed, thinking him just another sexy, if inappropriate, lover. I didn't yet realize that I had just met a character as outrageous as any I could have imagined; that—as a living character out of a Harlequin romance or a James Bond thriller—Jack, as he had finally told me was his given name, was to become an archetype in my research on the pure macho man. I didn't know that, over a period of time, I would fall in love with this self-described pirate who lived on a yacht off the South Carolina coast and drove a $42,000 Mercedes-Benz, who often showed up at my Savannah apartment sporting a black eye or broken bone, and who sometimes met me in the company of bodyguards. Nor was I aware that I was embarking on a relationship that would continue, off and on, for half a decade; or that, at one point, we would promise that no matter who else we were involved with, we would always sleep with each other—a promise I would break only when I met Zane.

It takes one macho man to intimidate, or garner the respect of, another; and that respect is directly related to such macho manifestations as biceps, guns, and don't-give-a-damn toughness. When the Pirate came by one day just after I had begun living with Zane, I mentioned that my new lover was teaching a class that afternoon on how to shoot a .45, but would soon be home, and how nice it would be for them to meet—they would have so much in common! It was the first time he ever unexpectedly popped in without hanging around till he had manipulated—or forced—me into bed.

"That's what *I* want to experience while I'm here," breathed the Radcliffe-educated New York screenwriter CBS had sent down to research her script on my oil-rig experience: "A real live Rhett Butler!" I was supposed to tell her what good ole boys are like in twenty-four hours or less, and had just described the scene in which the Pirate had phoned me to say he was coming to see me despite my protests, and the man sitting in my living room. "Get rid of 'im," he had commanded, "I'll be there in thirty minutes!" By the time he had arrived and had threatened to throw the terrified man down the stairs, he didn't have to: my other interest was already running, his unbuttoned shirt waving behind him, his shoes in his hand. For the rest of the night, the Pirate made passionate love to me, telling me over and over how much he loved me, asking whether I loved him, and saying he didn't want me to do things "like that"—that is, sleep with other men. Never mind that he had a wife at home on the yacht, and at least one other serious girl friend ("I always have three goin' at once—my wife and two others"), plus a continuous rotation of waitresses, barmaids, and other sexual receptacles: his first words to me each time we met, no matter how long it had been, were "Have you been faithful to me, girl?"

Yes, I seriously doubted whether a northeastern Cliffie, used to what novelist Rita Mae Brown calls "that distinct lack of sparkle, which Yankees call sincerity," would willingly put up with—on a day-to-day, or even hour-by-hour basis—the kinds of shenanigans common to such scoundrels. The Pirate, for example, reappeared unexpectedly every few weeks—or months! Basic to his mistrust of women, his commitment to total male dominance, he wouldn't participate in woman-initiated dates or plans, indeed hated to make plans at all. It was a quality convenient to a busy woman still in search of the "right" man; I could go away for a half-year to teach, and when I came back, our relationship resumed itself as though it had been yesterday—with a little extra romance thrown in because of the separation. And because of my rapport—probably induced by my Bible Belt background, the Holy Trinity, Christ's death at thirty-three, and all that—with the number three, it seemed to me an appropriate number of lovers for a God-man to have. I wasn't upset when I met him out with another woman, the other in his trilogy, because I was usually out with another man; then, too, it was a situation that reinforced fantasies of threesomes—two women and him, of course—that he liked to talk about in bed. One night, as we danced around, beside but not with each other, barely acknowledging one another's presence, at a local disco, I felt exhilarated rather than jealous. Because our attraction was disconnected from "real life," it felt like a junior high school crush in which one might at any time run into the skittish boy who was the object of one's affections—a kind of return to innocence, to spontaneous response that so often seems missing in adult life. It was as though he hung suspended for years in the delicately romantic "first stage" of a relationship.

I had read that fishermen who go to sea to return home only periodically have the most romantic marriages. For many macho men, such as the oil rigger or rodeo rider, such space is automatically built into his relationships (for instance, Otis the Welder planned to leave his wife and family back on the Mississippi home-place during a six-month gig on a rig at the South Pole); others go out of their way to create such distance by simply being unreliable, unpredictable. "I ust tuh tell my wife I wuz drivin' a car down to Flarda," explained a used-car dealer. "Then I'd hop a plane to the B'hamas, gamble. all night—never even see the damn ocean—'n' come home the next mo'nin' just as bushed as if I'd been workin'!" He grinned, pleased with himself at his ingenuity at outwitting the limitations of family life. The Pirate's deep-sea diving company, in addition to his other "work," provided travel up and down the Eastern seaboard to Miami, outward to the Caribbean Islands, and south to Colombia, but when he was in town, and his wife, Linda, knew it, he had realized that "If I just come home that night—even if it's five in the morning—it's okay. At lease she knows I'm not spending the *whole* night with another woman!" It's a style natural to the macho man, who considers any limitation on his comings and goings tantamount to psychological castration, who prefers to sentimentalize his relationships, which is naturally easier to do from a distance—and who doesn't wear too well up close anyway!

The fact that I rarely saw the Pirate meant that when I did, I could afford to turn geisha girl, scrubbing his back, washing his hair, pouring his wine while he made calls, did deals from my footed bathtub. As a deep-sea diver, water was his medium; I could ignore the wet towels he flung around my apartment like a tomcat flinging his spray, leaving his mark, and could even adapt myself to his demand that I not use birth control. Blinding myself to what a pregnancy by such a renegade—married, to boot—could mean, I often relied on the Russian-roulette infrequency of our lovemaking.

"I just don't want *any*thing between us, baby," he whispered urgently, jerking my diaphragm out and flinging it across the room, barely missing a beat. It was the most macho thing a man had ever done to me (in fact, this happened twice: first with Jack; then with a blue-eyed sailor from Istanbul who couldn't speak English, and didn't even comment on his act). If the Pirate's unpredictability was one part of his bad-boy charm, another was his outrageousness—an attitude with sexual frenzy as its goal. Vibrators, beer bottles, belts, bedposts (as in, "How would you like to fuck this bedpost, baby?")—any things, substances, places, positions, or orifices were tools toward the passion we both held paramount. Indeed, it was our mutual commitment to the sexual nature of our relationship that bound us. We usually began our sex play within five minutes—or five seconds—of his knock on my door, as in the time he pushed me down to the foyer carpet, shoving the neck of the half-full bottle of St. Pauli's Girl he had been drinking beneath my pushed-up skirt, into my vagina, as we fell together to the floor. He didn't have to know about the G-spot—he was bound to hit it by accident.

Nor did it matter if I had other guests: "At *least* let me shut the door," I pleaded, as he tugged me down to the bed. "Just get 'em to come on in here with us," he said, laughing at my shock. There was one thing I should have learned by then: there was no use appealing to his sense of propriety, or even something as universal as the incest taboo. "I'm just an animal, I guess"—accompanied by a self-satisfied grin—was his favorite boast.

Frequently, with what seemed a genuine—and joyous—animal awareness, the Pirate applied just the right degree of gut wrench, the perfect jab of emotional S & M to jazz up our passion. There was the time we visited my friend Madge, and he spent the whole evening persistently and systematically coming on to her—sitting close to her on the couch, holding her hand in his, murmuring in a low voice how he now suffered from tremors of his thighs from being under water so much—as she looked embarrassed and I glared at him from across the room. By the time we walked down her stairs toward his pickup, I was in a mute fury. "What's the matter, Rosemary?" he taunted, "you don't mind if I make it with your girl friend, do you?" Through visits to two bars, and a discotheque, I snarled as he smirked, the smile of a man who has achieved his ends playing at his lips. Back at my apartment, as he made love to me lustily if not tenderly, conjuring images of Madge in bed with us, I responded excitedly in spite of, because of, my spent rage.

Or the evening he called to demand that I meet him in the bar at the Savannah Hyatt: I arrived to find him with another woman —"An old girl friend, just ran into 'er," he explained, smoothing my hair possessively as the other woman stared at me coldly —and the kind of entourage with which macho men—from good ole boys in their pool halls to "businessmen" surrounded by their bodyguards—love to encircle themselves. "That guy's the richest Cuban in Miami," he whispered confidentially, "and the other two—the gunmen—always ride in the car behind him when he's down there."

He turned his attention back to the woman. "'N' Penny used to live on the yacht with Linda 'n' me when she was redecoratin' it for us. . . ." I felt a jab of envy. I had begun having strange fantasies— that I was Linda, she, me—of her, the Pirate, and me living together, bound by a polygamous love. "What's she like?" I asked. "I always wondered what kind of woman could live with Jack." "She's kinda quiet, doesn't say too much," Penny replied sulkily, as I envisioned a woman mute, powerless in the face of the outrageous infidelities her husband played out just beneath her nose. It made me think of what I had heard about Ted Turner's skirt chasing, the bruised look his wife, Janie, wore in the pages of *Time* magazine. "Yeah," the Pirate laughed. "I just sent her 'n' the kids off to Texas to visit 'er mother—whether she wanted to go or not!"

As the group rose in the glass elevator toward the rooms they had taken for the night, I covertly took in Penny's frizzy perm, T-shirt, cotton drawstring pants, Chinese Mary Janes, comparing them with my high-heeled sandals, slit skirt, low-necked blouse. Who was supposed to sleep with whom, I wondered. In the Pirate's room, we sat on the double beds, sharing tokes and sniffing lines of coke as he ordered quarts of Chivas Regal and Black Jack from room service. When he had introduced everyone, he divided his attention equally between Penny and me, an attitude she apparently didn't appreciate: when the others decided to hit the bars on River Street below the hotel, she left with them.

At three in the morning, after the Pirate and I had made love twice, and watched *Fort Apache, the Bronx* on the color Magnavox,

Penny tiptoed back into the darkened room and began to undress. "That other guy, that Cuban—I didn't want to sleep with him. That's the only reason I came back in here," I heard her explaining crossly. As she climbed into the other bed, the Pirate got out of ours, and into hers, caressing her stiffly held back. "Go back to your friend," she said angrily, her voice muffled in her pillow. Watching him cajole her, fondle her long breasts, I noticed with unsisterly satisfaction that they weren't as nice as mine, and felt at the same time that strange titillation—a combination of fascination and jealousy—that is part of seeing someone with whom one is intimate, being intimate with someone else. When dawn turned the hotel windows to rose, and faint snores replaced the sexual sounds from the other side of the room, I passed the other bed to dress, and the Pirate pulled me down toward him, kissing me tenderly. "Last night was wonderful," he breathed, as though the whole evening had been a romantic encounter between just the two of us.

I kissed him back because by then I knew to protest would have been as futile as Jackie O., then Kennedy, trying to cure that other Jack of his womanizing. Nor did it do any good to try to outfuck or outrage him. My dates with other men, my continuing search for the "right" man, merely inflamed his sexual interest, and made him say things like, "I hope his balls fall off!" None of them, he told me from the bathtub, were good enough for me. I should marry a wealthy man. When I snapped a Polaroid of him as he stood naked, my menstrual blood dripping from his still-stiff penis—producing an image that would have sent many men's testicles recoiling inside their bodies—he was unperturbed: throwing the photo impatiently onto the bed table, he pulled me back toward the sheets.

I knew in my heart of hearts that my relationship with the Pirate was sick. But as long as I was uncommitted, I felt I could afford it; because he was rarely available, or available only out of season (in season being marriage, the long run, and all that), I could gluttonize myself when I had the chance. Besides, it was fun to play out in caricature the roles I had been brought up as a Southern woman to fulfill. It felt *right* for me to sit beside the bathtub, scrubbing his back as he talked. *Right*—despite his lack of interest in my life, career, problems—for me to listen as he obsessed about his smuggling, business deals, even his wife. *Right*—though he rarely reciprocated—for me to massage the tension from his calves, spasming from too many deep-sea dives. *Right* for him to come to my apartment, fling my towels around, drink my booze, fuck me, and then leave.

According to the proprietor of a California S & M club interviewed on "Donahue," his clients are mostly high achieving, responsible men who seek relief from decision making, being in control. I, too, found my temporary subservience relaxing, a release from thinking about myself, the introspection of writing. Nothing was too sexual or outré for him to say or do, no service or sexual position was too submissive for me to assume. We each had our parts down pat and, sharing an unspoken pact about the nature of the drama, played them tongue in cheek.

Naturally, since he treated me so badly, I began to fall in love, imagining I wanted the flung towels on a more regular basis. "Well, what do you think about that?" I demanded. We were lying in bed; I had just said a lot of things about my growing dissatisfaction with our relationship, its chaotic, uncommitted style. "About what?" "About all those things I just *said*," I snapped, imagining I was about to get one of those stories about a-man-who-met-a-dog with which Southern men evade serious—read, Yankee or "pussy"— discussions. But the Pirate wasn't even into that minor diversion. "Oh, I just think you were talkin' that *woman* talk," he answered lazily, pushing my head back down toward his penis, where, in his view, it belonged.

Yet his sexual audacity was just a reflection of his personality as a whole. To the Pirate, the concrete world—matter, money, women —were simply fields for manipulation, or the Big Game. Indeed, the same detachment, the same love of the sport, that made him a wild lover, made him a risk-taking entrepreneur as well. What could be called sociopathology seemed so at one with his boyish charm, his pleasure in his life, his effervescent energy and enthusiasm, that it was hard to fault him. "Every morning, I wake up thinking how I can make money that day!" he told me with obvious relish. While he might complain that he had to come up with $4,000 by the next day to make the payment on the shipyard he had just bought, the same fun-loving dash would fill his voice as he called his bank from my bathtub. "The secret of dealin' with banks is to owe 'em a *lot*," he advised with an irascible grin as he waited for his connection to the bank president he had manipulated, by the sheer amount of his debt, into becoming his patron.

Since I was so unworldly in one of the two areas he considered the most important in life—sex and money—he liked to advise me. "Get as many credit cards as you can, borrow as much as you can on 'em, pay it back quick the *first* time, get 'em to raise your limit, then borrow on *that*—you can always leave town; they can't make you pay—and oh, yes, when you do get some CDs, borrow against them, too, as much as you can, and invest *that*. . . ."

To me it was like a song in a foreign language, but it wouldn't have been any use to try to educate him about *my* interests. Things as schoolteacherish as book-learning and writing were woman stuff, similar to woman talk, something cute that women—their heads permanently in perfumed clouds of unreality—do. "How many books a week do you read?" he asked once, looking at the stack tilting precariously on my bed table. When I answered "three— plus bits and pieces of others," he laughed. "That's about as many as I've read in my whole life! The best one was *Snow Blind*"—a story of cocaine smuggling—"but yours is good to jerk off with." His last remark was designed to irritate me. Yet he did enjoy my writing about *him*. "Maybe you *can* use my real name," he mused, his desire for notoriety battling with his need for a low profile as he read a page stuck into my typewriter.

"It's just a business, like any other," he said when I asked him whether or not he was afraid. "Like goin' to the bank or the law firm, bein' a banker or lawyer. . . . Yet I guess I'll get nabbed someday," he went on cheerfully as I toweled his back, ignoring the fact that he had already been to a federal prison on work-release for six months of the time we had known one another. It was the only time I had seen him disconcerted, depressed—once, even *impotent*. "But then, that's what St. Barts and the Dominican Republic are for. I wonder what I'll do there?" he asked himself, as though he were talking about what he might do when he grew up. "Maybe I *will* become a lawyer or banker. But I've got to make a couple more million first."

"But those people could *kill* you," I anguished, rubbing the hard curves of his ass, the perpetual tan between his shoulder blades. Every time the *Savannah News-Press* chronicled yet another drug bust or slaying, my eyes raced to the names. "Right *there*," he writhed in pleasure, adding, when I paused, "I'll kill you if you stop!" Then went on to answer me: "Just have to shoot 'em first, I guess," he said grinning. Although short—five-seven or so—he didn't carry a gun himself, "because guns get you killed."

While he talked, he buttoned the lower three buttons of a fluorescent-green Hawaiian shirt, pulled up the khaki camp shorts he planned to wear to the board meeting at the Savannah Bank & Trust—ever the sartorial bad boy, he was now in his tropical phase. While shampooing his white-blond hair, I had noticed how much grayer it had gone since we met; his thick beard, his chest curls, were silvery now, too. The crinkles at the corners of his mischievous blue eyes, the white lines in his tanned face, had deepened through the years as well, yet his expression was more boyish than when we had met.

As he buckled his belt, slid bare feet into canvas deck shoes, I picked up my Polaroid camera to capture the way the electric-lime shirt turned his baby blues green. But now, since he was a success—just as surely as a bank president or judge—in the coastal underworld, he must have suddenly felt he had something to lose. "Don't do that," he flared, like a primitive afraid of the camera; "If you do, I'll kill you."

He spoke that phrase—"I'll kill you!"—more and more often now, I noticed. Yet his apparent pleasure in his life, his oneness with it, made it hard to judge either his criminality or his womanizing; like Jack Kennedy in regard to the latter, he was driven, energetic. In fact, when I exclaimed, as driven by his extremities I often did, "Jack, you're incorrigible!" he grinned as though I had given him an ultimate compliment. It was as though he had been born to the role of outlaw, and while his vocation was anarchy, nonconformity, it was one he cheerfully and willingly fulfilled, like a priest who retains a lifelong enthusiasm for his faith, his vows.

It had all started when he tilted the edge of a plastic wading pool in a variety store at nine, wedging a beach ball beneath it to release the rabbits displayed inside it, then opened the doors to cages containing birds, snakes, hamsters, gerbils, and guinea pigs—"Parakeets were still flyin' around in there a month later!" he laughed. While I was selling hand-scribbled poems on Peachtree Street, and dealing in black-market bubble gum, my pirate-lover was beginning his career by illicitly hawking Tootsie Rolls in grammar school, "takin' in ten or fifteen dollars a day, in a time when a dollar was a lot of money. I always know exactly what I wanted, never had any doubts at all," he went on, explaining his singlemindedness in pursuing his destiny as rebel. At fourteen, he dropped out of high school, left home to live in a shack near the Charleston docks, started his own deep-sea diving company at fifteen, then went on to accumulate tugs, ferrys, motorboats, yachts, seaplanes, automobiles, shipyards, bars, a trade, and a reputation. "Wherever the Pirate goes, there goes trouble!" laughed a fellow sailor, describing the time Jack had steered his barge the wrong way up the Savannah River, and had been stopped by the Coast Guard; "And he had so much grass growin' on it that it was a goddamn *lawn!*"

The very extent of the Pirate's outrageousness made just being with him a party, like someone continually tickling your funny bone. As a Southerner and macho man, the Pirate insisted on *fun*, indeed, was committed to it, and could turn even the worst experience into the kind of story with which such men love to regale one another. Such as the time he landed his ailing helicopter on Key Biscayne Boulevard in Miami, to escape the Coast Guard on foot. Or another, when he crashed his seaplane into a sea wall, the girl with him yelling, " 'If we get killed, I'll kill you!'—then she pissed in her pants and passed out!" Or when he opened a bar with a male strip show during which "I danced out during the first number wearing a raincoat with nothing on under it—just as I opened it up, the cops came in the door!" To hear Jack tell it, even the six months he had spent—after plea bargaining to reduce his sentence—in a federal work-release program had been fun. "They had us staying in this Salvation Army dormitory, 'n' we'd get girls to come in 'n' sleep with us, right there in those flimsy bunks with all those old drunks fartin' around us," Jack chuckled, then shook his head. "I don't know *why*—but the girls just loved it!"

In fact, he admired the kind of woman who was as wild as he was. "When I married Linda, I had been fuckin' Reena for a while. 'N' she didn't wanna give it up just because I got married. A week after the weddin', she came to the door with two tickets for a rock concert, and asked Linda, 'Where's Jack? I wanna take 'im to a concert.' Now *that's* a gutsy woman," he said admiringly. Indeed, he had married Linda instead of another woman he had simultaneously impregnated, "because I thought she'd be more *fun*"—and even *that* was funny. "They were both in the hospital at the same time, and when I walked out with Linda 'n' the baby, there was that other girl, her daddy pushin' 'er out in a wheelchair with my *other* baby. Hell, baby, if looks cudda killed, I wouldn't be here with you right now . . . !"

When he called to invite me to a party to celebrate his purchase of the oldest house on a private island off the coast of Georgia, I had begun living with Zane, and was determined to resist his charms, break our sexual bond. But I wanted to observe Flash Gordon on his own turf; and to see the woman I had fantasized, empathized with, even imagined myself to be. He had moved Linda and the children to the island—I thought again of Ted Turner, moving his wife, Janie, to the isolated plantation outside Charleston—along with Uncle John, a pockmarked Sicilian "employee." "She can't complain when I'm gone all night," Jack gloated. "It's a *lot* harder to get home when you have to drive forty-five minutes by motorboat. 'N' then, there'll be *lots* of bad weather!"

But the day of the party was dazzling, and as we sped across the water in the boat he chauffeured back and forth to the island, I noticed the sparkle in his eyes at his role as host, the way the wind swept his gray-blond hair and beard backward, his new Hawaiian shirt—blue, this time—away from his chest. While we rode by van up the dirt road from the dock, the junglelike foliage darkening the island around us, I saw that his other guests ranged from preppily dressed yachtsmen and -women, through post-hippies in cutoff Levis and stringy hair, to a woman who looked as though she had spent a lifetime as a Huddle House waitress, and a man who wore the Rock, crossed shovels under it, symbolizing Alcatraz, tattooed on a bicep beneath a rolled-up T-shirt sleeve. Wandering around the cleared area that surrounded the two-story frame house, they swatted the mosquitoes and guzzled what seemed an endless supply of Budweiser, gobbled the barbecued ribs, fried catfish, and deviled blue crabs—local specialties constantly being carried from the kitchen on huge trays by a crew of black gullah women, who spoke in the near-foreign dialect of the island.

"Now don't act funny when you meet Linda," the Pirate warned, suddenly serious, as we sat side by side on the wooden steps to the verandah. He was holding a plate on his tan knees, eating the limas and ham hocks with his fingers. But when a rangy faded blonde— raggedly, rather than chicly, pretty—walked toward us, a beautiful, white-blonde child with Jack's long-lashed eyes tagging along behind her, he jumped as though he had been caught by the Georgia Bureau of Investigation. Linda, I noticed, wore a wary, yet passive look, like a woman worn down by the need for constant surveillance. I tried to imagine the scenes he had described: Linda, hitting him over the head with a frying pan; he, tying her to the bed with her stockings and fucking her—"It's the only way to make her shut up!" he had said, expressing an attitude I was to find too soon that Zane shared; she, drunkenly accosting him in bed with another woman—"a high school principal, she almost lost 'er job over it. That's the one thing I hate about Linda—she can be a real mean drunk!"

Yet, as they stood discussing some party detail, my bad-boy lover turned Godfather before my eyes. "Now share your toys," I heard him say firmly to the little girl, who, a crown of wild flowers atop her cotton-colored hair, was tugging her hula hoop from the hands of a black island child. For the rest of the day, as everyone else grew drunker, more stoned, he divided himself impartially among his guests, joking but not flirting, filling their needs with a subdued largesse, while Linda moved stoically between kitchen and children, or among the revelers, taking photos. For a family album? I wondered, excited by Jack's ability to play both patriarch and wild man. Upstairs, I had seen my favorite of his shirts, the electric green one, blazing from a knob in an austere white bedroom, and had longed to caress it. Now, as a country-rock band played on the verandah, I watched him at the edge of the woods in the distance, unzipping his jeans to piss into the foliage, and felt that old surge of desire. The following week, I saw him in the foyer of a Savannah restaurant. He stood in profile to where I sat, the same subdued look on his face. He wore the fluorescent shirt, this time buttoned farther up, the woman with him was his wife. But I still felt that sexual rush, as excited by his domestic pose as by his outrageousness. He cut as romantic a figure as Daddy ever had, yet could still provide that protection a woman sometimes craved.

A month later, he called me as I lay in bed, a laminaria stick dilating my cervix in preparation for an abortion the next day. "I got me a new baby-blue Mercedes, four-door, another boat—God, I've spent a million this past month!" he enthused. "You know, I think I'm the happiest I've ever been. . . ." "I'm glad," I groaned, "but I really can't talk now." I had already reassured him that the fetus was Zane's, couldn't possibly be his. Otherwise, he might take a contract out on me.

As I hung up, gunshots and sex whirled in the delirium caused by the cramps in my groin. I was just beginning to understand. Despite my fantasies of that other Jack and Robert, my envy of

Jacqueline and Ethel, I was not, never could be, a Linda, a passive wife to a wilder mate. For if Flaubert *was* Madame Bovary, I was the Pirate, he, the man I would have been, my masculine twin, acting out my secret wildness, my hidden desires for anarchy. It was not Linda I envied, but him—his ability to move freely in the world, to enjoy both a sailor's bar like "Jaw's Tavern" and a suite in the Hyatt Hotel, to make his living through his wits and his energy, while enjoying both the stability of a home and a life of sexual adventure.

The first person to make me laugh after my abortion, a period of morbid melancholy, was the Pirate. When he called to ask how I was, I answered that I had been depressed since my recent surgery. "What do you mean?" he replied with characteristic outrageousness. "Since you killed your baby? There should've been a headline in the *Savannah News-Press*—'Authoress Murders Small Child!'" I had become obsessed with violence during the time when I had to make the decision, I went on to explain. "Aw, come off it! You know you love all that stuff!" he kidded. "Why, the one thing that would make you come back to me"—he referred to my new lover, my new commitment—"would be if I chopped somebody's head off and left it on your doorstep!" As I giggled in spite of myself, I realized that, if nothing else, Jack had permanently killed off my desire for the comfortable boredom of bourgeois life with the kind of conventional lover Mother would have called the right man!

PART FOUR

CONSORTING

WITH

THE

ENEMY

"It's snowin' up on the mountain, so you better brang yore toothbrush."

During my years of living alone, I met many such rogues as Jack.

Tonight, I was being entertained by a teacher at the school in the north Georgia mountains where I was working as poet-in-residence. She and her husband lived on the side of a private mountain, where the only other house, a half-mile farther up the slope, belonged to her sister and her sister's lover, a land developer who was responsible for their all moving there in the first place.

The developer, whose named turned out to be Randy, had driven down the mountain with my friend's spouse to pick me up at the little three-room cottage I had rented for the duration. Because of the deepening snow, they had come in Randy's four-wheel-drive vehicle. As I walked toward the Ranger jeep with Tony, whom I had met before, Randy rose to meet us. He was football-player big, beefily handsome, with the kind of baby face common to Southern men with Scotch-Irish backgrounds. As our brown eyes met, I felt a flash of recognition, a sure sexual excitement. I also instantly knew from my blood-sisterhood to such men, that this was one who preferred, indeed, required quarts of Jack Daniel's Black Label, hours in the woods with hunting dogs, sex that was raw rather than prettified, and stacks of gospel hymns on the stereo. "Sometimes he gets in that *mood*," his girl friend, Lila, a Yankee from New Jersey, would tell me later. "He just gets himself a bottle, plops down in his recliner, and listens to those records he likes so much." As we vibrated up the mountain over curved dirt roads, he enthusiastically talked over his CB radio, described the good hunting around us, and stared, whenever he could, at what body parts he could discern through my antique fur coat.

"Randy and I met right after I had been divorced from my first husband, a psychotherapist," Lila, a blandly pretty blonde psychologist, who worked at the nearby state prison for young male offenders, told me during dinner. "He was at a girl friend's apartment—we spent that night together, 'n' have been together ever since. Then he got tired of Atlanta, the city, 'n' moved up here. I followed 'im, then Judy 'n' Tony came. I tried to open a psychotherapy office in the town where you're livin'"—Demorest, Georgia;

population 300, with a law still on the books that prohibits blacks in the town after nightfall—"but had to close it: everybody thought it was a *massage* parlor!"

We had just enjoyed seafood crepes and a banana soufflé, incongruously washed down with quantities of the Black Jack with which Southerners will accompany almost anything. Yet it turned out that Randy was also that kind of good ole boy who could enjoy the "finer" things of life, such as expensive weekends at Hilton Head, flights to London for good theater. As we drank the Nassau Royale he and Lila had bought by the case during a recent trip to the islands, I told them about my wild life on the oil rig and how I had recently been photographed by the *Atlanta Journal-Constitution* for an article for the Sunday supplement on bourbon drinkers in the state. Sitting in a four-poster bed wearing an antique silk bed jacket, I had sipped Black Jack, delicately nibbled at barbecued ribs and chocolate-chip cookies, from a lace-topped bed table.

When Lila, Randy, and I at last stumbled, giggling, through the snow toward his jeep to drive up the mountain to their house— where, since we were now snowed in, it had been decided I would sleep—I felt barely conscious. The last things I remembered about the evening were sitting on a living-room couch with Randy and Lila, drinking more Nassau Royale, then suddenly becoming aware that Randy was pushing my head down toward his engorged penis, now protruding from his unzipped khakis, whispering, "You know you want it," while I futilely protested, "But what about Lila?" During the ensuing struggle, I heard—from my bent position, to my terror—Lila, who must have wandered off to bed during my unconscious phase—open a door from somewhere behind me to call out, "Randy? Are you comin' to bed?".

The next morning, I woke in a pleasant guest room, sunlight reflecting brightly—too brightly for my liquor-stewed brain—off the snow through white ruffle-curtained windows. I was naked between sheets I didn't recall sliding into, and, with horror, I noticed the male clothes flung about the small room, a heavy gold signet ring on the carpet. Here I was, stranded on a mountain, with a man who had raped me—who I had *wanted* to rape me—and a woman who might well be ready to kill me. I shuddered, imagining the butcher knife through my rib cage, my blood trickling into the snow. . . .

"How 'bout some coffee?" Randy said brightly, opening the door. As he spoke, he deftly retrieved his clothes and the signet ring without even looking at them. "Here's a little sumpthin'," he added, handing me an opaque flowered peignoir, playing the perfect host. "The bathroom's to the left; we're all out in the kitchen. . . ."

A few minutes later, clad in the peignoir, I wandered tremulously into the kitchen, wondering what might happen to me at Lila's hands. But as I joined Lila, Tony, Judy, and Randy at the kitchen table where they sat drinking coffee, everyone smiled and said "Good morning." We could have been at some kind of perverted garden party. "I really must have hung one on," I dissembled in the best Southern tradition. "I can't remember a *thing* that happened after we left your house." "Me, too," Randy said shamefacedly. Lila stood at the kitchen counter, her back to us, pouring more coffee and separating bacon slices. "Well, if you don't know what you were doin', I'm sure not goin' to tell you!" she said evenly, only a hint of an edge in her bland voice. As Randy walked over to her, kissed the nape of her stiff neck in the best guilty-husband manner, I shivered with relief that I was apparently not to be hacked to pieces or shot. For the rest of the day, as the snow melted enough for the drive down the mountain, we chatted lackadaisically, Randy and I avoiding one another's eyes. When we left, the two women—cheerily suggesting a tour of the local sights—drove me back into town.

That evening, back in my little rented house in the village, I collapsed on my bed with relief, and with a lot of weird feelings about myself. While Randy could be said to have raped me, I also knew that—beyond my feelings of sisterhood, the need for courtesy—I had wanted him to. If the macho man at his worst was truly an uncivilized animal, then I was his female correlative.

A week later, Randy stood at my cottage door, a red rose in one fist, a bottle of Black Jack in the other. He had come to apologize, he said. Yet within minutes, we were fucking atop the rose afghan I had just bought from a mountain craftswoman. "What did Lila say?" I asked after a while. "Nothin'—she's a good woman, she knows I git crazy when I git tuh drinkin'. . . ." As he left, he insisted I call if I ever needed "it" once I got back to Savannah. "I'll fly anywhere to give it to you," he enthused. "I do it fur lots of girls—why, jes' last week, I took care 'a five of 'em—the girls in my office, a woman up in Etlanta. . . ."

Several months afterward, he, Lila, Judy, and Tony drove to Atlanta for a book party for *Fatal Flowers* at my sister Anne's house. As the group trooped in, we all hugged, then Randy handed me a package. "It's a record of me singin' Christmas carols, 'Edelweiss' 'n' all that stuff," he said. "That's me, 'n' those are the girls who work in my office." There on an album cover complete with a misspelling that read "Edillwess" stood Randy, dressed in lederhosen, in the center of a group of women clad in black dresses and white peasant aprons, in front of the Hansel-and-Gretel-style building that housed his office in the fake Bavarian village of Helen, Georgia.

Next he unbuttoned his suit vest, ripped open three buttons of his pin-striped shirt to reveal a Superman T-shirt, then chortled like Tarzan. For the rest of the evening, he intermittently opened his shirt to the Superman image, emitted jungle sounds, and cornered and kissed my women friends, while Lila, her back perpetually turned, chatted pleasantly with the other guests. "Who *is* that man?" an attractive, recently divorced woman asked. "I don't know *why*, but I just let him take me out to his van and fuck me!" "Sh-sh," I whispered urgently, "that's the woman he lives with right there in the blue dress. I'll explain later. . . ."

That is, if I—or any woman—*can*, I thought.

.   .   .

"We sure don't have nothin' like you out here!" exclaimed the weathered blond man as he opened the door of his red pickup and I stepped up into it.

Just before coming to Wyoming, I had had my hair cut Chinese-style—bobbed with thick bangs—then hennaed a fiery vermilion. I *was* wearing boots and a denim skirt, but the shoes were high-heeled Italian numbers and the skirt a midi with a designer label. Even my faded blue denim jacket had forties-ish shoulder pads, a nipped waist, a Saks Fifth Avenue label.

As my blind date drove me away from my motel, I saw that he was no sartorial slouch, either. As heavily mustached and lined-of-eye as the original Marlboro Man (who, I had already learned, had been discovered in nearby—by Wyoming standards—Riverton). He wore an elegant three-piece pin-striped suit, yet the worn snakeskin cowboy boots through which he pressed the gas pedal, the clutch, kept him looking like the gen-u-wine Western lawyer–sheep rancher–topless-bar owner that he was.

I had been in Gillette, a boomtown made up of jerry-built one-story wooden structures and the land rigs and strip mines that gave it one of the highest per capita incomes in the United States, for two days when I met Gary through Claire. A brunette Dolly Parton dressed in cowboy boots and jodhpurs, dark curls cascading down her back despite her thirty-eight years, Claire had appeared in the back of the classroom where I stood reading poems to fifth graders. As the class ended, she joined me in admiring the rattlesnake-skin earrings which a ten-year-old—"Daddy made 'em for me outta a snake he kilt over'n the Badlands"—displayed in her pierced ears, then Claire explained that she had heard of me and asked whether I'd like to have lunch. When I said yes, I didn't know that I was about to become—for the rest of the week, with her as guide—part of the Gillette Syndrome, a phenomenon in which one hangs out in bars so long that one loses track of day and night. "'N' too bad it's weekdays," she would later say proudly. "The blood *really* flows on Saturday night!"

Now she had set me up with Gary, an old friend of hers who alternately glanced down the bumpy road ahead of us, barking indecipherable messages over a CB radio, and stared down the throat of my blue silk shirt as though I were a creature of some other species. At a roadhouse twenty miles down the highway, we met Claire and her ex-husband—still her lover—Billy. Throughout our meal of bloody steaks—vegetarianism is an unofficial crime in the state—Billy talked about money and mineral rights, mineral rights and money, as though they were the words to a country-western song, and his one refrain, aside from allusions to our looks or his sexual prowess. Indeed, I wondered if Claire was in love with him or with his idea of himself as future millionaire. Though her former spouse's intermittent trips to a pay phone to make calls to other women brought tears to her lovely mascaraed eyes, she wasn't sure if the relationship was practical. "At my age," she whispered, "I don't want to get involved with any men who're not really rich."

In between Claire's confidences, and Billy's sex-and-money lyrics, Gary fed me French-fried Rocky Mountain oysters, describing to me as I vainly tried to swallow how he himself castrated calves out on the ranch. "We just throw 'em on the fire like hot dawgs, eat 'em right then 'n' there!"

"In Wyoming, men are men, and sheep are nervous," goes a joke about the state. For the next twenty-four hours, Gary drove me around in his red pickup, showed off his law office, with its dusty wooden file cabinets, broad oak desk, and beehive-coiffed secretary, and bragged about his extensive cousinhood to Wild Bill Cody and other outlaws. When he described to me the Devil's Tower, an eight-hundred-foot phallic jet of rock spewed up from the earth fifty million years ago in the northeastern part of the state, it seemed an appropriate symbol of the culture. "Sex is our fun out here," he explained. "We don't believe in all that 'love' stuff." Nor in hygiene either, I thought disloyally, recalling the sour taste of his uncircumcised cock the night before. Then repressed my musings, recalling the poetry collage he had drunkenly stayed up all night to make for me. *To a Southern Lady from her Cowboy Lover* read the lavender Pentel scrawl across the flattened brown paper bag. Among the words, he had cartooned himself—cowboy hat and boots, pistol and holster at his hip, a long-stemmed pink rose between his teeth, and had glued on Western artifacts—a bullet, a bit of snakeskin, even a flat fossil imprinted with a fish skeleton from a mesa that had been the bottom of a sea when Wyoming was under water millions of years before.

Thanks to generations of role models, a lifetime of practice, Gary's sentimentality existed, I learned, in easy camaraderie with his callousness. Indeed, he could have been said to be a fitting descendant of Liver-Eatin' Johnson, who consumed the livers of the Sioux he killed in retaliation for the murder of his wife. (The film *Jeremiah Johnson* is a prettified version of his story. Johnson, along with Butch Cassidy and the Sundance Kid, is a part of Wyoming mythology, and is revered by subscribers to the Western mystique.)

That midnight, in yet another bar, Gary suddenly stood up to leave "for Denver with mah pod'ner" to interview strippers for his bar. "I'll be down to Lar'me"—my next week's destination—"to meet ya," he promised, nuzzling my neck with his mouth, his mustache, putting his rough hand down the front of my blouse familiarly. "Don't count on it!" Claire whispered from behind me.

From her, I was finding that Western women are tough as well. Yet it was a toughness that facilitated, rather than interfered with, having a good time. During the rest of my stay in Gillette, Claire and I cruised more juke joints, weighing propositions while two-stepping with miners and cowboys, until, in the middle of the third—or was it the fourth?—night, she stood up as abruptly as Gary had, and announced she had to go. Where? "To South Dakota to see my race horses—it's only a four- or five-hour drive." As we walked out to the parking lot together, Claire stopped to talk baby talk to two snarling dogs in the back of a pickup. "Aren't they the cutest thangs, guardin' the truck like that?" she cooed while I shuddered, imagining her driving into the night through infinite space and blackness, on roads like roller coasters over the Rocky Mountains. But the next morning, through the throbbing of my dehydrated brain, I heard the phone ring. "Hi!" said Claire brightly. "Some dude left an orange down jacket over in my room at the Ramada Inn. Pick it up for me, will yuh? I'll get back to you next week in Laramie. . . ."

Though Claire did send one of her many men friends to my motel in Laramie to pick up the coat, that was the last time I heard from her; nor, as she had predicted, did Gary appear. But by that time, a full week later, I didn't care anymore. I had met a six-foot-five rancher with whom I had danced—or "stomped"—at the Brass Boot in Cody. In Cheyenne, we had shared bad Chinese food and sweet Polynesian drinks in plastic coconuts topped by purple plastic orchids—probably the misplaced legacy of the Orientals who had come West to work on the Union Pacific. At a roadhouse in what seemed the dead center of nowhere, we had washed down bloody steaks with straight Black Jack, served by an unlikely girl in high-heeled sandals, a Southern-sweet organza blouse, while Willie Nelson sang "Georgia on my Mind" on the jukebox. And now he was about to drive five hard hours one way, five hours back the next dawn to his working ranch, just to sleep with me for one night—demonstrating the passion that—while just as brief—can wash away a woman's anger like a flash flood hollowing out gullies. Yes, even if they were often insensitive, sexist, mendacious, Western men *did* seem to put first things—like good booze, good times, good sex—first.

Four years later, in Wyoming for a poetry reading, I was approached by a vaguely familiar man with a weathered face, wearing a Stetson, accompanied by a large man with a paunch. "Don't you remember me from Gillette?" he asked mournfully, as though disappointed by the lack of recognition in my face. "Gary!" I exclaimed, suddenly recalling—not altogether with pleasure—his sour cock, the poem on the brown paper bag. It was time for me to go onstage, but after my performance, I came down into the audience, and for old times' sake—and to make up for any hurt I had caused by forgetting something as impressive as his penis, much less his face—sat down with Gary and the fat man. "Do you wanna ride a Caterpillar with me in the mawnin'?" the latter asked, regarding me with interest as Gary scribbled something on the edges of his program.

Macho Thoughts, I read, when he handed the program to me: *you speak so much of the perfidy of man and your Raw desolation of Female Sexuality But I as a man am also born of woman I also care!*

· · ·

"Are you gay?" asks the stocky, sandy-haired man in wire-rimmed glasses. I'm not surprised. For while I am wearing a clingy, low-necked blouse, a full, flowered-cotton skirt, and high-heeled sandals, I am also standing alone at the bar in Bananas, Savannah's one lesbian bar.

I am there because I have grown bored down the street at Who's Who, the other gay disco, where I have gone earlier in the evening with my friend, Robert John. Robert John, a skinny gay with an aversion to fat, much less fat females, believed in saturation therapy. To cure himself of his twin phobias, and because he despised avoirdupois so much, he lived with two dykes, who, weighing in at at least 250 pounds each, liked to walk around the house naked. And tonight, when he had spied the peroxide blonde with the double folds beneath her bare midriff blouse, the beyond-wobbly thighs quivering out of hot pants, shakin', rattlin', 'n' rollin' across the dance floor, he had felt compelled to ask her for every dance—till she had finally sashayed over to where I sat to ask me breathlessly, desperately, "That guy—I think he's fallin' in *love* with me! Ain't there a *wimmen's* bar around here??" I knew the groundlessness of her fear, but since I fancied walking down the street myself, said I would show her the way.

Now, as I stood at the bar, sipping a white-wine spritzer, watching women—including the happy-at-last fat lady—dance through purple strobe lights before mirrors that illumined every fleshy wiggle, the well-built man moved closer so we could talk above the sounds of the Sisters Sledge singing "We Are Family." "No—I'm sorry to disappoint you," I answered, implying that I knew why—voyeurism, a turn-on—*he* was there. "Came with some friends from Statesboro," he said, indicating a town north of Savannah as though to clear himself of the charge, waving a hand toward several suburban-looking couples at the other end of the bar. He added, "Ah'm a buildin' contractor up there."

It would be two years before Beau would tell me the full story of what had happened that day. He and his buddies had rented rooms the night before at the Savannah Inn and Country Club, where they had left their women that morning to go off into the country hunting quail. When their van had broken down outside town, they had commiserated the chilly dawn away over a bottle of Wild Turkey. Then Beau had volunteered to stand out on the highway to flag down help, which had arrived in the form of a Volkswagen bug full of "stoned bull dykes on their way into Savannah for a wild weekend." The women had grudgingly agreed to give him a ride into town, but their driver—a muscular woman at least as large as he—had driven so recklessly that he had complained, in fear for his life, further irritating a group who already considered him the enemy. "Aw*right*, macho man, *you* drive!" their leader had screeched, swerving the car onto the shoulder of the road. For the remaining fifty miles, he had tremulously steered, the nose of the stoned woman's .38 pressing into his rib cage.

"Goddamn, those wimmen were tough!" he exclaimed when he finally told the story. It was probably *his* toughness that had turned the women off, I thought as he related the story, by now turned into the kind of funny tale Southerners, particularly good ole boys, love to tell over and over, further embellishing them with each telling. Beau exuded the air of a man unmistakably high in testosterone and, while not conventionally handsome—his broad nose bent inward like a boxer's, gold wire-rimmed glassed framed his small eyes—he looked stolidly, undeniably masculine.

It was his ruggedness that had attracted me enough that first night to make me agree to play tour guide to him and his friends. Soon we were back at the other gay disco, where I sat with them while they gawked at the six-foot man dressed, in a long white sequined dress and a white-feather headdress that added another foot to his height, as Helen Traubel—"Helen *Trouble*, my dear!" he said, swooping down to kiss my hand.

"You're a witch with a way with words!" one of the men in our group, a professor with a state university, a black patch over one eye, told me, holding my palm in his as, around us on the dance floor, men kissed open-mouthed, thrusting poppers to nostrils, while bodies never missed a beat. He's a psychic, Beau whispered of his friend above the music. When the man guessed my age exactly, and my profession as a writer, I was impressed. But I was mildly surprised when—considering our lack of real attraction— the others said good night, and Beau said good night to them, too, apparently assuming we would go home together.

But, as Keith Carradine sings, I was "as easy as Sunday morning," and the next day was the Sabbath. At my apartment, where we had driven in his pickup, we made drunken, indifferent love. The next morning, I woke to see him jumping into his khakis. "Goddamn!" he exclaimed. "I left three thousand dollars out in the truck, 'n' didn't even lock the goddamn fuckin' door! 'N' in *this* goddamn neighborhood, too!" he added, referring to the Victorian district—the fringe area populated by whites in vaguely renovated town houses, and blacks in ramshackle, if architecturally ravishing, structures—in which I lived. "'N' there's a bunch of goddamned niggers around here, too!"

The money was still in its pouch under the dash, but there didn't seem to be much reason for Beau to hang around. Macho men experience more fusion with the women with whom they sleep than other men, I had read in *Cosmopolitan* magazine, but my and Beau's encounter had been mutually passionless. I enjoyed him more as we sat discussing books for a few polite minutes before he left—he was surprisingly literate, though his favorite subjects were those good-ole-boy specialties, world and military history—and gourmet cooking, macho-style—that is, the best ways to roast oysters, venison, or quail and how to make the hottest, most authentic Tex-Mex chili.

In fact, it was while speaking of hunting that he became the most poetic. As he talked of the upkeep of the dogs, teaching them to point, the meticulous details required in hunting quail with them, he warmed to his subject with a feeling that had been missing during our night in bed. Embroidering his usually monosyllabic speech, he spoke of the birds rising from the fog at dawn, the sound of the hen call, the boom of the guns, the taste of the George Dickel White Label kept in a breast pocket against the chill, then the taste of the freshly roasted fowl.

Yet just as in other sports—with polo, sailing, skiing, tennis at one end of the spectrum, and bowling, football, and basketball at the other—there are class distinctions in what a man hunts, with quail, ducks, wild turkeys—and creatures one must travel to reach, such as elk or moose—as prey more elite than the more readily available rabbits, deer, 'coons, and boars.

When he grew up on Hilton Head, Beau told me wistfully, it had been "country." There had only been a few houses and some shacks for the "niggers"—and plenty of them to clean the birds. It would have been as futile to confront his linguistic crudeness, his bigotry, as it would have been to try to change a quail's protective coloring. For despite—because of—it, I recognized him as an example of the failed aristocratic good ole boy, the man described in a poem by Mississippian James Seay: *The way it works is this:/ we devote ourselves to an image/ we can't live with and try to kill/ anything that suggests it would be otherwise.*

But though we sometimes met on Savannah streets and even slept together a few more times, it would be a couple of years before I suspected the other source of his melancholy. It was on the last occasion of sex between us, as lacking in sparkle as the others, that he hinted at the pain that held him in thrall. I had long suspected his failed marriage to "a good-lookin' airline stewardess," but now he mentioned Vietnam for the first time. He had been a captain, a company commander for two years, he explained, staring at the round light fixture on the high ceiling of my bedroom as I fooled with the curls on his chest. "Things happened there"—he paused, closed his eyes—"'n' when I came back, nothin' that people care about here had any meanin' to me anymore. The things that happened there—they were so bad that nothin' could ever be that bad again—not losin' my wife, *anything*. . . ."

We lay in silence. Though I hadn't yet heard of Post-Traumatic

Stress Syndrome, I had experienced the kinds of shocks that leave one emotionally razed, cored of feeling, unable to communicate. Was that the same sadness, deadness, I now heard in his voice?

A few months after I met Zane, Beau called to ask me out. I explained that I was now living with someone, but—sensing that the two men might like each other—invited him over anyway. From then on, he dropped by more frequently than he ever had when I lived alone. He and Zane drank and talked about guns and war and jumping from planes and war and history and war and football and war, until finally the bourbon would run out, and Beau would leave for home.

"I don't know *what* we were doin' over there," he said to Zane that first evening, referring to Vietnam with proper liberal sentiment. But by his next visit, he had realized Zane's militarism, and felt free to express his own. As the three of us sat in the living room drinking Jack Daniel's, the two men first excused the three Army Rangers who had recently stomped a homosexual businessman to death outside a porn shop a few blocks away by convincing themselves that "he probably asked for it." They went on to discuss the atrocities in which Beau had been involved in Vietnam, including the time he had had the North Vietnamese boy with his arms shot off injected with adrenaline. "We *had* to do it, it wasn't *torture!*" they chorused when I demurred. In their eyes, I could see, in addition to their rejection of my feminine—or "pussy"—response, an air of male bonding as solid as a brick shit house. Was this what the language—the *goddamns* and *motherfuckers* and *sons of bitches*—was all about? Instead of the drip of pain I had imagined, was it really a leak from an endless reservoir of rage, aggression?

The week before, I had had the abortion. Now I ran from the room, nauseated, to hide my head beneath my pillow in bed, to block out the sounds of their coarse male voices, the image of the armless Vietnamese body—somebody's son—and of the fetus I had dreamed male, so recently carved by a male doctor from my womb.

A few months later, the three of us—still friends—sat in a downtown café at happy hour, and the two men were relating their macho tales again. We were about to leave for Who's Who—the best place in town to dance—when Beau told the story about the dyke with the gun, his forced drive into Savannah. "Beau, I'm definitely writing you into my book on macho men with *that* one," I laughed.

"I'm not macho!" he protested. But I wasn't surprised. I had already found out that macho men object to the term, while non-machos are insulted at not being included. "Well, why do you talk about that stuff—guns 'n' army 'n' huntin'—so much, then?" "Because *Zane* likes to," he explained petulantly. I knew the feeling. As a Southern woman taught to listen politely, indeed, draw one's man out on the subject of his choice, no matter how bored one might be, I had sometimes found my eyes glazing over as I tried to focus on monologues on the best football plays, ways to spit-polish a boot, or even how to dismantle an M-1.

Yet as I started to nod in agreement, Zane looked at me and winked. "You don't believe *that* for a minute, do you?" he asked, grinning.

SLEEPING WITH SOLDIERS, OR THE LONELINESS OF THE HANDSOME TEST PILOT.

Not long after I met Beau, I became acquainted with the two career officers who would begin my military education.

That year, my twenty-one-year-old daughter Laura had taken time off from graduate school to live and work in Savannah. Her apartment was a block from mine and on Friday nights we often went together to a local bar to dance and flirt, or just talk to each other.

The laboratory where Laura worked testing the metal content of helicopter fuel was part of a local military base where she was constantly surrounded by soldiers. True, Savannah was full of Army Rangers, who were recognizable by their shaved heads, amazing physiques, and general look of horny longing—an expression undoubtedly agitated by the fact that few local women would go out with them ("except Rangerettes—that's what we call wimmen who hanker after Rangers—'n' they're mostly dawgs," a soldier told me). And if one did date military, it was better to go out with officers—they had more money to spend, were more worldly. The pilots were especially dashing with their flight suits, their air of difference. Sometimes at first one wasn't even aware the officers were military. They were well dressed, drove Mercedeses and Jaguars (one popular man-about-town owned *two*), and generally fit inconspicuously into the local singles scene.

But since I wasn't the Debra Winger character in *An Officer and a Gentleman*, looking for a husband, a way out of the factory, I hadn't given Army officers much thought before the night the pleasant-looking, slender man with brown hair and mustache asked me to dance. The beat of the Village People, the purple strobe lights crossing our bodies, the many-colored lights flashing beneath the Plexiglas surface under our feet, kept us twirling until we finally left the dance floor sweaty and laughing. When Laura and I said we were leaving, he introduced himself as Jay, and asked for a ride back to his motel. He was in town for six weeks to train Cobra—or fighter—helicopter pilots, he told us as Laura drove. In the ritual that, in the singles world, means practically nothing, he politely asked for my number.

Indeed, I'd almost forgotten our meeting when he phoned a week later. As he asked if I'd like to have dinner, I vaguely conjured up the pleasant face, the brown mustache. He had been nicely dressed, I recalled, remembering the obviously expensive tweed jacket, the subtle tie—different from the sailors and construction workers, or wild men like the Pirate, with whom I usually went out.

My memory of his style was borne out at our next meeting. He carefully had planned drinks at one of the more elegant hotels, then dinner at the only half-decent Italian restaurant in town. Over stuffed artichokes, the best veal dish on the menu, his conversation was refined, even his sexual innuendos veiled, delicate. As we walked down River Street along the Savannah River after dinner, we passed a huge yacht; through its windows, we could see a chef in his white pleated hat, tall vases of pink gladiolas, skinny, well-dressed people sipping what looked like champagne. "That *must* belong to Jacqueline Kennedy!" Jay joked. Indeed, the next day I learned from the front page of the *Savannah News-Press* that the boat did, indeed, belong to Jackie O.'s Palm Beach beau, that she *had* been aboard, and the next day had toured the city, offering to buy a house, with its entire contents, belonging to a local antique dealer.

Glimpsing the yacht, driving with Jay through Savannah's cobbled streets, sharing his pleasure in the town's historic architecture seemed to set the tone for our relationship. "Now, *that's* a beautiful car," he commented as we passed a quaint yellow Austin-Healey Here was a man with taste, restraint, I thought—not like the Pirate, or the truck drivers who wanted to fuck even *before* the first date. After years of being thrown to the rug by men like Jack, or raped by blues guitar players, how could I not warm to such a man? As we listened to jazz over Irish coffee in another night spot, he tentatively put his arm around my shoulder, yet gave no indication that sex was any more on his mind than good talk.

He had been an Air Force pilot—following in his father's footsteps—since nineteen, he told me. In fact, as a teenager in Kansas, he had had his own monowing plane, which he flew over farms and ranches, landing in wheat fields and pastures. Though he was thirty-three, he had never married because of his transient lifestyle. He had kept moving from base to base across the country— "for *too* long," he said, adding that though he was lonely, he no longer liked going out with his fellow pilots, looking for women night after night, that instead he often stayed in his motel room, playing his guitar, composing songs. As he spoke, I imagined that his detachment—the romantic solitude of the test pilot—echoed mine as writer. When we undressed to go to bed together later that night, he whispered shyly that he couldn't believe I had let him stay. While we made love, I dreamed I sensed in him, his whole slender yet well-formed body, an extraordinary sensitivity, an elegant eroticism.

When we met the next night, Jay talked about Death the Big Turn-On—about the dangers of his job, how the smallest mistake—"a bit of sand in a fuel line"—could cause his own demise. Of how, in Nam, his job had been to transport snipers, mercenaries, men who looked like they might do *anything*, to the center of jungles, drop them out, return for them at a certain time, then promptly leave again, no matter how many had not showed. He spoke of how one had to block one's mind if one was to survive that sort of thing, and of sex, desperate sex, between soldiers and the women of an occupied country. . . . At last, he put his hand over his eyes as though he couldn't go on, and pulled me close to him. "I can't tell you how much it means just to be able to talk to you," he whispered, his hand between my thighs again.

"There's something I want to tell you, something I've never told *any* woman," he said pensively at our third meeting. We sat on the bed in his room in the Days Inn, he still in his khaki flight suit, me in blouse and panties, my skirt off. A bottle of Dom Perignon stood open on the bed table, beside the two stemmed glasses he had bought for the occasion. He had just played several melancholy songs for me on his guitar—the kind of songs that, because of my Bible Belt upbringing, often gave me a gut wrench, brought tears to my eyes. This time my feelings had been heightened by my awareness of Jay's imminent departure from Savannah.

Was it *love* he was about to speak of, I wondered, looking deeply into his hazel eyes. No, it was something else. "There are a *lot* of things I feel guilty about. Like in Nam, the women there . . ." Here he hesitated, then went hastily on. "And some of the things that happened in college, in my fraternity. For instance, our frat house was right next door to where a young Methodist minister and his wife lived. A lot of the guys wanted to get into her pants; they were always talkin' about it, about how she went out in the yard in shorts, 'n' so on.

"Well, one night, we were all sittin' around in the livin' room drinkin' beer, 'n' somebody yelled, 'Hey, look at that!' We went over to the window—'n' there she was, sittin' behind *her* window in bra 'n' panties, lookin' like she was lookin' back at us over the edge of the book she was readin'. And her husband's car wasn't even there. We nudged each other 'n' laughed, 'n' kept on drinkin', 'n' finally convinced ourselves that she was doin' it on purpose, that she *wanted* us to see. . . .

"So a couple of the guys went over, 'n' came back 'n' said, Yeah, she'd been drinking, wouldn't care. They went back across the yard 'n' fucked 'er, then came back to tell the rest of us, even though we already knew—we'd watched it through the window. . . .

"Well, that started it, 'n' before long there was a line up to her back door, all of us fightin' 'n' waitin' to fuck 'er. They—we—kept givin' her more to drink, holdin' a bottle of Scotch to 'er lips—I guess she just wasn't used to drinkin' or somethin'—'n' treatin' her like an animal, fuckin' her every way possible—we were all laughin' like crazy, makin' fun—when we heard her husband's car in the driveway. Then we all got out of there, *fast!* She was left lyin' there, the whole room torn up, blood 'n' come all over the sheets, even in her hair. . . .

"The next day, they moved. Just disappeared. I never *have* been able to get it out of my mind—that, 'n' some other things. . . ."

As he concluded, he unzipped his flight suit, stepped out of it, lay down beside me. Reaching for a bottle of Jergens lotion in the drawer of the bed table, he uncapped it to slosh the almond-scented cream on his now-erect penis, between my legs. "Now, you know *all* my secrets," he whispered, massaging the substance into my anus, replacing his fingers with his prick. . . .

But how could I object, opened up as I was by his pain?

Two mornings later, at the bottom of the steps to my apartment, Jay passionately kissed me good-bye, murmuring poignantly that what had happened between us was unlike anything that had ever happened in his life, that "as soon as I'm back from my furlough to see my folks in Kansas 'n' settled at the new base, I'll write for you. . . ." As I clung to his neck, pressing the rough buttons of his uniform, his chest, to my breasts through the pink silk of my nightgown, I imagined our future together: me, played by Claudette Colbert, in a romance worthy of a Second World War movie, flying to meet my heroic mate, our passion enflamed by separation.

When a month passed without a message, I wondered tearily what I had done wrong; next, whether the "folks" had really been a wife and four kids, rather than the doddering mother and father he had described. After a while, I just assumed I had met the most subtle specimen yet in the genre macho man.

Two years later, the phone rang and, to my amazement, the speaker identified himself as Jay. He was in Savannah for a weekend, and would like to see me. As I reluctantly explained that that would be impossible, that I was now living with Zane, I thought—perversely—of my daughter Darcy, who had moved to Savannah just a few months before, was between boyfriends, and in need of fun. Perhaps he would like to meet her after her shift at the restaurant where she was working, I suggested, maybe take her out for drinks or dancing. . . .

The next morning, the phone rang again, and Darcy's voice came crossly over the line. "I'm getting sick 'n' tired of standing in for you with your drudgy ole ex-boyfriends. And I don't know why you said he was so nice. He wasn't even that good-lookin', and as far as I could see, all he wanted was to get laid.

"Besides," she went on scornfully, adding the coup de grâce: "He's just an average dancer—and wasn't even that good in bed!"

MORE SLEEPING WITH SOLDIERS, OR WHAT WE WERE REALLY DOING IN VIETNAM.

"Moth-ah! You're *not* going to do *that* again, are you?!" Laura asked a few months after Jay's first leave-taking. Afterward, she thought she had explained to me in detail the characteristics of military men, as garnered from her army-base job. Yet here I was, standing at the same bar where I had met Jay, looking with interest at the ruggedly handsome blond man seated beside me in a uniform covered with ribbons and patches I didn't understand.

"*He's* the worst kind of all," she went on, following my glance, "a commander—a lieutenant colonel, for God's sake"—she had learned to read the patches, the insignia that were a foreign language to me—"of a *Ranger* battalion!" she exclaimed, referring to the local common perception of Rangers and Green Berets as brutes, sheer, shave-headed brutes, who—though one might occasionally dance with one, just for the feel of rock beneath skin— weren't for socializing with. Besides, they were always leaving—for Iran to try to save hostages, or overseas to do secret things for the CIA. "*He's* probably an *animal*, no tellin' *what* he did in Nam," she said, calling on all her powers of persuasion, trying to dim the attraction in my eyes.

"But don't you remember how, when you and Darcy were little, I tried every way I could imagine—cabinets, bookshelves, hidden alcoves—to store your toys, beside the obvious one?" I asked, still looking at the handsome brute from beneath my mascaraed lashes, while she looked at me, puzzled. What I was trying to explain was something that she, as my daughter, should have known about me by now, my fatal inability to learn anything except by experience— *repeated* experience. After all, why did she think I had been married three times? It was something I had learned to accept in myself. In fact, I considered this bullheadedness both my weakness and my strength, giving me a ready excuse to do what I wanted to do anyway. It also reinforced my notion that while I may have failed with one soldier, I might succeed with this one.

Thus, giving myself permission to further delight—and possibly torment—myself through the auspices of the U.S. military, I reached into my purse, pulled out one of the little Somaliland cigars I carried for the purpose, and leaned over to ask my objective for a light. Two hours later, we had dropped a sulky, disgusted Laura at her apartment, and were in mine, doing what I had had in mind since I had first laid eyes on his insignia-laden biceps.

"When I woke up the next morning, I realized I'd rather chew my arm off than wake 'er up!" goes a joke about casual sex and a woman who was "coyote-ugly." But while my pickup was far from physically repugnant, indeed, lived up to his promised muscular development, I realized by morning that I had taken the risk basic to one-night stands—that of waking up beside someone by whom one is repulsed—and had lost.

The night before, Barry had described himself as an attorney by profession, now a lieutenant colonel and general's adjutant, "just travelin' with the general, takin' care of his affairs." With this, he had looked at me as though I should be impressed, but he was unaware of how little I knew of the military class system. And while I *had* heard the arrogance, the self-satisfaction in his voice, I had overlooked it in favor of my own desires.

Now we lay in my four-poster bed, his hard, blond length amid my flowered sheets, talking in the desultory way of people who have just had sex, but barely know each other. As he spoke of Vietnam, where he had been a commander, I was struck by his harshness. He sounded crude, even cruel. "If we drove a Ranger patch through a man's skull with a nail, 'n' hung his body from a tree in the village where he lived, it kept us from havin' to kill more people—kept the problem down, you might say."

"But what about that man's mother or daughter?" I shuddered, queasy at the thought of my counterpart, this small woman on the other side of the world, *her* world suddenly destroyed by this handsome American, this firm body on whom I had recently fed my own lust.

"I guess she just went crazy, ran out into the jungle, became one of those crazy little old ladies carryin' hand grenades," he said crossly, irritated by my lack of comprehension. "Listen, you get *used* to seein' people die. We did the things we did because we *had* to."

"What about the women?" I persisted. "Did you have a Vietnamese lover?"

"I never fucked one of those gooks!" he said indignantly. "They're all whores, you know." Well, what about my friend who had married one, I wondered aloud. "She must have been a whore," he said impatiently. Yet he had asked for a second assignment to Nam, he went on, preferred it, in fact, to civilian life—and to the women in the U.S.

The conversation was disintegrating in a way that is disconcerting when one is naked. Besides, I felt myself in danger of having to face something—I didn't yet know what—that I didn't want to confront. Surreptitiously pulling the corner of a pink sheet up toward my breasts, I tried for the reporterlike detachment I found useful in situations that had gone out of my control. "What about the films *The Deer Hunter* and *Apocalypse Now*?" I asked in what I hoped was a neutral tone. "Were they accurate to your experience?"

Barry laughed bitterly. "There was a guy in our platoon, he was afraid all the time—wettin' his pants, shiverin' like a scared puppy ever time we got into some fire." Inside, I shivered empathetically. "Well, we had some chinks for questionin'. And I told this jerk to cut one gook's throat if he wouldn't talk—what I really meant was, intimidate 'im by *threatenin'* to cut 'is throat. Well, the gook resisted, 'n' this stupid motherfucker just *cut his goddamned throat* —thought that's what I *meant* for 'im to do. 'N' then he got down on his knees, started runnin' around the body on all fours, barkin' like a dog—like somethin' had snapped in his head. But you know, after that, he was okay, gung ho, always volunteered for the dangerous stuff. . . ."

He looked at me challengingly, then laughed at what he saw in my face. "Now, do you believe that for a minute?" Then a shadow crossed his own features: "But don't you go writin' this stuff down!" To change the subject, he reached between my legs. I was in bed with a woman-hater and a murderer, but I noted to my revulsion that my body was responding, whether my head was or not.

Indeed, I was receiving disturbing messages from the interior, the first hints of my own heart of the heart of darkness. "There is nothing one man will not do to another," wrote poet Carolyn Forché. And despite accounts I had read, films I had seen, I couldn't imagine a female SS officer, or women dealing out to one another the same tortures, inflictions, men routinely perpetrated upon each other. The very idea of it rang perverse, sexual, a variation of homosexual S and M—as perhaps it did among men as well.

Yet the body is often where people give up control, I thought with disgust, closing my eyes against the craggily handsome face moving above mine, the feeling of imminent—now inevitable— orgasm rising in my loins. Still suspended in my fog of liberal superiority, I wasn't yet ready to admit that these men—Bobby, jumping from planes on acid and aiming a high-powered sniper's rifle in Vietnam; Jack, outrunning the Coast Guard, showing up with his arm in a cast and with a bodyguard; Jay, testing fighter helicopters and playing fraternity-boy rapist—were really my blood brothers, my male self made manifest, that they acted out the risks, the violence, that permitted me, a genteelly if weirdly reared Southern woman to own tenderness, beauty, and freedom from guilt, if not original sin. It would be a long while before I would admit my own addiction—already being acted out in the sexual arena—to the adrenaline rush.

In fact, it would be more than two years before Peter Ross Range, who had served as *Time* correspondent in Saigon and profiled Lieutenant Calley for *Playboy*, would assert to me that "anybody—any one of us—can be corrupted within two days!" As a member of a Southern family that had included suicides, alcoholics, and other tragically wasted lives, and as a white, middle-class woman who had spent much of my life around oppressed blacks, I identified with the guilt of the survivor, the gut-level knowledge of real sins against humanity. A Methodist woman told me of meeting one of the young Army Rangers who had stomped a homosexual businessman to death in Savannah in 1979—none of whom had spent more than six months in prison. "He was in our prayer group, asked if there was *any*thing—he didn't tell us what —that we thought couldn't be forgiven." She paused, adding as an afterthought, "He seemed like such a *sweet* boy, too." Was this what Beau, Jay, Barry, and the others had wanted from me in bed? Forgiveness for the failure to make moral choices in the midst of evil, absolution through the laying on of hands, breasts, thighs? Or just understanding—and the confirmation that they were still human, whatever their sins?

When I talked with an Atlanta psychotherapist who specialized in treating Post-Traumatic Stress Syndrome, he described the primary effect of the Vietnam experience as "an inability to relate to women as peers. These guys, maybe eighteen, nineteen years old at the time—some couldn't even buy a beer in this country—usually from working-class backgrounds, stomped through the jungles carrying guns, feeling like gods. They felt omnipotent, powerful, experienced a mastery previously missing in their young lives." (An article in *Rolling Stone* on the SDS Weathermen cited the end of the war as affecting that group in much the same way as it had the vets: though they'd vehemently opposed the war, its conclusion took away their raison d'être.)

I already had heard firsthand of an incident in which the younger women in a Vietnamese village had been taken out under a tree away from the other villagers, their American captors implying that if the women had sex with them, they wouldn't be killed like the rest of the villagers, but after the women had acquiesced, they shot them anyway. "And the women in Nam were the *lowest*," the therapist explained, "—to be raped, killed, bartered for drugs— lower than gooks even. What they did to those women was terrible! And they came back to this country totally unable to relate to women as people with needs of their own."

Yet when I met Barry, I understood none of this, only that his callous cynicism made his company uncomfortable, even repugnant. For the next few weeks after our meeting, he called, made more aggressive by my refusals to see him again. Finally, he phoned with the suggestion that I fly with him cross-country— Savannah to San Francisco, a weekend jaunt to the West Coast—in his Piper Cub. Though my brother-in-law, Larry, a Delta Airlines captain, had warned me against flying in anything single-engine, I was titillated by images of the fear I knew I would feel—of sailing over the Grand Canyon, the Rocky Mountains, in a plane nearly as light as a bird. Drawn by my fantasy of a new kind of adrenaline rush, I agreed to a dinner date the next night to discuss it. He would pick me up at seven.

The following evening at eight-thirty, I had been dressed for an hour and a half, but Barry hadn't arrived. "Colonel Smith checked out today," replied the desk clerk when I called his motel. "No, he didn't leave any messages." I shouldn't have been surprised. A man who could drive a nail through another man's skull certainly wouldn't feel much compunction about social civility toward a mere *woman*.

Laura told me a few days later, "You know that guy you met, the one with all the insignia? Well, I saw a soldier at the base wearing a similar patch while waiting outside the Drug and Alcohol Clinic and stopped and asked him what it meant. It stands for the Americal division, nicknamed the 'Baby Killers'—the same one Calley was in!"

She shuddered in a mother-daughter role reversal. "I sure am glad you didn't get mixed up with *him!*"

.   .   .

Reality is for people who can't deal with drugs! someone had scrawled in orchid lipstick across the mirror in Sean's Danish-modern bedroom. A coke-driven, post-hippie businessman, Sean sported a consistent *Gentlemen's Quarterly* style and had paid for the extensive plastic surgery—nose and boobs tilted, belly tightened—that had turned his ex-wife into a "Ten" just before she left him for his best friend. When we met, he was blotting out his rage with chemicals and sex with as many women as possible, preferably several at a time. Since I, too, was trudging the postdivorce desert, we shared a mutual quest for sensation, oblivion.

During our first night together, he rubbed my feet till I lay de-boned in the marshmallow folds of his white linen couch, the jelly lights from his stereo. "That thing cost a bundle, but I just had to have it," he said, describing its superior components. I would soon learn that, in addition to what could be ingested, luxurious gadgets and furnishings were Sean's weakness. "I just *have* to have the best," he would assert, throwing aside envelopes containing the latest importunings of American Express, MasterCard, Visa, and various collection agencies.

After that evening, however much my insteps craved that hard pressure of thumb and forefinger, he never rubbed my feet again, instead insisting, husbandlike, that after orgasm, I lean down to rub *his*. Like a salesman who gave free samples, he expected a return for his initial investment, and this was his method with his avocation as well. A walking *Physicians' Desk Reference*, he gave me my first real lessons in illicit pharmaceuticals—dope, coke, meth, vitamin Q—and when he deemed me ripe for conversion, persuaded me to take my one and only acid trip. "Don't do it," my sister, Anne, for many years a nurse, had advised, "you're too unstable." But when my friend Robert John, veteran of many hallucinogenic sorties, told me, "Yeah, sure, do it—you're so stable, it won't hurt *you*," I decided to take the risk, cop a new sensation.

Sean's best buddy, Carl, a German with an unlikely Alabama twang whose father had defected during World War II to build U.S. bombs in Huntsville, was to be our sober—that is, stoned only on marijuana and booze—guide for the journey. Early one Saturday evening, the three of us passed around a couple of joints and Sean brought out the small white tabs, which he swallowed easily, I, in trepidation at irreversible brain damage. Then Carl drove us in his van to Captain D's Fish House to fuel up for the next twelve hours.

As I look up from the styrofoam plate of greasy fish 'n' chips, the foot-high plaster fishermen—modishly decked out in red raincoats, caps, and waders, the symbol of the restaurant chain—become tiny crucified men, writhing on the fake dining-room rafters from which they hang. Their terrible suffering makes me want to cry. Instead, I giggle uncontrollably. As we walk back out to the van, the concrete surface of the parking lot shifts precariously far from my feet. I take giant steps, like a child playing "Mother, may I?"

At Sean's house, he turns on the stereo, then goes out on the porch to look at the moon. I huddle into the white couch, which now sucks me into its crevices like a starving amoeba. As Carl silently lights a Camel, walks across the room toward me, a Nazi cruelty informs his blond features. I now know Sean and Carl are both CIA agents, that they have deliberately drugged me in order to torture and murder me (my crime, I know well: writing sexual— and therefore, anarchist—material). When he nears the couch, I slide to my knees, hold up my clasped hands, beg him not to kill me, then burst into more giggles. My brain is divided into two distinct halves, one of which is dominated by nauseating terror, the other of which knows this is an amusing dream.

"You've got to look at this!" Sean calls from beyond the front door. I don't think I can walk that far, but know I have to obey his command, because of the invisible string binding us together. It is delicate, a spider's silver cord, and I must not let it break. I crawl the five feet through the door, where Sean lifts me up to look out through distant pines at something blinding, fluorescent, white.

The word "moon" quivers in the air around his mouth, hangs there as though struck by a giant gong.

When he goes inside, I lean—still paralyzed by the white—against the stone façade of the doorway, and one irregular stone at the middle of my back begins to pulsate, mold its contours to my shoulder blades, vertebrae, flanks, which are as squishy, as malleable, as the boneless lady I have seen in a book of freaks. As I move to embrace the stone in return, it is warm, alive. I am at one with this stone, more in love than I ever have been in my life; I never again want to live apart from this rock.

"You've just found your magic spot," Sean explains indulgently as, back inside, I babble of my new relationship. My ecstasy is like multiple orgasms of the mind. Why have I ever feared insanity or death? And why aren't all my friends—all those I love—doing acid every minute, every day, *this* day? Sean walks toward the mantel for a cigarette, the room tilts. I call out for him to be careful, not to stretch the thread too far, then crawl through what feels like acres of living white shag toward the den, where I see the telephone on the floor. At the doorjamb, I stop to strike its curved wooden grain, which arches, shivers, rises to meet my hand like the back of a striped cat. Now, despite the coy movements of the Princess phone, I hold it still long enough to dial Laura's number.

"I'm taking all my savings, flying to Morocco to do drugs for the rest of my life," I say when she answers. "Moth-ah! What are you doing this time?!" she asks suspiciously. "I just dropped acid, and I'm the happiest I've ever been in my life." I'm giggling so hard I can't talk anymore, and she laughs, too, then turns stern. "But when *I* did it, you messed up my trip—yelling at me, saying, 'What's wrong with you?'" "I'm sorry," I giggle apologetically, "I just didn't realize how wonderful it was."

As I hang up, Laura is a woman of twenty-one, sitting in her own apartment, poring over chemistry texts, the convolutions of molecules. . . . But she is also distending my vagina, sliding into the world at this very moment, lying on my belly, her umbilical cord still winding up inside me, her apricot-fuzzed infant skull pulsing beneath my hand for the first time, a moment that had been, is, will be. And like multicolored rockets—red, blue, green—the simultaneous births and adulthoods of my other children, David and Darcy, burst in my brain as well. "I made three people *be!*" I scream to Sean and Carl, the power of this realization knocking me backward into the sea of shag. "And the *best* thing—that means that I don't ever have to take any shit off them again! Because *I* made them!"

I feel a grin split my face; I may smile like this forever. From the couch, Carl glows, his face now angelic. The white linen folds swell around him like an affectionate marshmallow. Sean sits on the rug beside me, his hand on my stomach a metronome, carrying the beat of the rock music through my whole body. I fondle a conch shell from a dish on the coffee table, and it quivers like a small animal, bristling tiny hairs. The glass table on which it lay melts like Dali's watch, liquefies. The jelly lights from the stereo are soundless fireworks, popping, popping. . . .

After a while, I change into a long flowered crepe dress with a plunging neckline, throw a fake black feather boa around my throat. "Outrageous!" Sean yelps with delight. Now Carl chauffeurs us to an after-hours bar where crowds of men—dressed as huge white rabbits, as Scarlett O'Haras, or brides, in leather that looks permanently bonded to leather-brown skin, clanking keys, and flashing tattoos—mill in place like the cells of one giant animal. It's Easter eve. At the glass counter in the lobby, I look at the *Cruise* magazines, which I now realize are religious publications, and admire a black velveteen pillow fringed in gold satin yarn, inscribed *Mother* inside a heart in gold metallic paint. When a hand or leg brushes mine, I feel the electricity leap from my flesh, a charge almost visible in the air, a cartoon jolt.

As Sean and I dance, I boogie all over the floor, high-stepping, tossing the boa. He laughs, his aura glows like a beacon. The thread that binds us keeps us in perfect sync. His hand on my breast inside the neck of the crepe dress is fluorescent, cool, blue-white. As a dry-ice fog rises around our knees, silver tinsel descends from the ceiling, strobe lights dot-dash our motion, I'm following better than I ever have in my life. . . .

But when he leaves me, moves through the crowd toward the bar for beer, the cord stretches uncomfortably taut. Abandoned, I sit on a dais beside the dance floor, my brain pounding to the beat of the music, terrified, now certain, of permanent brain damage. But, miraculously, Sean is back, two dewy Heinekens in his hands, and I realize my head is throbbing because I am seated directly beside the enormous speakers, the magnified sounds of the Village People.

We find another seat on a grimy bench near a pool table and watch the dancers. It is as though my eyes can't drink in enough of this beauty, this panorama. Everyone who walks by falls speechlessly into my eyes. Three people—two men and a woman so coolly elegant I am sure they are European royalty, or at least jet-setters—stop to play pool. In the middle of their game, the younger of the two men—slender, James Dean-handsome—suddenly kneels at my feet, wordlessly kisses my hand, then goes back to his game.

It's seven a.m., time to go, our trip is almost over, Sean says. Out in the van, Carl smokes a joint. An incredibly fragile pink dawn comes up over the filthy parking lot, the aged-looking men trickling from the warehouse doorway. Back at Sean's house, the two of us fall into bed, make at sex with what feels like dead flesh, but neither of us can come. I go into the bathroom, look into the mirror, and see that I am a hundred years old. My eyes are sunken into my skull, every drink I have ever taken, every carbohydrate and fat calorie I have ever consumed, are indelibly engraved on my flesh, which hangs from my body in aged white flaps.

Yet at ten, I awake, manically happy. It is Easter Sunday, the sun is shining, and I know something new: the Secret of the Universe. That afternoon, I try to explain my experience to Anne. "You sound like every cliché ever used to describe an LSD trip," she says acidly. It's clear that I haven't been able to convey my new sense that we need never fear madness, disease, death again, that all of us and everything—from a cracked dish to a Tampax box to a gnu on an African veld—are infinitely connected in a way usually invisible to us because of our limited perception. . . .

"And you know, Larry and I were talking," she goes on, referring to my brother-in-law. "He thinks—and I agree—that you really *must* start taking better care of yourself—stop drinking and doing those drugs. And lose ten pounds—*that's* what's keeping you from attracting a really *nice* man, somebody you could marry. . . ."

I may have seen God, but at least Anne and I had shared one insight. It was exactly what I *had* known, looking at my dying flesh in the mirror that morning—that I needed to lose ten pounds!

The foot massages, the acid visions, were not enough to keep Sean and me more than occasional friends. Though I sometimes traveled to Atlanta, where he lived, I hadn't seen or touched my rock for a year. His love of gadgets and cocaine, mine of books and bourbon, stretched further and further apart, till the silver cord was finally broken.

Another twelve months passed before the answering machine in my Savannah apartment recorded a call from him in a voice surprisingly taut. A few days later, Carl phoned me as well, urgently requesting that I return his call. "Sean's in Houston, havin' tests," he said when I reached him. "He thought he had some little ole thing, a bladder infection, but it turned out to be somethin' else—" he paused, his voice lowered, "somethin' that when they cut it out, he won't be able to fuck anymore. . . ."

A week later, Sean himself rang, pain ragging his usually mellow tones. "Well, it was either the surgery or bite the bullet," he groaned bitterly, going on to describe in graphic detail the malignancy around the neck of his urethra, how he constantly had to piss a bloody flux, but that to do so was so excruciating that to make himself urinate, he had to stick his finger up his ass. The surgery, in which his entire bladder would be removed, leaving him with a limp cock, a bag taped to his abdomen—I thought of his smooth olive skin, the swirl of jet hair—was scheduled for Christmas week. "I just hope I can get enough good sinsemilla to keep me goin'—'n' I've got some pills stashed in case things don't work out."

During the holidays, I called the hospital to ask about his condition, but was told no such patient existed. "He's in there incognito," Carl explained when I reached him. "Some woman's husband is out to kill 'im!" We both involuntarily chuckled. Flashes of pure Sean—unconscious beneath his hospital sheets, hooked up to blood, IVs, catheters, yet with a frothing, irate husband, held back only by nubile nurses, beating down his door—leaped through the long-distance line. . . .

Six weeks after his surgery, Sean and I agreed to meet at an Atlanta pub, where I would be with a group of friends. As I sat drinking beer, I felt anxious, not knowing what to expect from a friend who had just gone through the kind of crisis of body and spirit that I had not yet had to endure. Yet as Sean walked through the swinging door into the saloon's dim light—thinner, much thinner, but spiffily dressed in a three-piece gray tweed suit that set off his newly salt-and-pepper curls, his recently grown beard—he leaned on the arm of a tall, striking brunette, directing a cane with his other hand as though it were simply an accoutrement to make him look more debonair.

"She's gay," he whispered in my ear from his seat beside me. "I feel less threatened by women like that right now. A Delta stewardess, too. We might just get married so she'll have somebody to show her parents 'n' I'll get all those free airline passes. And besides, she's got a great little body!" he said more loudly, pinching Nella, his intended, appreciatively on the ass till she erupted in a froth of Southern-accented giggles that didn't quite fit her height or elegant looks.

Despite the fact that he had just met several of the people at the table, Sean went on to describe his recent experience, the effects of his surgery, as though it were an adventure as catastrophically exotic as a trip alone down the Amazon, being captured by cannibals, castrated by crocodiles. The others sat mesmerized, looking with interest at this man who had gone where they most feared going, yet who had somehow come back alive.

When his monologue had run its course, he leaned suddenly, heavily, against my shoulder, and what came next was a real wail. "See that gorgeous girl over there!" he moaned, indicating a particularly pretty blonde. "Succulence—pure succulence. But I can never—*never*—just go up to a girl like that again at a party 'n' just put it to 'er, say 'How 'bout it?' And do you realize that that last time *we* made love was prob'bly the last time we *ever* will? But do you know what?" he went on urgently, ignoring the tears now streaming down my face. "Just because it's dead doesn't mean I feel one bit different about women, need them any less"—I swallowed, recalling that original need, how considerable it had been—"just because I had this—this *operation*. . . ."

We were already holding hands tightly under the table; I squeezed as hard as I could, hoping to draw some of the anguish out of his body into my own. Images of Sean—boogying his head off that night in the gay bar, his yelp of delight at my low-necked dress, his happy dive in bed toward my pubis—flashed through my mind. I thought of my own ravages of the flesh—how I had bravely had to deal with bleeding and estrogen imbalances, cellulite and stretch marks—and of the *real* devastation of women friends who had had breasts removed, even one who had had cancer of the vagina. I recalled the passages that had made me cry in Ron Kovic's book, *Born on the Fourth of July*. Paralyzed from the chest down by a Vietcong bullet, he had still craved the physical love of women so much that he had traveled to Mexico to live with whores, the only women he had found who would accept him, tubes and all. . . .

"And *that's* why I want you to go home with me 'n' Nella tonight!" Sean beamed, interrupting my masturbatory musings. "Maybe Annie, too," he went on, indicating my friend at the other end of the table.

"Sean!" I protested, "*that* was all over between us long before *this!*" True, I was an aficionado of scars, but what had happened to him was too much. My imagination, recoiling from seeing the damage done, had already conveniently airbrushed his body from ribcage to genitals. Besides, I was involved with the Pirate, and was also on the prowl for the Right Man again.

"Oh, come on, sweet thing," he grinned persuasively, the old Sean squeezing my hand once more, but this time in a distinctly sexual manner. "I may not be able to do much, but it sure would do *me* some good to lie up in the sack with all that nice juicy pussy."

"Sean! I'm not a *nurse*, for God's sake!" I whispered, angrily pulling my hand away. Here I was, enraged despite myself with a sick man, one who had barely cheated death, had paid an excruciating price to do so.

Yet two hours later, my slight virtue dissolved by some good Hawaiian gold, a vitamin Q, I lay—with the other two women—in his king-size bed, amid his tan plaid sheets again. Aside from the broad elastic bandage covering a slight bulge above his belly, everything else looked, if less prominent, the same. "If we were goin' to sleep, I would have to get hooked up," he explained, "but since we're not. . . ."

Sean was my suffering friend, I suddenly realized, and what my friend needed more than anything was touch. For the rest of the night, Nella, Annie, and I gave ourselves over to his wish to bury his face in our vaginas, to lie till dawn between our breasts.

"I'm getting bandages printed up with full-color album covers—AC/DC, Toto, Blondie—to cover my contraption!" Sean told me a few weeks later. We were speeding down Georgia Highway 16 toward Savannah in my Fiat. As a part of his R & R program, he had accepted my invitation to visit during the city's Saint Patrick's Day Festival, a twenty-four-hour all-out bash that was one of the largest in the nation, thus right up Sean's pleasure-loving alley.

When I met him at the airport, he had been sporting a new Sony Walkman, a raccoon overcoat, and was leaning on the dashing cane. "Do you think my clothes fit as well as they did?" he asked anxiously. "And what if I meet a woman while I'm here—how can I explain *that*?" he now went on, passing me a joint in the car. "But it won't be for long—they said I can have the operation for a prosthesis in less than a year. 'N' then I'll be better than ever—a little bulb down there I can press to make it stay up as long as I want!"

At my apartment, he spent an hour in the bathroom, readjusting the unfamiliar device—"I'm just learnin' it." Then we did a couple of lines of coke and hit the crowded streets. As we wandered past drunks waving sequined green banners, strangers kissing green-shirted strangers, couples dancing on the sidewalks and in the streets to outdoor bands, he leaned on my arm, the cane, and prudently joined the long restroom lines at each bar we passed in order to release the urine accumulated in his new appendage. But he also chatted jovially with every friend to whom I introduced him and kissed every pretty girl who bumped into him. A hedonist, it was turning out, faced death as well as anyone else—maybe even better, I thought. At least, he knew what the body was for!

That night, as we rested up for the next round of our carousing, the phone rang. Before I could even say that I had company, the Pirate told me that he was driving from Hilton Head, would spend the night in Savannah on his way south to Saint Simon's Island, and hung up. I answered the doorbell an hour later, and he had already shoved me up against the foyer wall, twisting my mouth beneath his, his hand already on the zipper of his Levis, when he saw Sean, elegant in his yellow cashmere pullover and pleated trousers, at the top of the stairs.

"Who's *that*?" he growled jealously. "Haven't I told you I don't want you fuckin' anybody else?"

"Just a friend from Atlanta—"

"Well, get rid of 'im. We're gonna fuck!" He closed his mouth over mine again, till I struggled free, still trying to explain. "He's an old *friend*, not a lover"—I suddenly had visions of Jack punching Sean out in the area of the bladder bag—"and he just had a *serious* operation."

"Okay, okay, but just tell 'im we're goin' into the bedroom for a while. . . ."

After introducing the two men, I tentatively explained to Sean that the Pirate and I might retire for a little while. Would he just make himself comfortable?

"Yeah," Jack grinned, "we're gonna fuck. She said you've been sick or somethin'. But if you wanna come on in with us, feel free, man," he added, obviously having decided, out of some private male code unknown to me, that Sean was an okay guy.

"No thanks, man, I'm a little under the weather—just think I'll sit this one out, smoke me a joint," Sean demurred, grinning back.

The Pirate had not even allowed me time to close the bedroom door. Within moments, my legs were clamped over his shoulders. As Sean had forgotten his dope box, he walked through the room to retrieve it. "Come on, guy, don't you want some?" Jack offered, raising his face from between my thighs as I futilely tried to cover parts of myself. "It's good stuff." "No thanks, not this time," Sean answered jovially, closing the door behind him.

A half hour later, back in the living room, Sean got out the foil-wrapped cube. "Did you ever do this—scrub your gums with bicarbonate of soda, smear the coke on 'em?" In the bathroom, laughing, we rubbed first the soda, then the white powder into our mouths. Soon we stood among the revelers in a crowded bar, giggling, floating on our coke high, each of our mouths feeling as huge, as swollen, as Al Jolson's.

"Say, man, what kind of operation was that you had, that you didn't even wanna get it on?" the Pirate asked convivially, and something inside me clutched. How would he respond to another man who had experienced the kind of wound that he, as a compulsive womanizer, would undoubtedly dread most?

But Sean apparently had no such fears. In graphic detail, he described his condition, its onset, the result. And as we stood there in the crush of people on a three-day drunk, the two well-dressed men—the Pirate in his designer jeans, a soft chamois shirt, his curly, gray-blond beard; Sean in his usual *Gentlemen's Quarterly* splendor—looked into one another's eyes soberly, intently. It seemed they had something more in common than an interest in good dope and sartorial flash. For while they were not emotions he had often wasted on me, what I saw in Jack's eyes were empathy, respect, identification. I felt like an outsider to a moment of pure male bonding.

"Now when we get back to the house, he can sleep with us if he wants to," Jack told me authoritatively, peeling the top hundred off a roll to pay our bill in a fancy hamburger joint while Sean found the rest room. "That poor guy's been through hell, he's really sufferin'." I once more felt like the Eskimo's spouse, offered up like a bowl of whale blubber, but now the motivation seemed different.

Back at my apartment, the three of us listened to the stereo, passed a joint. I poured wine for the two men, then rubbed their shoulders as they talked. As I sat down on the rug at their feet, Sean lay back in the leather sling chair across from me, pale with fatigue. I noticed the stain spreading across the lower front of his yellow cashmere sweater, the elegant eggshell trousers. "Fuck it!" he said wearily, "I'm just gonna let 'er leak!" That he trusted us that much felt like tangible love, and the love was as much between the two men as between me and them.

"I don't think so, man, I'm beat," Sean said, declining the Pirate's offer again that he sleep with us. "I'll just sack out here on the couch." When he had readied himself for bed, I tucked him under a pink quilt, pulled it up to his chin, and kissed him on the cheek. Then each of us—two wild men, one outrageous woman—went off to sleep with the feeling of children to whom something good had happened.

"Yeah, that was one for the memory books," Sean chuckled two years later at a party in Atlanta. "Yes, indeedy—I sure wrote *that* one in 'dear diary'!" I knew about the loss of his presurgery job and the switch in drug dealing from avocation to vocation, about the medical bills, the second surgery, the move from the house to an apartment. He had just gotten back from a trip by van through the Rockies, and looked as handsome as ever in his Indian gauze shirt, but thin, too thin.

But he had had the prosthesis operation and "It works great, just great, doesn't it, hon?" he asked, turning to the pretty, long-haired hippie-type, imported from Jackson Hole, standing beside him— "a reflexologist," he had told me. I had seen her demonstrating her skills on several eager party guests. Now I marveled at the way

Sean had managed to build into his life both his love of foot massage, and his predilection for gadgetry. "I just press this little bulb in my groin, it swells right up and stays that way. And ya-hoo! I can last forever! You tell Jack when you see 'im!"

A few weeks later, in Atlanta again, I was to drop by Sean's "for old times' sake," but it turned out to be the only night I could interview an outspoken and political local prostitute. "Carl's here —he'll be disappointed, 'n' so am I, hon," he said when I called to break our date. "I've got some long-stemmed yellow roses, a bottle of French champagne. But I'll just put it all on hold till you come back. . . ."

As I hung up, I was first flooded by what could have been that night—the roses, the champagne, the flicker of firelight, maybe even a foot massage, then by all that Sean had taught me—about friendship, true class, heroism. "It is in the extremities of evil circumstance that the possibilities of grace are more clearly perceived," Flannery O'Connor wrote. "There is nothing that can cure the soul but the senses," Oscar Wilde said. And I had once written in a poem that "Only the sensual are innocent." But it had taken Sean to make me fully believe it, to disabuse me of the pie-in-the-sky, Bible Belt imprint that says the real baddies in life are best dealt with through self-denial rather than pleasure.

He and the Pirate had also contradicted my long held feminine notion that men never really supported or nurtured one another in times of duress, and the equally spurious idea that being a man has anything to do with having a functioning penis.

As a child, I had always sided with put-upon Mother, and rejected failed-macho Daddy as Bad Guy, the cause of all our troubles. With each of my three husbands, and many of my lovers along the way, I had confirmed my female chauvinistic values. But now—through my lark on the oil rig, my carelessly undertaken liaisons with the Pirate, Randy, Gary, Jay, Barry, Sean, and the rest—I had learned that while men—especially *some* men—were not perfect, they were not that imperfect, either.

And ironically—since I had picked these lovers for reasons of pleasure rather than shared values—I found myself in clear danger: that of liking and respecting the other sex for the first time in my life.

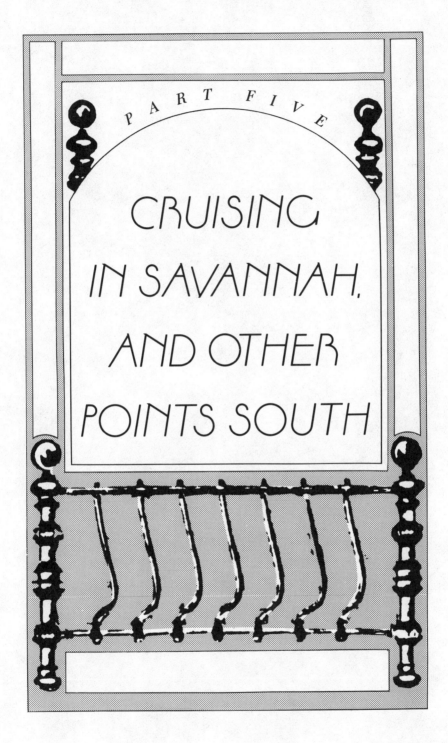

PART FIVE

CRUISING IN SAVANNAH, AND OTHER POINTS SOUTH

CRUISING. OR ONE WEEK IN THE LIFE
OF A SEXUALLY ADVENTUROUS,
OR SOME WOULD SAY PROMISCUOUS
AND TRASHY, WOMAN.

Monday morning: From my bedroom window, I notice again that shirtless and steel-washboard-bellied carpenter, renovating the house next door. From his perch on a lower floor, he looks up at me as well.

Monday night: Ten p.m. I drive to my friend Bobby's house. An ex–University of Georgia jock twenty years my junior, Bobby still wears a letter jacket and last year trekked the Appalachian Trail from Georgia to Maine. He has a big, affectionate Alaskan husky that resembles him remarkably. Though his domicile is so full of hockey pucks, ski equipment, smelly sweatshirts, empty Pabst cans, that one can barely walk, and though the husky sleeps in bed with us all night, lapping my face off and on, Bobby and I have an unspoken agreement that whenever convenient—that is, when it doesn't interfere with Real Life—we will supply sex to one another on call. He likes my reassurance that he's not too fat, his penis is not too small; I like his enthusiasm in making sure I'm satisfied.

Wednesday evening: I go to a downtown lounge for a cock-tail with a woman friend and after several—when my eyes have fully opened to what is around me—notice the muscularly hand-some yet melancholy-looking man my age in Stetson and business suit staring across the bar. The bartender sets up the drinks the stranger has sent to my friend and me and I smile. When he comes around to talk, he tells me that he's part-owner of a local country-western radio station and is regularly in Savannah on business. Later, sadly, he says that he "has family," but that he and his wife are separated: "Ev-ry mornin', ah wake up 'n' reach fur 'er 'n' she's not there." It sounded like the lyrics to one of the songs played by his network, but he looked down into his bourbon as though he might cry. That night, in my four-poster bed, he reaches for my body like a blind man, burrows into my flesh, clings to me as though he is drowning. I know what he is feeling, our imprints are the same: roots, family, sex, violence. Grief.

Friday night: Halloween. I dress as a French maid—short black skirt and leotard, a minute white organdy apron, organdy frills for my wrists and hair, a black garter belt that shows beneath the short black skirt, black-seamed stockings and black high-heeled sandals. At the top of one of my bare white thighs, I press a fake tattoo from a decal, a red rose with green leaves. Laura, costumed in a backless Danskin and jeans, a fencing mask over her face, her foil at her hip, has me press a rose onto her bare shoulder blade.

We first go to a private party, where a photographer for the *Savannah News-Press* snaps me bending over a couch, then gives me his card, asking me to call. Next, at the gay disco, I recognize beneath his Lone Ranger mask, the carpenter from the house next door, just leaving. I introduce myself—his name is Jimmy—and hand him my telephone number, then stand on a balcony overlooking the strobe-lit dance floor, the gyrating bodies, and choose a roughly attractive blond man, his cigarette pack rolled over a biceps in his white T-shirt sleeve. I give him eye contact, until, as though tugged by an unseen cord, he crosses the room, comes up the few steps to where I stand. I notice that the cigarettes in his sleeve are Lucky Strikes, that the knuckles on each hand are tattooed in blue letters, L-O-V-E and H-A-T-E, complementing his worn pants, his rough brogans. "Nice costume!" I say. "Costume?!" he exclaims. "Hell, ah didn't even know it wuz Halloween till ah stopped down here fur a drink!" He lights a Lucky behind one palm. In the flicker of the match, I see the deep lines radiating from the sides of his blue eyes. "Jes' drivin' me a load a' hogs down to Jacksonville, jes' thought ah'd see whut wuz happenin' down on ole River Street. . . ." Still, he allows as how, if he finds some reason, he just might stay overnight. . . .

Saturday afternoon: Jimmy the Carpenter calls, asks me to have dinner with him on Monday.

Saturday night: Laura and I drive out to a shrimpers' dive on the marina for boiled blue crabs, then go to a night-spot where the tunes are all Mickey Gilley and Hank Williams, Jr., and Savannahians in Hawaiian shirts and docksiders crowd to compete on the mechanical bull. Pushing toward the bar for a Miller Lite, I bump into Kenny, who is the same age as Bobby and with whom I have the same understanding. But Kenny is working-class, a pipe fitter grateful to have the job that supplies the money for his red pickup truck and stereo, the tight body shirts and Levis that look so good on his hard lithe body, the cowboy boots and the beads he wears around his bronzed neck. Quaaludes and dope—and the support shared with his policemen-brothers of the mother who for years has been in and out of mental hospitals.

Kenny is also the most sensuous dancer I have ever known. As he twirls me around the dance floor in a perfect two-step, his blond hair glistening like melted butter in the dimmed lights, he bends my groin inward with a firm hand to meet his. But tonight, because of all the other nights, I don't want to sleep with him, and that, like everything else in the world, is okay with Kenny, too. He grunts, nods affirmatively, affectionately kisses me on the cheek.

The first time we met—in the same bar—Laura also had been with me then. "I have to see her home safely first," I whispered to him after I had agreed to go with him. "She's my daughter, you see." "*Wondered* why . . . ," he murmured, referring to my unusual concern for someone who looked to him like another grown woman. But he didn't sound like he wondered much. Kenny is a man of few words—except when he comes, and then he screams, "ORGASM, ORGASM!"

Sunday night: A blind date with a Georgia Bureau of Investigation officer arranged by a friend who says he is "*very* sexy." When I walk into the restaurant where we are to meet, I spy him across the room, and see that she may be right—a shock of prematurely white curls above a sulky yet boyish tanned face, a well-filled-out plaid flannel shirt, faded Levis, and cowboy boots.

Over bourbon and a sausage-and-onion pizza, Larry fills me in on his job. He's cross, it seems, about a book written celebrating the drug busts of another GBI agent. *He*, he tells me, has busted more dealers than anyone in the country and wants me to write a book about him. As he elaborates on the details and dangers of his work—ingratiating himself with smugglers, then arresting them, soliciting prostitutes, having them undress, then showing his badge—I become mute, afraid that the name of the Pirate or another of my illicit pals will trip involuntarily from my lips.

As good ole boys will, he takes my silence for coyness, a challenge to be overcome, preferably sexually, and suggests stopping by the Holiday Inn to hear a country singer, who, he is sure, will "sing some sad songs"—in other words, turn me on. But when, drunker still on Jack Daniel's, I argue with the vocalist about whether Waylon Jennings professes to still wearin' jeans at over age thirty or forty in the country-western song "Amanda," I can tell the evening isn't turning out as Larry had planned. Yet the only thing to do with a man like him is to fuck him, I decide, putting my hand on his thick, denim-clad thighs, smiling up at him sweetly. . . .

Later, as I undress, he glances at the rose tattoo, still unfaded from my thigh, without comment, as though he assumes me to be the kind of woman who might permanently wear such a thing, then grabs me around the waist, tugs me to the bed, begins to make love to me in a way consistent with the cruel lines at the corners of his voluptuous mouth.

Monday evening: Shades of incestuous Savannah. Jimmy picks me up at seven, drives me to the apartment he shares with his sister, who turns out to be the former wife of my former lover. The other guests are a man in his twenties—whose well-off parents, whom I have met socially, are my age—and whose picture I have recently seen on the front page of the *Savannah News-Press* as a witness in a locally celebrated murder trial; and Marie, the blonde-frizzed live-in lover of Madge's pre-oil-rig boyfriend, with whom she has an open relationship.

"Ole Steve invited me over one night for pork chops 'n' gravy— 'n' the next thang I know, I'm in bed with 'em!" Jimmy tells me. I know what he means. When they had lived next door to me, they had unexpectedly dropped in as I entertained a date. Steve had played his guitar for a while, then he and Marie had suddenly disrobed and fucked on the rug before us. The motion of their limbs had been lovely, a slowed-down ballet in peaches, pinks. Only my knowledge that my friend Madge would feel betrayed had made me breathlessly whisper *no, no* as they had tugged at my and my date's clothes.

Yet tonight, Steve is not here, and after steak grilled on the apartment balcony and Breyer's ice cream with Gold Brick sauce, Marie, Jimmy, and I go to the gay disco, where Marie and I take turns dancing with Jimmy and each other. As Marie and I dance together, our breasts brush sensuously, but as we leave, I hear Jimmy whisper to her, "No, you *can't* go home with us."

I don't mean to get involved in a long-term relationship, but I'm so impressed with his monogamous impulses that for a few weeks— well, almost till Thanksgiving!—Jimmy and I keep company.

It was a life-style that wouldn't do for the choosy, but for a while, it was mine. During the same period I had been indulging myself with Jack, Sean, and the rest, I had also been enjoying numerous other men. And if, as humorist Florence King wrote, "a lady always keeps count," I definitely wasn't a lady anymore. But then, a lady—as demonstrated by my corseted school and Sunday-school teachers, my grandmothers, aunts, and especially my suicided mother—had never struck me as a very amusing thing to be.

Twenty years before, I had never heard of the Zipless Fuck, yet I had stood one morning in the shower, a bloodied diaphragm in my hand, an earnest young husband in boxer shorts in the bedroom, three hungry toddlers screaming for breakfast in the kitchen, and had briefly flashed a life of faraway travel, delicious sex with mysterious strangers.

Now it was as though my marital fiascos and my depression over them had led me not toward lesbianism, as it had several of my friends, or a rejection of men and relationships with them altogether, but toward my own form of saturation therapy. It was more fun to be a lover than a wife, I had discovered—and often even more to be the lover of several men rather than only one. I had almost given up the idea of being taken care of by a man, or finding the Right one—and with the shedding of the hope had come relief. I was no longer looking for intellectual stimulation, social contacts, career facilitation, or economic security, to be bought a diamond ring, or even taken out to dinner. In fact, I had taken as my own mission feminist Dorothy Dinnerstein's dictum that in order to free themselves, women must learn, as men have long been taught, to separate sex from love. To cut flowers, hardback books, chocolate-chip cookies, Jack Daniel's Black Label, and a good night's sleep, I had now added to my small but satisfying list of affordable luxuries, sport-fucking with handsome men, younger men, irresponsible men, wild-living, tomcatting, fun-loving men, all the types Mother —and my own censorious left brain—would have rejected out of hand as permanent mates.

I was indulging in something like raspberries out of season or mussels imported from France, something once enjoyed only by the rich and/or unencumbered: sex without love, sex in the daytime, sex with whomever-I-pleased. And since this period extended over several years, whomever-I-pleased became a considerable list: a potential ritual, a cosy rosary for my old age—had I only been able to recall them all. Indeed, their only common de-nominator seemed to be that they were *inappropriate*—from the Beaufort crabber who had courted me—for a couple of hours—by quoting Browning in a rowdy seaman's bar, and the ex-mercenary soldier who lived in a luxury apartment suspiciously full of constantly changing antique furniture, through the movie-star handsome German sailboat captain, Rommel's nephew, who had pursued me even in the company of other men till I had given in, but who then confessed, in his thick accent, that "I haf to haf new vimmen—for instant, last week, I haf seventeen," to the well-off, thrice-wed playboy who went barefoot to middle-class boîtes, and once—still barefooted—stole the decorative mannequin from Savannah's one chic restaurant to bend it to him in a sensuous foxtrot on the dance floor of a nearby hotel.

Outrageous, yes, but how could I fault them? By association I had become as roguish, notorious as they. For during my de-layed—or was it perpetual?—adolescence, I was more like a wild eighteen-year-old boy than the suburban housewife I had once been.

THE CHARM OF THE YOUNGER MAN.

When Jason and I met, our eyes fused with a perfect empathy, what the Spanish call "skin," or a sense in the first split-second of meeting of everything that the relationship will hold. I had just arrived at his grandmother's house, where I would be visiting for two weeks, working as poet-in-residence at the small Georgia high school where Maude was curriculum director in English. And Jason, Maude would later explain, had just come for a lengthy visit from Texas, a time away from his drug abuse, heavy drinking, suicide attempts—and his inability to get along with his stern rancher-father, her son. Yet as I walked into the kitchen for the first time with my satchel of poetry books and my suitcase, what I saw was a well-built young blond man, deliciously filling a black T-shirt and jeans, tan arms already thick from years of pitching hay, who looked at me with piercing, yet somehow clouded, blue eyes in which flickered an instant of recognition, which I, as a woman more than twice his age, felt but didn't understand.

At the dinner table, as his grandmother, his young aunt, and I discussed feminism, the moment recurred. "Feminism might be good for *women*, but is it good for the family?" Maude began in the familiar refrain, wrinkling her forehead at the notion of her own sex enjoying itself, while reiterating the sentiment I had heard repeatedly throughout the South.

As Jason reached a butter-downed forearm across the lace tablecloth for the bowl of fried okra, our eyes met again, and the corner of his full lips turned up in a faint, sardonic smile. "That trashy thang!" Maude snorted, when her husband, Jim, a graying professor at a small state college, timidly asked if I would read his novel-in-progress. "I don't know *why* you'd want to bore her with *that*! 'Fact, I don't even know how you can write such stuff!" Again, my and Jason's glances locked.

Maude's household included four generations: Jason, her daughter, who had come home in her mid-twenties after a bad marriage, Maude, her husband, and her elderly parents. She ran the household punctiliously, rising early before we left for school each day to attend to chores, menus, her senile and ailing mother's needs, then visited her terminally ill father in the hospital in the afternoon, and, if necessary, stopped off at the supermarket or cleaner's. Yet one morning when I went into the kitchen for coffee, as she was hurrying back and forth in her tailored workday suit, her crimped gray coiffure, she stopped to turn to me and cry, a note of real pain in her voice, "I didn't *mean* life to get so gray. . . ." It was as though my presence there as divorcée, poet, free woman, was an affront, affirming the values of her wild grandson, her pornography-obsessed spouse, rather than those to which she had sacrificed her life. For my part, I marveled at her total dedication to "doing the right thing" from the distant perspective from which I had always admired the perfectly stoic—and often perfectly stony—subservience of the most perfect Southern lady I had ever known, Mother's mother, Grandmother Lee.

I understood Jim better: his nearly unreadable manuscript was the story of an aging professor in the latter stages of a disappointing career at a small colorless college, a professor much like Jim, who discovers that he has the power, if he only kisses a woman's hand—any woman, no matter how desirable or beautiful or young—to make her fall into sex with him, do anything he desires. As I discussed the story's potential as a pulp novel with him at the kitchen table, he gazed at me with gratitude at my acceptance of his fantasies. When he rose to make another cup of tea, my and Jason's eyes met; the quiver of black humor touched his eyes and the corners of his mouth again.

Each morning, Jason carried my books to the high school for me; each afternoon, he was a student in one of my classes, writing a dark poetry that, because of what I knew from Maude, made me fear for him. But we remained formal, appropriately teacher and student in our conversation. What I felt between us must be my imagination, I told myself the second week, the fantasy of a woman nearing middle age, as useless as Jim's. Jason was the handsome new-boy-in-town, and in my class, I saw the surreptitious glances given him from beneath the lashes of cheerleaders in pink tights with pink bows in their long blond hair, of voluptuous brunette sweater girls with blue-lined eyes and twenty-three-inch waists. Besides, while I had toyed with the idea—indeed, controlled high school classes, disruptive jocks, with the same kind of eye contact I used to pick up adult men—I had never, during a decade of work in the public schools, had sex with a student, nor did I intend to begin now.

Even the fast lane has its code, I reassured myself that second Wednesday afternoon as I lay reading students' poems. Yet when Jason knocked at my bedroom door, I promptly invited him inside, offering him a swig from the bottle of Mount Gay rum in my suitcase. For the next two hours, I poured more rum, and he poured out his feelings of hatred for his harsh father, his frustrating relationships with girls, and, repeatedly, his hopeless sense of his future, his desire to do himself in: "I just wanna drive my pickup out into the middle of the range, take some pills 'n' wash 'em down with Weller's," he said, referring to Texas's most popular bourbon. From the far end of the house, I heard Maude, returning from the hospital, and whispered, "You'd better leave my room now." "Why?" he asked, surprised. "Granny's not *that* uptight." True, there had been nothing sexual in our talk. But that night, I slept restlessly, alternately dreaming of licking what seemed an endless flow of tears from Jason's tan cheeks and clouded blue eyes, then of kissing his lids closed as the lower parts of our bodies moved together.

I was glad when Friday came, time for me to escape these uncomfortable fantasies. I packed my bags right after school, then went into the kitchen to have tea with Jim, who had written out his special recipe for jalapeño cornbread for me. As he handed me my cup of tea, he put his large freckled hand over mine. "Let me carry your bags out for you when you're ready," he said wistfully. In a few minutes, Jason came into the room, poured a cup of tea for himself, and joined us at the table. "Just come on down when you're ready, I'll take your suitcases out," he offered, referring to the basement room, opening onto the driveway, in which he slept.

I put the small items in my Fiat, then paused at the bottom of the staircase. Should I ask Jim or Jason to help me with my luggage? Through Jason's door, I saw him lying on his stomach on his bed, his jeans taut over his curved ass, reading what looked like *Penthouse*. As I walked into the room, he jumped, dropping the naked centerfold onto the floor. Before I could speak, he had crossed the space between us, grabbed me in his arms, kissing me passionately on the neck, the mouth. "I've been wantin' to do that ever since you got here," he mumbled into my throat, pulling me backward toward his bunk. "Gawd, I've *dreamed* of you up there in yore room, of just comin' up in the middle of the night, gittin' in bed with you. . . ." "No, no," I whispered breathlessly, "your grand-daddy's upstairs, he expects me to come up and say good-bye. . . ." But by now, my resolution not to sleep with a student had dissolved as though it had never been. "You know the McDonald's near the college?" I asked, still the teacher as well as Compleat Scarlet Woman. "Meet me there in twenty minutes."

An hour later, we were at the local Holiday Inn, sitting up against the motel pillows, passing the bottle of Mount Gay rum back and forth. His scuffed cowboy boots, my Italian ones lay beside one of the room's double beds. His feet in socks had a curvaceous arch that complemented the rest of his small yet muscle-curved body. I crossed my still-stockinged legs primly, in sudden shocked awareness of what I was doing. "I can't believe this is happening!" I kept saying as he kissed my neck, unbuttoned my silk blouse. It was a sensation that had grown as I had gone into the motel office, presented my MasterCard. "Hell, it's not *that* unusual!" he protested, once more ignoring our twenty-five-year age difference to roll over on top of me, aggressively grasping my ankles. "I had an affair with another teacher once," he said in a muffled voice, his face buried in my belly. "My art teacher—she understood me just the way you do. . . ."

I flashed Bill the Tool Pusher, fucking his seventh-grade teacher behind the auditorium curtains, an event he had described to me on the oil rig. But only for a moment, for beyond his youthful enthusiasm, Jason was turning out to be more man than boy, making love to me with a finesse, a control, that I hadn't imagined. Where does it come from, I wondered through a cloud of poignant pleasure. And how could anyone who dwelled with such knowledge, in such a body, want to kill it? It was as though he had lived before, his angst so deeply rooted that it could only have come from a previous life. In his skillful dominance, I sensed a despair, as if he were clinging to life itself. . . .

As we soaped one another in the motel shower, I admired at close range the black dot I had seen floating in the iris of one of his blue eyes, and saw that his compact body was as perfect as it had felt. "But I'm fat," I said, patting my tummy. "You're *supposed* to be—you're a *woman*," he crooned sweetly, sketching a silvery stretch mark with a fingertip before becoming the sardonic, mocking teenager again. I watched reluctantly as he dressed. At ten o'clock, with one blind hand on my breast, he kissed me hard, as though drawing life from my mouth, and left for the senior prom, where the girls in pink rosettes and new net strapless dresses with the twenty-three-inch waists and the pink-tipped, cone-shaped breasts—where Maude, as chaperone—all awaited him.

Off and on, during the next two years, Jason called me, usually in the middle of the night. He had moved back home to the ranch near Waco. He was having fights with his father. He had been arrested and jailed on a drug charge, wanted to leave home, but was on probation. He wanted to go to Galveston, get a job on an offshore oil rig. Repeatedly he said that he wished to kill himself.

The next Christmas, after a long silence, I received a card from Maude and Jim, inscribed with a note. Jason had been driving his fiancée home from a date. The girl had been unhurt, he had been killed instantly. . . . At my desk in Savannah, I closed my eyes against the endless ribbon of highway in the dark middle of Texas, the twenty-year-old desperado lurching drunkenly behind the wheel; the swerve, the skid, the girl's scream—and the beautiful body smashed, the mocking smile stilled, the cloudy blue eyes staring at nothing at last. . . .

"Our Jason liked you so much . . . treasured the book of poems you sent him," Maude had written in a newly shaky hand. "But maybe it was a blessing, he had suffered so in his short life. Anyway, I just thought you'd like to know. . . ." I wondered how much she suspected of the true nature of our relationship. I knew she didn't approve, as a proper Southern matron, of my poetry, its sexual imagery, or my status as a triple divorcée. Yet had she intuitively known we both cared for her grandson, and in much the same way?

"What are you anyway? A social worker?" a therapist pal asked when I described my need to be gentle with young men even as I fucked them. A psychoanalytically obsessed friend had once asserted, obviously incorrectly, that because of the Oedipus taboo, I would never be able to sleep with a man younger than my own son. Yet expressing tenderness to younger men somehow eased the ache caused by my relationship with my son, David, which—despite an intensely loving, even symbiotic, beginning, had become over the years conflicted, pain-filled.

"I woke up this morning feeling like a sixteen-year-old—but there wasn't one around!" quipped the fat mistress of ceremonies in an Atlanta strip joint, making light of the middle-aged predilection for young flesh. It was the younger men, still struggling with their male identities, the difficulties of conforming to the macho images projected by society and strong fathers, who tugged at my maternal impulses, touched me the most of my lovers. Besides, I admired scars—psychic or physical—and theirs had not yet become keratoid.

Donald, a young graphic artist who was the youngest of six children, confided that he had seen, from his crib, his father forcing his mother to go down on another man. "And I *know* she was pregnant when they got married," he said, adding that "I've never told anybody about this in my life." We were sitting beside the campfire at a Savannah pig roast—a macho party where men do the kind of cooking men do: roasting whole hogs, throwing unwrapped potatoes and raw oysters onto the fire. One guest, a Vietnam vet, had been hacking wildly at the marsh grass with what looked like a machete; now he impaled the boar's head on a piece of bamboo, carved off the snout, and tried to feed it to the women cringing at the fire's edge. Our host had a reputation for taking his clothes off at social events; Donald and I were doing lines of coke, awaiting the denouement.

"It'll be wonderful sleeping with you tonight," he whispered between whiffs. "You'll be the mother I never had." As he caressed the arch of my sandaled foot with his hand, telegraphing the sensation upward toward my groin, my heartstrings twanged maternally.

The next morning, as we lay in bed, his phone rang. "My mother just told me she loved me, for the first time in my life!" he said with amazement as he hung up. I was writing a synopsis of a novel about a mother-and-son relationship and felt faint with recognition. "See what luck you are?" he went on. That afternoon, he tried to interest me in going to bed with his best friend, a tall skinny sky diver who kept an apartment full of uncaged birds—the stuff of the unconscious, the reenactment of the "unfaithful mother" scene. But I declined, and Donald and I never had sex again.

Moose, a twenty-three-year-old steel foreman, son of a steel foreman whom I met around the same time, was far less Freudian, but at least as touching. "Daddy keeps sayin' I'll git ust to it," he said, speaking of the day-in, day-out tedium of his job in Texas City. His blue-collar gig paid for the nights at Gilley's, where we had just met, his gen-u-wine lizard cowboy boots, an assortment of cowboy hats with feathered bands, and the shiny new pickup with the great stereo. Yet despite his *Urban Cowboy* accoutrements, his ability to swirl me around the dance floor in a two-step at least as adept as John Travolta's, Moose looked—with his sensitive pallor, his horn-rimmed glasses—as though he might be more at home in a library. When Moose had used the de rigueur words "nigger" and "queer" in the first minutes of our conversation, I had asked why, with his obvious intelligence, he felt compelled to use such language. "Thet's jes' the way we tawk down here," he said. "Hell, he'd worry more if I *didn't* do it," he went on later, when I asked whether his father would be upset if he knew about his sleeping with a woman so much older than he: "Cows, sheep, girls, wimmen—*any*thang, jes' so long's it's *fe*-male. Hell, 'bout the only thang he *couldn't* understand would be if I went queer—then he'd beat the hell outta me for sure!"

I met Raymond as we both stood among the crowd in a gay disco that jostled and hooted beneath the stage during a "buns" contest—a chorus line of jockey-shorted or G-string-clad contestants who pranced backward across the stage, jiggling their backsides. As the applause melted, he took my elbow, asked if I'd like to dance. I looked up, way up, into liquid black eyes fringed by long sooty lashes. As we moved around the floor, it was as though all the grace in the world had magically flown into his lanky six-foot body. Following him left me breathless but exhilarated. "I'm twenty-eight," he confided over breakfast at a fast-food spot after the disco had closed at three. "How old are you?" "Thirty-six," I lied, easily lopping off six of my forty-two years. "And at my age, I don't go out with anyone over three times unless there's a chance of a long-term relationship. And just now, I think that would have to mean someone with money." "Don't worry 'bout it," he said to my surprise, "I've got thirty thou in a trust fund."

By the time I found out he was actually eighteen and unemployed—indeed, was back in high school after an abortive stint in the army—we had already slept together several times. On the most recent occasion, I had admired, like a seamstress admiring a fine piece of shirring, the puckered scar from navel to groin ("Kidney surgery—if I ever have to go through *that* again, I'll just kill myself") that marked his otherwise China-silken body. He had burrowed into me, holding my wrists to the pillow as Mother's Finest sang, "Tie Your Mother Down" from the FM radio. "That reminds me," he blurted into my ear, "I'm not really twenty-eight like you thought. . . ."

Since I now knew his true age, I invited him to sit outside on the porch when he stopped by after his high school classes. I wanted to avoid the wrestling match toward my bed, the teasing and pleading and nipping that made him seem like a cute but annoying puppy, that would inevitably take place if I asked him inside. Determined to redirect my emotions toward the maternal—feeling, since I was older, responsible for both our sexual impulses—I listened supportively—all the while, admiring his black-lashed eyes, set like gigantic onyxes within his eggshell face, his perfect Grecian profile—as he talked about school, his "other" girl friends, and repeatedly, his problems with his engineer father, his straitlaced mother, his preppy siblings. An orchid in a field of crabgrass, I thought. I had once given him a ride to his parents' house in the suburbs. He had directed me to an ugly, sprawling split-level on a vast but shrubless lawn. A graying crew-cut man in a droopy sport shirt had stared warily at me from over his power mower, a woman with a crimped beauty-parlor wave, a red-and-white-checked apron around her puffy middle, had stepped out into the carport to see who had arrived. "I sleep in a room off the kitchen," Raymond had told me. "It's sort of like I'm not really part of the family. In fact, I used to think—to wish—I was adopted."

He was different from them, he said—he wanted to travel, do things, meet people, maybe even become a male model, or go on the stage. He had run away to New York once, he told me, where he had hung out around Times Square, performed in a couple of porn films—from his exhibitionistic dancing, his fancy fucking, this was easy to imagine. Finally, he had been picked up by "a man in a black leather coat—the only man I ever fell in love with. We lived together at his apartment; he bought me a coat just like his—that black one I have now. Then one day, he ran out into the street, got hit by a cab. . . ."

Like his fantasy finances, his imagined thirty thousand dollars, Raymond's past was an extravagance, a creation, as was his personal style. He dressed with a flash, a flair, common to Savannah blacks and gays, yet rare in straight white Southerners. Sometimes he duded himself up in a black leather jacket with a tiger painted on the back, black leather pants, black leather wristbands studded in steel. Other times he affected a three-piece mint-green suit— "Don't I look like one of the bro's?" he asked proudly. In his vest pocket, he stashed a half-pint bottle of Maddog 20-20 from which he occasionally swigged as I primly sipped Bloody Marys or gimlets over lunch in middle-class restaurants.

"Where did you get *him*?" Anne asked when I met her at a Savannah airport with Raymond in tow. He was walking ahead of us, carrying her bags, dressed in the black leather jacket, the steel-studded black wristbands, his glistening black waves slicked back in a satiny ducktail. I could tell she wondered if he was dangerous. "But really, he reminds me of a motherless puppy," she laughed after he had eagerly shaken her hand, jumped out of the car at a downtown intersection, and, waving good-bye over and over, had loped backward down the sidewalk like a gangly black Labrador retriever.

"You're just like an actress—you get right down on his level," accused another woman visitor after going dancing with us. "Well, of course!" I said, amazed that she found anything unusual in my behavior, in my consorting with an eighteen-year-old. "You don't expect *him* to get on *my* level, do you?" Indeed, right then, maturity meant sadness, the past, to me. Pleasure was my primary value—and Raymond was by far the best dancer in Savannah, moving through strobe lights like liquid mercury, leaving me too breathless to live in any but the present moment.

A Southern writer once told me the story of what he and his teenage buddies had done to a girl when he was growing up in Chattanooga: in order to be liked and accepted, twelve- or thirteen-year-old Lucille allowed all the boys in his gang to have sex with her. One day, out of compassion, he had taken her aside to say, "You don't have to do this—*I* like you *now*. 'N' there's somebody else who always loves you, too—*Jesus*." To his gang's dismay, Lucille had taken my friend's words to heart, changed her ways. But then one day when he had been particularly horny, he had taken her aside again. "Jesus's changed his mind, 'n' so have I," he said, leading her toward her bedroom.

It was the attitude I took with Raymond. When I didn't want or need him sexually, I considered his best interests, but when I did, I indulged myself, as though he were a box of Godiva chocolates I only occasionally took down from the shelf. In fact, I used him as coolly as any rake ever had a woman and, during the periods of my renewed interest, Raymond's romantic hopes flared, just like a girl's at the hands of such a man. When he at last got a job—as a clerk in a pornography shop—and his own little apartment downtown, he invited me over for supper.

As he puttered in the kitchen, I sat on the couch, my feet propped on a crate, flipping through the stacks of hard-core porn magazines that lined every wall of the tiny living room, feeling, for a moment, that power to which men must be accustomed and are often so reluctant to give up. It was a sense that had begun when I had walked in to see the snapshot of me enlarged to eight by ten, framed in a ten-cent-store frame, and placed on the fake mantelpiece. "How do you like it?" he had asked hesitantly, like a woman who hopes to please her lover.

"Do you think I put too much salt in the mashed potatoes?" he now asked anxiously as we ate at the Goodwill dinette set. He had laid out flowered paper towels folded as napkins, and in deference to my refined tastes a half-gallon of Gallo Chablis Blanc sat on the formica tabletop amid the serving dishes. As a roach climbed the rusty aluminum table leg, he quickly whisked it from sight. When his new puppy—a Heinz 57-Variety mongrel he had rescued from the street—nibbled affectionately at the ties of my rope sandals, then peed near my foot, Raymond jumped up with more paper towels.

After he had cleared the dishes, we went to "bed"—a mattress on the floor covered with a frayed army blanket—to watch the "Tuesday Night Movie of the Week." Above us, life-size women in full-color GYN shots loomed down from every wall, competing with the nine-inch black-and-white TV. As the plot thickened, Raymond chomped through three boxes of Mallomars, pausing only to sop up the puppy's new messes. When we finally made love, the Mallomar crumbs rolled beneath my shoulder blades; the dog scampered over and between us, nipping off my plastic Timex watchband, nibbling at my nipple till I yelped. "Do you think we could get married?" Raymond whispered tremulously after he came.

Early the next morning, just as I had rolled over on top of him, cupped his cock in my hand, someone knocked hard at the apartment door. "Oh, my God!" Raymond groaned. "It's Roseanne—I forgot I told her she could come over today!" He jumped up, throwing my dress at me. I knew he had girl friends, multiples of them, in fact—but I had never before met one, I realized, as I disappeared into the tiny bathroom, pulled the dress on wrong side out, and bent over to tie my espadrilles. "Excuse me, I'm just leaving," I explained to the plump, freckle-faced teenage girl who stared at me with an angry, tear-stained face as I entered the living room, then, closing the door behind me, walked down the hall toward sunlight.

A year later, I opened a local newspaper to see a picture of Raymond—dressed only in a black G-string, his beautiful scar revealed to the world—cavorting across a small stage, smiling happily down at what looked like the heads of a group of middle-aged women, covering the front page of section two. "Savannah's First Male Stripper," read the caption. "There's standing room only at the Gator Lounge each Wednesday night as Savannah women crowd to place dollar bills in this young man's G-string. . . ." "Do you want to go?" the woman who had questioned my maturity in dating an eighteen-year-old called to ask me excitedly.

In two years, I saw him again. Eating a box of Mallomars, dressed in the suit of an exterminator of roaches, he waited at the front of the supermarket, for a dim, freckled woman—Roseanne? —who stood in line behind a loaded cart. Where had his exotic beauty gone, I wondered. His hair was as dark and sleek as ever, his skin as silken, his eyes as wondrously lashed, but there was something different in his lanky frame: a stoop of defeat. "I got married, got me a house trailer out near Mom 'n' Dad," he explained defensively, looking away from my eyes, and down at the gray poplin uniform with its embroidered pocket that read "Orkins." In that moment, I wanted to take him in my arms again—not as a lover or mother, but to breathe back into his body his dreams, his old verve.

THE PLEASURES OF PLEASURE, WITH A SPECIAL NOTE ON THE PLEASURES OF THE FLESH

At the time, I could have used Raymond's services regularly. In my unrenovated Victorian apartment, roaches ran in frantic droves up, down, across the kitchen walls, dug their way through the rotting rubber gasket of the old refrigerator, dripped steaming from the kettle each morning that I forgot to replace the water before heating it for my cup of instant coffee. But, as Mary Douglas wrote in *Purity and Danger*, "Dirt is matter out of place." I had totally lost interest in housekeeping, indeed, didn't even care anymore whether I got fat.

"You always sounded like you were having so much *fun* over there," a next-door neighbor said with a sly twinkle in his eye, referring to the fact that his second-story window was opposite mine. True, the apartment I occupied during my period of loose living was heated only by one small gas heater, but there were two decorative, if unusable, fireplaces, the twelve-foot ceilings were iced with crown moldings, and my randy neighbor and I often kept our windows open to Savannah's balmy breezes as well as the sounds of one another's intimacies.

"I think what I like best about Southerners," wrote former New

Yorker Neil Shister in *Atlanta* magazine, ". . . is their seemingly limitless capacity for 'fun.' In the North 'fun' is something of a suspect word; to use it too often is to run the real risk of being thought frivolous and less than trustworthy. Down here . . . one is not only excused for having fun, but periodically expected to seek it out. . . ."

"Yeah, we sure did have fun," Laura recalled of her two-year hiatus in Savannah, our time of mutual bar-hopping. There were pig roasts and oyster roasts and crab feasts that, liberally laced by booze, coke, and dope, seemed to slide on all weekend. There was the annual Georgia Day festival, in which drunk grown-ups, watched by children and other drunk grown-ups, dressed as Indians and settlers in order to reenact General Oglethorpe's landing on the Savannah River, his meeting with Chief Tomochichi. There was the "First Saturday" on River Street, fronting the Savannah River, a monthly bash with outdoor bands, street vendors, and artists, and seasonal motifs. There was the yearly Saint Patrick's Day orgy during which we roamed the streets, passing back and forth a half-pint of Jack Daniel's in a brown paper sack, French-kissing strangers in green, and watching out-of-towners make fools of themselves in the streets. There was the regular Wednesday-night happy hour, margaritas three-for-one, at our favorite singles bar; and every weekend, and in between, bar-hopping along River Street, watching the desultory progress of enormous ocean liners down the Savannah River; perusing—perhaps cruising—the handsome Swedish, French, Italian, and Greek seamen who filled our favorite drinking establishments. I, Laura, and the rest of our local friends were wasting away in old Savannah, if not Margaritaville, and for a long while, it felt delicious.

And some kinds of fun, I was discovering in my new freedom, had long been the secret domain of men—and women outside society. "One's pretty lively when ruined," says the London maid to her country counterpart upon the latter's amazement at her fine clothes, her sleek ways, in Thomas Hardy's poem "The Ruined Maid." As nobody's wife or lover, as the mother of adult children, I could hang out at sleazy bars, hold no societal obligations other than those I chose. When I was arrested in Atlanta for Driving Under the Influence—was photographed, fingerprinted, frisked—

the incident was not an embarrassment, but simply an annoyance that became a funny story to tell my barroom buddies ("Take it off, *all* off," yelled the men from the holding cell as the just-arrested hookers grinned from the bleachers, and a policewoman felt down my sweater and skirt).

"In many ways, she's a lot like me—she don't give a damn about so-ci-e-tee," sings Hank Williams, Jr., in what could have been my theme song. "She likes to get high 'n' listen to the band. She likes to make love with her kind of man. . . ." Like the "Outlaw Woman" of the tune's title, I lived in a state of pubescent exhilaration, expectation, of not knowing exactly what, or who, might happen next. "A married woman gets tired of one man all the time," goes a black blues song from the thirties, but in my new life, there was never time for this to happen. Yet it was not the number of sex partners, or the frequency of lovemaking—actually, I had sex less often than when I had been married—that was heady: it was the sense of anticipation. Was this why men sometimes *seemed* more open sexually than women, I wondered, because they move around the world with more ease, and thus experience a more generalized excitement? Freedom was an aphrodisiac, turning the tap of my eroticism toward the polymorphous perverse. Glossy-faced young women in a gay bar, beautiful women kissing and swaying on a dance floor, excited me just as did the well-muscled macho men I now favored.

"I may have stopped counting my lovers at a hundred," a woman friend near my age told me primly, pointedly, "but I've *never* had group sex, sex with a woman, or picked up a man in a bar." To me, she sounded like Polly in my favorite girlhood novel, *An Old Fashioned Girl*. By then, if I could have said such a thing, it would have been with dismay. For while I believed in a moral scheme of sorts, that one should try to live in a way on which one could look back from one's deathbed with some satisfaction, I also believed that the things one had *not* done were just as likely to be the things one might regret.

By the time I was into what I would later think of as my third year of fucking around, I had become, without meaning to, or realizing it, an adventuress, an explorer of sorts. Instasex had become my recreation, my distraction, my adrenaline rush, my connection, my fix. Indeed, my cruising had become as complex, as convoluted—as much a total life-style—as the bar life of confirmed homosexuals. As the daughter of a nouveau-poor Southern belle and a drunken, improvident father, I hadn't been brought up to ski, sail, or play tennis, but sport-fucking, it turned out, was a pastime I, as a Southern woman, had a knack for. Nor did it require special equipment or expertise. I had only to apply a little perfume, don a slit skirt, put a flower in my hair, enter a room, look around, make eye contact—and the man of my choice would be tugged—however circuitously—to my side and later, if I was in the mood, into my bed. After a while, I began to feel that my selection of a man was a magical act, the equivalent of drawing him within the circle of my body space as by a magnet.

Soon, it was a skill for which I became known among my women friends, several of whom suggested that I teach a course or write a book—sure to be more profitable than my literary poetry and prose—on the "Art of Flirting." "It's just an old-fashioned flower scent, a low-necked blouse, high-heeled sandals, a smile," I demurred, ignoring the fact that it was probably my very ordinariness—my height of five feet five; my curvaceous, rather than slender, figure; my heart-shaped, freckle-sprinkled face; and my long auburn-brown hair—that men liked, and giving away the easy secret—that men are primarily visual, olfactory, tactile in their sexuality—that, as a self-respecting feminist, I should have rejected out of hand.

"Now watch Mother," Laura told her visiting college roommates as we walked into a Savannah singles bar. "By the time we leave, she'll have any man she wants with her." But there was another element as well, I explained to my daughter, still in the throes of the quest for True Love. As I wasn't looking for a relationship—indeed, didn't really care about any one man in particular—I automatically focused only on those I sensed to be receptive, thus saving myself from rejection. Since the pain of my third divorce, my abortive attempts at relationships with my male peers, rejection had not yet become a feeling I was willing to risk again. In this simple, transient world—unlike the worlds of the proper suburban matron or the woman writer caught in the web of the male literary establishment—I felt easily powerful. Wherever I went, there were willing takers, men who obviously shared my need to parry, to conquer or be conquered, finally, to mingle bodies in an intimacy that—however much the intimacy of combatants, contestants, adventurers engaged in mutual risk, however brisk, however inconsequential—was still intimacy.

Yet my attitude toward that intimacy had changed. When a woman friend referred to a sexual encounter with a man who didn't want involvement as "humiliating," I realized I felt differently—in fact, more like a man who uses such encounters to maintain his own emotional independence (or like Germaine Greer, who exuberantly announced on national television that "I'm the most faithful woman I know—I still sleep with the first man I ever had sex with!"). The very characteristics the old-style male was trying to abandon, according to Shere Hite in an article in *Family Weekly* in November 1982, "The New Sensitive Male"—"to deny, mistrust and suppress feeling, to always be rational, strong and competitive. In other words, to be, or at least to appear to be—insensitive . . ."—were those I wished, to a degree, to adopt: to give up the excessive nurturing of, and overreliance on, others; the lack of regard for my own needs and ambitions; and the overindulgence in such feelings as dependency and anxiety that I, like almost every other woman I had known, had been brought up to accept in ourselves.

While still a teary, hysterical young housewife—puzzled at why, when I had everything I had been taught would make me happy, I was so miserable—I had gone to a therapist who, on my initial visit, had had me make two drawings: one of a woman, another of a man. My sketch of the woman showed her sitting outdoors in a feminine dress, her skirt and long hair blowing in the breeze, "pregnant with thought," I had written in description. My other drawing was that of a man dressed to travel, suitcase in hand, "off to New York to visit his many old friends and lovers."

As a child, I had been deeply disturbed by my recurrent image of an embedded penis, emblematic of what must be the grotesque male part of myself, hidden deep within my body and psyche. When the therapist pointed out that the two drawings revealed my internalized images of my male and female halves, I slowly realized that the woman, gestating ideas, was my creative self, the part of me that wanted to write, or nurture others; that the man, moving freely, expansively, about the world, was my aggressive, risk-taking self.

Now, in my new double life—my feminine demeanor opposed

by my active cruising, my solitary writing days matched by my adventurous nights—I felt for the first time that both parts of myself were being given play at once. In fact, for a while I became so masculinized that I thought of men as a commodity, as males to have sex with in much the same way I thought of money, as in *I need twelve hundred dollars a month, and ten good fucks*. To keep myself financially aware, I jotted my expenditures in a notebook; to make sure I could provide for myself sexually, I marked the days of the month when I had had sex with an *X* and my partner's first name. Some days would bear two *X*'s, some weeks five, other weeks none at all. (Later, looking through these notebooks, I would find with chagrin that I couldn't recall the faces, the bodies, to match the names and *X*'s.)

When I was just divorced from my third husband, Ben, I was terrified both of not being able to take care of myself financially and of doing without the sensual life to which I had been accustomed since marrying for the first time at sixteen. The bottom line of freedom, I had long suspected, was economic and sexual. The notebooks were an effort to reassure myself that I could be truly independent.

Gradually, I began to lose my usual discomfort at eating alone in strange restaurants in strange cities, and now, if I felt like it, I could visit the hotel bar and meet a man with whom to provide for myself sexually as well. I found I could more and more easily fuck without love and that in that fucking there was a power, an exhilaration in knowing I could provide for myself sensually as well as materially. Like my transsexual friend, Cherry Delight, I was part woman, part man, but because I was acting out the masculine half of myself, I ironically felt more feminine—and less angry—than I ever had in my life. There was no one else to blame for my mistakes, yet in that knowledge, I felt a great relief from my past, lifelong burden of dependency. The discomforts I had accepted as part of life as a daughter, wife, and mother—conflicts with intimates, recurrent anger, struggles for power—dissolved completely during my period of dissipation. Indeed, what was dissipating was not, as one might expect, my body, character, or spirit, but the pain of Mother's suicide, Daddy's death, and my three divorces. For me, at least, the Buddhist diagram that describes experience as a circle in which either hedonism or asceticism can lead to nirvana, or heightened consciousness, was proving true.

I had once fancied that my alter ego, had she been given her head, would choose an old maid's existence—cats, books, and hot cocoa in bed. I loved the novels of Barbara Pym, in which, as *New York Times* reviewer Michael Gorra claimed, "Almost everything . . . takes place across a middle-class tea table"—usually in an Anglican vicarage. Now, like an unexpected rainbow, my wanton life flared with another, just as pristine, kind of purity. The body, it was turning out, was more reliable, less deceptive, in its knowledge than the conscious brain. But I was learning that knowledge was more like that of the collective unconscious—that it didn't belong to any one individual, any one body. And as country-western singer T. G. Sheppard titled a song about a lifetime of lovers, "I Loved 'Em Every One," that was the way I felt about the men—and on occasion, women—with whom I had slept.

Though my sexual experimentation seemed random, there was a point at which aesthetic selection took over, revealing more and more clearly the sensitivity, intelligence, and character of each potential lover. (It was a period, I would later realize, that had greatly enhanced my extrasensory powers, my psychic perception, my "street" sense.) Often, as I talked to or made love with a stranger, I suddenly sensed—acutely, even painfully—the inner life behind the veil of conversation and touch. I felt myself to be giving a gift of myself, or even absolution, as I had with Jay, Barry, Sean.

A Catholic friend had said to me that she thought priests should be permitted sex, but not marriage. And casual sex interfered no more with my basic commitment to writing than such a priest's casual liaisons supposedly would with his vows. Through public television, I had learned that among certain Indians of South America, a pubescent girl is cloistered for three years from the time of her first menstrual period, but that she can, if she wishes, sneak out of the family hut under cover of darkness. In my single life, I felt just as cloistered. "Some women are like sieves, or the Virgin Mary—forever untouched, no matter how many lovers they have had," my third husband, Ben, told me tenderly at the beginning of our relationship. "Someday I'll write a true photograph of Rosemary, the little girl who never learned how not to love," my gay friend, Robert John, said to me fondly during one of our evenings on the town.

At eleven and twelve, I had imagined sex to be an event so powerful, so unbelievable in its sheer spiritual and animal intimacy—and, of course, filth—that those who shared one another's bodies through intercourse were inevitably, eternally bound, like a mother to her child, or criminals by their crime. Instead I was finding that the communications of flesh could be as delicate, as ephemeral, as snowflakes or soap bubbles, that sex could be as inconsequential as a sugar rush or enjoying a new dress or pair of shoes. It had been excessive dependency, proximity, that had created anger, ugliness. In cruising, there was an excitement that was similar to falling in love over and over again—and an adrenaline rush it would be as hard for me to give up as for Jack to give up his smuggling or Zane his skydiving.

But each intimacy was also a sudden, blinding break, a leak in the vacuum of isolation. One night, I dreamed of a hummingbird, poised close to a blossom, so quick as to be nearly invisible; yet singing, its bird throat full, vibrating with gorgeous song. Another time, of a yellow bird, suddenly descending from a flock to huddle between my chin and collarbone, pulsating against my throat—a moment of pure ecstasy till the bird rose and swiftly flew toward the horizon.

And with each brush of transient flesh, there was that sweetness, that innocence, a brush of the eternal, like the brush of the bird's wing.

•   •   •

As a former born-again Southern Baptist, thoroughly washed in the Blood of the Lamb and rewashed in it, I knew, of course, that there had to be punishment for all this harmless fun. In the Bible Belt Georgia town where I grew up, I had thought the stories in the *Ladies' Home Journal* risqué and had tormented myself with guilt after every post-prayer-meeting parking session, writhed in nightmares of hellfire after every backseat or drive-in-movie encounter. Now I was forty-five, had written two books full of sexual images, smoked little cigars, and had had more lovers than I could recall— but something still clutched in my gut when I read in the *Savannah Evening News* that Billy Graham was to speak on network television on "Herpes, Sex and the Bible."

"Women were made for pain and poverty," William Faulkner had written in words that described the code with which I had been indoctrinated since childhood. As a teenager during the fifties, prior to the women's, birth-control, and humanistic-psychology revolutions, I couldn't have imagined my life as a sexually free woman. But now I was like Temple, in Faulkner's *Sanctuary*. A society debutante who is raped by the uncivilized Popeye, then kidnapped to a Memphis whorehouse for his pleasure, Temple finds that she prefers her new life to her old. (In the novel's sequel, *Requiem for a Nun*, Temple—rescued and turned respectable matron—leaves home again, obviously yearning for her previous life of debauchery, and it's clear that Faulkner holds her, rather than her trauma at the hands of the rapist, Popeye, responsible for her predilections.)

"Marriage is designed for the sexual repression of women," psychologist Wilhelm Reich wrote long before I had ever heard of him. "Yes, marriage definitely is designed for the benefit of men," a woman sex therapist asserted as we chatted at a party in Greenville, South Carolina. "Research shows that when couples experience conflicts, married men are the least concerned, married women the most, while unmarried lovers are equally involved."

Freud wrote that the history of the world could be stated in one word: repression. But now it seemed that even the most unlikely were liberating themselves. During a "Donahue" show on male strippers, Midwestern housewives, pregnant matrons, and grandmothers in polyester pantsuits hooted, clapped, hollered, as several harmless-looking young men jiggled and bounced around the stage. But just after a grandmother of seven had gigglingly accepted as a gift the garter and satin boxer shorts worn by one of them, a young woman with a face free of makeup, long straight hair, and a stern expression rose to announce herself a born-again Christian, to denounce the Sin! the Sin!—the terrible temptations of the Devil, the Flesh.

A few minutes later, when a second group of strippers gyrated onto the stage—this time, two blacks and an Oriental, in costumes involving camouflage, pistols, cowboy boots, whips, and chains, dancers whose undulations were genuinely erotic, even malevolent—the grandmothers and matrons fell suddenly silent, disapproving, dark. Yet when the camera panned to the face of the born-again Christian, she looked as rapt, as mesmerized, as I was. To the rest of the women in the audience, sex was about as interesting as a game show, but to us, it was important, the dark part of the soul. Would she, too, soon feel a sense of betrayal like that of homosexuals, who, after years of persecution, suddenly became *chic*? Would she, like me, feel disillusioned when she realized that while she had lain in her teenage bed, writhing in fear of hellfire for her simple desire to touch her own body, the other members of her church, yes, even the preacher himself, whose shouted sermons had been the source of her torment, had been secretly, discreetly fucking?

During the early eighties, *Playboy*, *Cosmopolitan*, and the *Ladies' Home Journal* did near-simultaneous surveys on the sex lives of American women, predictably revealing that the readers of the first two publications were slightly more adventurous, those of the latter more monogamous. (In a previous study, the *Ladies' Home Journal* had already shown that "changing" women experienced less depression, sadness, loneliness—or feelings of being too fat— than did "traditional" women.) In her featherweight philosophical tome, *Having It All*, Helen Gurley Brown advised single women to "have a smorgasbord. . . . Sleeping with more than one man on the same day or in the same week could be considered promiscuous, I suppose, yet I think you can do quite a lot of that and *not* be. . . . When I was single, it never occurred to me not to have plenty of this pleasurable thing . . . ," she confessed breathily, breezily—in italics, of course—despite the fact that Gurley on sex sounds not like sex at all, light-years from that primitive drive of the dark night, but an ad for some frilly new deodorant. And though a later article decries the miserable mental health of "The Bed Hopper," *Cosmopolitan*—under Gurley's editorship—tells, in "The Multi-Affair Girl," how to keep all those men happy at once. Indeed, it is a life-style with its own set of manners. "I went ahead and swallowed it," I overheard a young woman at the next table in a chain restaurant confide earnestly to her female companion. "I was afraid it would hurt his feelings if I didn't."

Yet while the new freedom of choice Ms. Gurley espoused was given lip service, Middle-Americans had not yet seen enough of it on television to fully buy it. People fear social change, particularly feminism, because they fear hedonism, claimed sociologist Daniel Yankelovich in an interview in the tenth-anniversary issue of *Ms.* For some, the hidden message in *Looking for Mr. Goodbar*, both the novel and the movie, was that women who assumed the sexual freedom usual to men would bring upon themselves an ultimate punishment—that such freedom was, for women, dangerous business. Just look what happened to Janis Joplin as played by Bette Midler in *The Rose*. And even if one escaped with one's sanity, there were sure to be other punishments: I CAN'T FIND MR. RIGHT—SHIRLEY MACLAINE ran a headline in *The Star*. "Lonely Shirley MacLaine has admitted that despite years of playing the field, she cannot find the perfect man to settle down with," claims the piece; it also quotes the actress as purportedly confessing that "'I don't think that kind of lasting relationship . . . has come to me because I've disregarded a lot of things society says are important. . . .'" "If you ever want to remarry, you'd better do it before this book comes out," a woman friend warned, implying that after my admission to a period of sexual freedom, I would be ruined, disenfranchised.

It was a fear that I, too, sometimes felt, for the double standard was obviously still in full force. When Burt Reynolds described in a *Playboy* interview a period after his divorce from Judy Carne during which he boozed it up and engaged in random sexual experiences of almost every kind, his confessions simply enhanced his image as a superstud; when Erica Jong was interviewed by the same publication after the success of *Fear of Flying*, she had quickly demurred on the subject of her own Zipless Fucks, saying she had really only sexually experienced a "very small" number of men.

"She wuz out runnin' 'round, givin' poetry readin's, neglectin' her chirren," an English professor at a small North Carolina college grumbled to a woman friend of mine after reading *Fatal Flowers*. "What about James Dickey?" my friend had asked. "Is it different for him because he's a *man*?" "Yeah," I mused as she repeated the conversation to me, "if I'd been leavin' my kids at home to support them by workin' the night shift at the chicken processin' plant, *that* would have been okay—just what *any* Good Christian Woman would've done!"

"Why do women, when they get liberated, take on all the worst traits of men?" a man friend grumbled. Indeed, it was my male peers who seemed to take my assumption of personal freedom most personally. "*You're* macho, too, you know!" another accused over dinner as we discussed the subject of macho men. In fact, in following through on my attraction to macho and other "unsuitable" men, I was simply assuming what middle-class men have long held, the privilege of erotically enjoying lovers whom they might not consider marrying—in their case, barmaids, waitresses, and prostitutes; in mine, construction workers, smugglers, and foreign sailors. And while I may have become a tough cookie, someone akin to novelist Reynolds Price's description of a Southern woman as a "Mack truck disguised as a powder puff," I had found valid few of the traditional feminine reasons for treading the sexual straight and narrow: I had not felt depressed or humiliated by sex that didn't lead to a relationship—instead, had experienced the opposite emotion, exhilaration; nor had I been unduly disturbed by my new separation of sex and love.

"It's not *right*," the fat computer expert who had admired the subservience of Moroccan women complained petulantly over the phone to Anne, just after he saw me joke on Atlanta television news about what I liked about working on the oil rig—even though my comment that I "had never pinched so many asses in my life" had been cut. "Well, that's convenient for *you!*" the same man had snorted months earlier, when I had told him how little regard I had for the double standard, or what people thought of me. He had apparently forgotten that at the beginning of our relationship, he had bragged to me that he frequently slept with a different woman every night for weeks on end—giving me an indication of the level of the sexual desperation of single women in America!

"Oh, people have written about those alienated groups," a sociologist and philandering suburban husband said smugly as he lay in my bed, brushing aside my comment that perhaps singles had not yet been seriously studied as a social group. I had just explained that I often found them to be among the most aware, involved people I knew—people who got out into the world, mingled, made things happen, rather than sitting home each night in front of Home Box Office (as he undoubtedly did); too, that I considered the risks repeatedly taken by this group—of rejection, not to mention murder or herpes—in their quest for intimacy to be the equivalent of traveling alone down the Amazon, Indian arrows flying over one's head. But there was little chance he would take my views seriously: overexperienced woman that I was, I had just failed at melting in his clumsy embrace—in fact, had been so underwhelmed by him sexually that I was more interested in talking about sociology than in my palpitations of illicit love. For I had become that thing men—and society—fear most: a sexually and intellectually free woman.

"There was an air about you then—that you could do anything,

weren't afraid of anything," said the woman who had warned me
that I should quickly remarry. But I had always had a faulty early-
warning system, and during my time of living dangerously, I did
have experiences that, for the more self-protective, would have
served as an immediate red light: a dinner date with a handsome
cabbie who had driven me politely from the airport, but who, at the
hotel restaurant, had demanded that I go to the ladies' room to
remove my lingerie "to prove you're a *real* woman"—who, after I
had refused, turned—walking me down the empty hotel corridor
toward my room—even more insolently, frighteningly dominant.
The pleasant-looking man in suit and tie who told me in the bar
where we met that he had made a warmly received pass at Jackie
Onassis in a New York elevator—a possible, if unusual story—but
who, sitting later in my living room, leaning stiffly forward, his eyes
glittering, rambled on in a way that convinced me he was certi-
fiably insane. A harmless-seeming, four a.m. chat with a black-
jacketed biker and his pals in a SoHo bar that quickly turned so
malevolent that my woman companion and I grabbed our coats,
fled the six blocks to her loft, and ran up six flights of stairs to
collapse behind her locked door gasping, sobbing in relief. "In all
the years I've lived in New York, I've never been more frightened!"
she confessed later.

SEXUAL SHAME, OR THE
MAN IN THE BLACK RAINCOAT.

One rainy spring night inside the gay disco, I accepted a drink from
a shaggy, bearded blond man in faded jeans, a black raincoat. My
friend Robert John, standing nearby, shook his head vigorously,
negatively, a signal of his disapproval, but I was high, horny, and
wanted to dance. During number after number, we twirled around
the dim strobe-lit floor, dancing closer and closer each time, his
hard-on pressing more and more persistently into my thigh. It was
only out under the streetlights that I saw the dirt beneath his fin-
gernails, saw how rough, how craggy, how lit by some bizarre light,
his face really was. But by then, it was too late—Robert John had
long since left for home, it was three a.m., and I was too drunk to
protest. What happened when we arrived at my apartment made it
clear I had made a mistake. As he shoved me down onto my bed,

hoarsely whispering sexual suggestions I had never even heard of, things that seemed to have to do with urinating into, and otherwise assaulting, my every orifice, I assumed the role of amiable geisha, hoping that subservience would help me talk him out of at least some of these and perhaps even get me safely through the night.

The next morning, as he reluctantly got out of my Fiat on River Street, I covered my tension by asking that he pick an azalea for me from one of the bushes that bloomed along the plaza, then drove off, waving gaily as I breathed with relief, certain I had seen the last of him. Yet a few weeks later, a persistent rattling and banging woke me from early morning sleep. When I tiptoed into the living room, peeked through the lace curtains, I saw the Man in the Black Raincoat. "I want to screw you," he yelled drunkenly for long minutes after I had tiptoed back to bed.

It was not the kind of behavior that was likely to be noticed in my neighborhood. There had recently been an attempted rape in the apartment above mine; a friend had been shot in the side, the bullet deflecting off a rib into his arm, in a recent mugging; across the street, blacks on welfare sat on their stoops till the early mornings of muggy Savannah days, escaping the heat of ramshackle, unair-conditioned Victorian apartments. Now sometimes as I typed beside a window at sidewalk level, the Man in the Black Raincoat appeared suddenly—leering, importuning, pressing his face to the glass, then moving back and forth to push the front doorbell like an insistent gorilla.

Months later, in Atlanta to visit friends, I stopped at a red light at a downtown intersection to hear a voice from the rattletrap car idling next to mine. "I *know* where you're stayin'," the Man in the Black Raincoat murmured intimately, leaning his scruffy elbow out the passenger side window. During a later trip, I went with friends into a package store in an unsavory section of the city to buy wine to take with us to the Korean restaurant next door. As I glanced backward toward the store front, I saw the Man in the Black Raincoat, his now even scragglier beard, his dirty blond features blunted further by the plate glass as he stared in at me from the dark sidewalk. "I keep thinking of being shot, the thrill of it," my friend kept saying over and over in my living room two days after his mugging. Now the same kind of thrill shot through me, a piercing realization of how often, during recent years, I had risked my life for the adrenaline rush of danger.

It was the same desire for sensation that made me live in the neighborhood where I lived, prefer the sleazy places where I hung out, choose the men friends with whom I now consorted—the same impulse that made my now macho lovers jump out of airplanes, smuggle drugs, drive race cars—an imperative that had become symbolized for me by the Man in the Black Raincoat.

.   .   .

THE LEGEND OF SILVER LEAF AND SILVER LEAF RENT.

One day, Silver Leaf was walking in the forest, and fell into a trap set by her own father. As it would have the animal he had intended to kill, a stake impaled her body through the center. Within moments, she was found by her horrified mother, who had her pulled from the spike.

Her father, shamed, fled the village. Silver Leaf lived, but her wound took two years to heal, and thereafter she was known as Silver Leaf Rent. She spent the following years going from tribe to tribe seducing the men, yet because of the scar near her heart, feeling nothing for them.

Until the day she lay down with the brave who wore her father's pain on the day he had left written across his face: when she arose, she saw that the scar had miraculously dissolved. . . .

After a while, I had slept with so many men that if I lay down alone in my pink and white Victorian bedroom to masturbate, I found myself unable to focus on any one man in particular. Yet, man-like, I could now also concentrate on almost any attractive male image, just as men are able to do with the images of unknown women in pornography; but perhaps unlike men, the sheer number and variety of my lovers had broken down any preconceived preference of body type. Instead, their various faces, bodies dissolved in my brain like soap bubbles—lovely, yet teasingly ephemeral, evanescent in their diversity, and with as little individual impact, flimsy figments that burst into rainbow colors, the Godiva chocolates of memory, melting at the edge of sleep or fantasy.

More disconcerting were the pictures, like Polaroid snapshots, that suddenly developed in my mind during the most ordinary activities—shopping for tomatoes, or driving to the post office—of nameless faces, cocks, postures. "Look at that handsome man!" I exclaimed to Laura as we passed a tall, silver-curled stranger, who was striding the sidewalk opposite my Fiat, then realized it was Larry, the GBI agent with whom I had long before slept. Sometimes there was something titillating—the wink across a crowded room, a special smile, the delicious sense of a shared secret—in running into a former one-night-stand at a party or in a public place, a sense that, if several were present at once, felt something like having a lot of money in the bank. But when I met a former bedmate with whom I shared such apathy or aversion that neither of us wanted to speak or even recognize the other, I tasted a piquant shame at having given myself so carelessly—or was it of not having really loved or cared? "Let's not go *there*," I began saying to women friends, leaving out my unspoken fear that I might run into too many men with whom I had slept.

CONSORTING WITH THE ENEMY.

"I never knew men were such shits until I became a woman," says the transsexual Roberta in John Irving's novel *The World According to Garp*. I had always known that they were; I had been dependent on them but had not really admired them. Now, for the first time, I could view a man as a person rather than a meal ticket, a power source, or a steady Saturday-night date. Though I still occasionally muttered, "I hate men!" as I watched a TV show on, say, rapists or the arms race, that bitterness had dissipated along with my dependency. Ironically, the more I liked men the less I had to fuck them.

In retrospect, I realized I had suffered my whole life from a profound ambivalence toward the other sex. On the one hand, I was an adventuress who had disrupted my own life—not to mention the lives of others—with multiple marriages, affairs, and one-night-stands; on the other, my compulsions had been fed by an underground stream of deep mistrust. Yet instead of adding to that feeling of distrust, my period of sexual randomness had had an unexpectedly tonic effect. In a few years, I had discovered more about men than I had in my whole previous life, and, in choosing and accepting lovers at the far end of the spectrum of macho, had also exorcised the embedded penis of my childhood nightmares. The word *promiscuity* didn't adequately cover what, for me, had been an incredible learning experience—a means to conciliation with the male half of myself and the other half of the human race. Whereas before I had seen men as cardboard cutouts—rakes, pirates, or wimps—I now saw them as partners in mutual need and pleasure, rather than figures I needed for social or economic reasons. And because of my own indulgence in "masculine" behavior, things that—had I been seeking a more dependent relationship—I would have found intolerable, I had begun to accept, even enjoy.

It was not that men were any less childish, difficult, or insensitive than I had previously believed, it was just that my attitude toward them had changed. What I had once considered puzzling or disgusting was now understandable, if still disagreeable. I had wondered at the loneliness of the desperado, but now I, too, feared the middle-class trap, the comforts—and the ennui—of suburbanism. I had been angered by the way they clung to the security of dull wives, fucking women like me on the side. Now I, too, had experienced sex without responsibility or love, as adventure or sport. I had snorted at their desire for younger lovers, but with Jason, Raymond, and others, I had felt the headiness—however reprehensible—of dominance, control, and the ability to detach oneself, walk away without a thought. When a man friend—a "sensitive" poet— beat on the side of his pickup, yelling, "I wanna fuck that!" as we passed a pretty pedestrian, I still didn't like it, but what could I say? Hadn't I assessed, if less vocally, the curve of an ass, the flex of a thigh or biceps?

Curiously, the better I understood male limitations, vulnerabilities, the more maternal I felt toward the men I saw struggling with their male roles. "How can you ask something from *him* you don't expect from yourself?" I asked a fashion-model-turned-housewife who had just tearfully complained to me that her husband— who had left his first wife and his five children for her when she became pregnant—wasn't supporting her in the style to which she had been accustomed, nor was he fucking her as much as he had during the first passionate years of their affair. Yet I knew how she felt. With Daddy, my son, my husbands, I had expected toughness, control, responsibility—they were *men*, weren't they?—and had been disappointed when I hadn't gotten it. But now, as an economically independent woman, I found it remarkable that men had managed over the years to assume as much responsibility for others as they had, and found their heartaches, heart attacks, and high blood pressure understandable.

Even sadder were the patterns I had observed in the oil riggers, and my other blue-collar boyfriends. Bobby, my roughneck lover, worked two weeks on, two weeks off, twelve hours a day to make the money he needed to live each month and foresaw no possible change in the future because of the limitations of his education and class. When we met, he was twenty-four, had been married, divorced, and had seen too much in Vietnam. The most he could expect of the future—if he were lucky—would be a house trailer, a pickup truck, a wife who would sometimes fuck him and would put him to bed without too much flak when he came home drunk. What the middle class depends on to soothe the psyche—art, books, travel, beautiful surroundings—all those comforts symbolized by Sunday mornings spent over croissants and *The New York Times*—were unknown and unavailable to him. Was it any wonder that he stayed high during his two weeks off, threw his bowie knife at the roses in my wallpaper, wanted to indulge in wild escapades—to forget, forget, forget?

I once walked with a male friend across the dry rock bed through which a dammed river sometimes poured, and seeing the dam wall rising ominously above us, had felt terrified. The man, one of the frustrating lovers I had before turning to macho men, was amused—as such men sometimes are at a woman's discomfort—by my desire to hurry to the other side. Now it seemed to me that the whole history of my life with men had been like that dam, looming over my head with the threat of the unresolved.

A neurosurgeon had described to me an anomaly of the brain, in which blood vessels cluster and press beneath the skull, affecting brain function, as a "nest of worms." Now I slowly realized that, through my experimentation, I had been unconsciously following an organic course of resolution: I had been untangling threads left from childhood, the throbbing nest of worms that was my relationship with my father.

"Neurosis is always a substitute for legitimate suffering," stated Carl Jung. And the wound that was my early life with Daddy was becoming obvious as the reason for my sexual flightiness, my three marriages, my problems with my son David during his teenage bouts with drugs and the law. Co-opted by Mother for her "side," I had never considered my relationship with my father important. But with Daddy—and later with David—there had been something missing at the center, something that should have been resolved before I became the mother of a son at eighteen.

As my career as a female Don Juan drew to a close, I found myself feeling the empathy that had been absent from my relationships with them—and with other men—for my whole life. It had taken Mother's death, years of therapy, and a period of sexual freedom for my love and tenderness, if not my rage, to surface at last.

Now, like the paint books I had as a child in which one brushed on water and a full-color image magically appeared, technicolor images developed to haunt me: Daddy's golf clubs, rusting outside the kitchen door; his failed life as a tire salesman, and Mother's endless complaints about money; his disappointment when he couldn't get into the Navy during the Second World War because of hemorrhoids; his compulsive drinking, his gambling debts; and, finally, our moves back to our grandparents' homes, Mother going out to work to support us—pictures of every scene that must have led up to his diminished sense of himself as a man. Since he was dead, I could only imagine, in retrospect, his misery: what it must have been like for this sensitive, artistic—if hell-bent—young man to gradually realize his inability to take care of his prize—his beautiful belle-bride.

With fresh pangs, I recalled the look on the face of my second husband, Paul, when he learned of my affair with the Famous Southern Poet, and the dark look on David's, as, pubescent, my son emerged from the shower to hear Paul shout, "I don't want another man's penis inside you, you hear?" I remembered a letter written to me by my third husband, Ben: "Do you realize that you have spent more time during the last six months with this other man than with me, your husband?" I thought of Bobby, crying drunkenly in the night at his memory of watching from his vantage as a sniper the disembowelment of a Marine major by Vietcong, of Jay's burden of guilt at his fraternity-boy rape, of Jason's inability to live up to his rancher-father's stern imperatives. In a way perhaps only a woman socially and economically independent of them can do, I was beginning to sense the tragedy of men's lives.

THE INVENTION OF THE KLEENEX, OR AFTER YOU ARE INTRODUCED TO DISPOSABLE TISSUES, WILL YOU STILL WANT A LINEN HANDKERCHIEF?

"The point is not to cross the desert but to be in it," Robyn David-son, author of *Tracks*, told *Town and Country* magazine. It was the way I felt about the men whom I had encountered during my pe-riod of loose living: I had wanted the experience of them, not the possession.

Yet if freedom was so heady and, at times, so instructive, why did I find myself voluntarily ending it?

Because I tired of waking hung-over in strange bedrooms, the knees of my designer stockings torn. . . . Because sleeping with so many people, however delicious each was, became like trudging through fields of chocolate-covered cherries. Like a child who had been allowed as much candy as she wishes, I had become sick of sweets. . . .

Because, one morning at three a.m., I drove down a Savannah street to see my transsexual friend, Cherry Delight, leaning for-ward in the rumble seat of a white convertible, moonlight lapping her pale curls, her white-white shirt, and felt, in the moment that we passed, how each of us was encapsulated in perfect loneliness, prisoners of our own freedom. . . .

Because, at the supermarket, I began to yearn to be part of two, to buy a lobster and cook it with someone I knew; someone with whom, even after sex, I might want to stay and talk awhile. . . . Because as soon as I took the notion, I was like somebody with the flu—all my previous excitements began, in the face of this new fever, to pale. . . .

Because one night I walked into a bar, looked at the smiling Stanley Kowalski–type leaning against the bar in cutoffs and T-shirt, beer held in a fist leading to a tattooed bicep, and felt it was time to test my new empathy in a one-on-one relationship with a man as wild as I was, the kind of man I had learned from my re-search that I liked best.

PART SIX

MAGNOLIA

AMONG

THE

MESAS

"What're *you* doin' here?" asks a fat, muscular man in kilts and fatigue shirt, a bagpipe over his large shoulder, peering at the press badge perched on the slope of my pink lamb's-wool sweater. When I explain that I'm here to observe the macho man, he glances around the lobby of the Charlotte, North Carolina, Holiday Inn. Around us mill hundreds of men in camouflage, a few in T-shirts with slogans like "Happiness Is a Confirmed Killer," and "I'd Rather Be Killing Commies," and several amputees in wheelchairs, their fatigues rolled where knees or elbows would have been. "I wonder if there's any around here," he says, puzzled.

The event is the annual *Soldier of Fortune* convention, subtitled "A Society of Professional Adventurers." The first time I saw an issue of the magazine that sponsored the convention had been when Laura—crying, "Mother! Look at this weird magazine!"— had fished a copy out of the trash barrel she shared with the policeman upstairs. When Phil Donahue had as guests on his show the magazine's editor and publisher, Robert Brown, and contributor and French Foreign Legion veteran, Bill Brooks, I agreed with his charge that the Soldiers of Fortune were "children—dangerous children." I had applauded the exchange in which Brooks said that the beauty of the Legion was "the discipline—they didn't question orders," to which Donahue countered, "they didn't in the Third Reich, either!" I enjoyed Donahue's accusation that—even though Robin Moore, author of *The Green Berets* and keynote speaker in 1980, had been asked to leave by the publisher because of racist comments from the podium—few blacks or Jews had attended the organization's most recent convention. I too had been appalled, along with the liberal Donahue, at the permanent-waved and pant-suited audience's apathy, even approval, in the face of such militarism.

Yet now I lived with a man who kept the magazine beside our bed! The first few times I opened one of Zane's copies, I slammed it shut, repelled by one advertisement after another for weapons of every evil kind and intent; what looked like picture after picture of glorified blood and gore, open wounds, and decapitation; and article after article on such handy subjects as, say, "How to Kill from Behind," "The Correct Execution of the Belgian Rear Takedown," and "The Head Smash, The Eye Gouge, The Two-Finger Strangle"—complete with detailed and instructive illustrations. But giving in to my magnetic attraction to the printed word in any form (also my own repressed aggressive impulses?), I continued to flip through them, as well as his copies of *Army Times*, *Guns and Ammo*, *Sky Diver*—and, of course, all his hard-core pornography—until, gradually, I had become desensitized. By the time *Soldier of Fortune* advertised its coming convention, it had simply become another raunchy rag, the *Hustler* magazine of violence. I was used to the imagery—and curious. Who—besides Zane—craved such literature? And what were the other women like who related to such men? Thinking that, in case I needed a bodyguard, Zane would accompany me, I called the publication's offices in Boulder and asked for a press pass.

But Zane, it turned out, had better things to do that weekend—such as be in the real Army and hang out at his favorite bars. Thus I found myself, one wet night in October, driving the six hours to Charlotte, North Carolina, alone, experiencing, though I was a frequent solitary traveler, more trepidation than I had expected. It was a feeling that was compounded as I twice erroneously exited the rain-smeared freeway—once to find myself at a muddy truck stop among milling men and semis full of oinking hogs and clucking chickens; the second time, to end up in a silent industrial area where huge factories and warehouses looked like the landscape of a deserted planet. When I finally found my way to the Days Inn across from the convention center where I had a reservation, man after man was being turned from the desk.

"Ev'ry motel in town's full cause 'a this thang!" the clerk said, adding that, miraculously, my own room had been held. Leaving behind a bass choir of voices offering to share my accommodations, I went back out to my Fiat for my pink Diane von Furstenberg luggage. As I self-consciously lugged it up to my second-floor balcony room, a chorus of whistles and "Hey, mamas" fell like persistent rain from the fatigue-clad men leaning on the rail. In my room at last, I secured every lock, collapsed on the bed with a glass of straight Black Jack, and wondered what I had gotten myself into this time.

Yet the next morning in the Holiday Inn, a pretty young woman in jeans smiled warmly, handed me a press badge and a press kit, and introduced me to other female members of the staff. Lou, a middle-aged woman with a kind face and intelligent eyes, manned the table where insignia, clothing, and other paraphernalia were on sale. She wore a *Soldier of Fortune* T-shirt, a green beret atop her dark knotted hair, as did her gray-haired, seventyish mother, standing beside her with a smile to match her daughter's. A senior editor, Lou is one of two staffers with doctorates in medieval drama. She spent a year at Oxford, another as an editor at Lippincott, and met her second husband, Bob Larson—a gentle-looking man seated beside her nodding beatifically—when he sent an article to the magazine describing his experiences as a prisoner of war captured on Corregidor during the Second World War.

The magazine is apparently a family affair for the rest of the staff as well, whom Lou describes as "a tight group of artistic and educated people." All have at least college degrees, she tells me. Another editor has a master's in Precambrian geology, and Bill Brooks, who has written extensively of his five years in the French Foreign Legion, was once a librarian. As we chat, a Warren Beatty–handsome man in black turtleneck, a camera slung over a shoulder, stops to say hello. "Dana Drenkowski—he used to be on the staff," Lou whispers.

Dana turns out to be another anomaly: an Air Force Academy graduate, Air Force captain, and fighter pilot, he also has a law degree, a master's degree in psychology, and worked for Congresswoman Pat Schroeder during her 1976 and 1978 campaigns. He served as an officer in three Miami-area chapters of NOW, and is on the board of directors for the organization in Florida and Colorado. "When I left the Air Force, I thought about which group—civil rights or women—would need the support of a white single male more, and decided the women would," he explained when I looked surprised. "It stemmed from my belief in individual rights. I was a professional soldier, but in Vietnam, I found I was literally martyring myself, covering up the corruption—our hands were tied behind our backs, operations were poorly planned and executed. I was with a unit that was annihilated—less than thirty planes left out of seventy-two. I went through three roommates, and suffered guilt at my survival," he went on, explaining why he had left the service. But he had been abroad in a nonmilitary capacity since.

"Rescues and so on," he said, adding quickly that "I served *in* foreign countries—but never *under* the flag of one, or of our armed services either. . . ." He looked at me intently, making certain that I had this clear. It was an exercise in the semantics I was soon to learn were an important part of the language here. ("But what do you *do?*" I would ask a grizzled-looking older man later that afternoon, imagining, when he handed me a card with the magazine's logo, the words "security officer," and his name, that he was a janitor. "Just put it this way," he said, looking at me slyly, self-importantly, "If there's a fire somewhere, I go put it out!")

"These people are active, do things," Lou emphasized as Lou's mother smiled benevolently, Dana walked away and into the open arms of women staffers eager to embrace him, and I fantasized the words "The Best of What It Is to Be American" emblazoned across his noble forehead, just beneath his curly forelock. "Their greatest fear," commented Lou, "is not being free, and they have mottoes to express that fear—such as the Marine saying, 'Freedom is not free.' Or 'Controlled violence to control violence.' And another thing we promote is a more positive view of America—our publication praised the Vietnam vet, the American military for doing a necessary dirty job. . . ." Her words recalled Zane's inevitable comment during our endless arguments about the U.S. Army: "Well, *somebody's* gotta do it!" he would finally cry in exasperation.

These sentiments were undoubtedly popular with the magazine's aficionados: 11 percent were law-enforcement officers, 12 percent active military, and 48 percent veterans—the same groups of men who have the highest rates of spouse abuse, I thought to myself, perusing the press-kit printout. I read on to learn that the average *Soldier of Fortune* reader has a college education and earns $23,000 per year. "But the best thing for us women on the staff is that they're so nonsexist," Lou was saying as I glanced farther down the page to read that *Soldier of Fortune's* writers and editors are "goers and doers rather than deskbound journalists. All *SOF* staff personnel, men and women alike, may volunteer for free firearms, scuba and parachute training. *SOF* staffers have reported on the scene from conflicts in South Africa, Angola, Afghanistan, El Salvador, Lebanon, Pakistan, Honduras, Guatemala, Philippines, Morocco, Thailand and Laos. . . ." "They even go overseas for stories sometimes," Lou continued. "For instance, one editor, Donna

DuVall, could've gotten killed when she took that cab to the airport in Beirut," she added as though speaking of a privilege.

"Hey, baby, what're *you* doin' here?" asked a tall blond—and yes, movie-star handsome—man with a wink, interrupting our conversation. It was only one of the several times I would be asked the same question that day. As he picked up two T-shirts and laid some bills on the table, he grinned flirtatiously, clenching his fat cigar between his teeth. "Dr. G.," said Lou. Then, when he turned to shake hands with yet another handsome—this time, as in tall, dark and—man: "And that's Dr. P.—good examples of the kind of people we get here." Which, I thought after I had walked over to ask if I could interview them together, is, to say the least, *competitive*: for the next fifteen minutes, macho phrases like "grew up in the ghetto . . . first outfit in Vietnam . . . crawled in shit, had to eat it. . . . Sixty-four Olympics, All Marine Corps boxing team . . . box sixteen-ounce gloves . . . shoot five-millimeter rounds . . . jump out of planes . . . lift weights . . . high-speed auto accidents . . . chase women . . . married gal with big bucks . . . was adviser in jungle . . . would volunteer for El Salvador," poured over my head like a tidal wave.

"One more question," I managed to interject as Dr. G. was explaining that while he had chosen to come to the *Soldier of Fortune* event rather than attend a White House cocktail party, he *had* chartered a jet for $6,000 "to take me later." "Do either of you consider yourselves macho?" "Of course!" Dr. G. exclaimed in an out-of-sync chorus to Dr. P.'s "Absolutely not!"

"By the way," Dr. P. went on, "What's the title of the book you're writing?"

"Just write this," he said authoritatively when I told him. "Soldiers don't sleep well!"

As I sat down in the motel coffee shop, I glimpsed Dr. G. at a nearby table, sitting across from the silent, wasp-thin blonde woman who had the distinct look of a wife petulantly indulging her boymate's whims. While I thought about the many times I had seen expressions such as hers before, a large bald man in camouflage, with what looked like the skeleton of a human hand hanging from a chain around his neck, approached the group in the booth next to mine. "Have you heard the sound of one hand clapping?" he asked jovially, flapping the bony pendant. "I love to shock those reporters." I had seen him earlier, sitting with a long-haired girl who had been earnestly scribbling in a notebook. "She asked the same old question they all do"—here he mimicked a falsetto voice—"'Are youall really like people think you are!' And she claims *her* name is Candy Barr!" The group laughed, and I noticed that they were dressed differently from the other conferees around us: an attractive, fortyish man wore a cowboy shirt machine-embroidered with roses; a plump pale man around the same age was preppily clad in V-neck sweater, pin-striped button-down shirt; and the woman had on a black cotton jumpsuit and high-heeled sandals. Their civilian softness in the midst of so much camouflage couture was appealing. "Do you mind if I sit with you and ask some questions?" I asked.

Ed, the man in the rose-embroidered shirt, introduced everyone to me, then asked if I was "the Daniell who had written a book." He was a writer, too, he said, did pieces for *Soldier of Fortune*, *High Times*, *Rolling Stone*. . . . "But first of all, he's a *soldier*," interjected his wife, Jennifer. The man in the sweater, also an Ed, said *he* was simply resident comedian (I would later learn he was a millionaire munitions dealer). He added—in a tone that assumed I would know the name, giving me my first indication that this was a world with its own stars—that the malevolent-looking man with the human-hand necklace was *John Donovan*, who, it turned out, was, as Jennifer put it, "America's foremost demolition expert—if you want anything blown up, John can do it!"

Ed-of-the-roses had served in Vietnam as a Special Forces major "in tactics and strategy. After which I was nuts for a decade—Nam took seventeen months of my life, but it now occupies seventy-five percent of my thinking. . . ." He had gone on to creative-writing school, wrote articles, wanted to write a book, but in his mind, was still military. "I don't *have* a political philosophy," he said when I asked. "I'm just a *soldier*. . . ." At forty-five, he ran thirteen miles and did an hour's yoga each day, to keep in shape—"and got really depressed when he couldn't keep up on a patrol not long ago!" Jennifer whispered confidentially.

I thought of what a psychologist friend who specialized in working with spouse batterers had told me—that the men among his clients who have a high investment in their physicality, their macho image, suffer a mid-life crisis of identity that is much like that experienced by an exceptionally beautiful woman who has depended on appearance for self-worth, then finds her looks naturally fading with age. Yet recently Ed had been to El Salvador as an adviser—"I can turn you on to some people down there if you want to go"—and had been one of the few non-Thais to parachute into Thailand from a hot-air balloon, where such vehicles are used as a training device.

Jennifer, who had taken the photographs of that jump that were used in the magazine, wore the wings he had received in honor of it on the blouse of what she told me were black Oriental pajamas—"I had them made in Bangkok." Even with little makeup, she was pretty, feminine-looking, with small bones, white, white skin, and curly, shoulder-length hair of a shade that, in the beauty business might be called "refined brown." But her conversation was peppered with references to the DMZ, "packin' it in" (being killed), and "carryin'" (a gun)—"She's been around *us* too much," her husband said laughingly to the other Ed, pleased. And though they had only been married a year—"my third marriage, Ed's fourth"—she had already been with him during that time to Lebanon, Israel, Cambodia, Thailand. Indeed, she had gone from Thailand into Cambodia to the front lines because Ed, as a journalist, had been too well known.

"Yeah, I was worried as hell about 'er!" Ed said. "It was a *lot* worse than going out, bein' shot at myself!"

"Well, the worst thing to *me*," Jennifer retorted, her giggle a girlish tinkle, "was that I got so *tired*. It was twelve kilometers out to the front lines, but before I realized how far that *was*, it was too late to go back, and Harry"—she indicated a Tom Selleck look-alike across the room—"certainly couldn't *carry* me all the way. . . ."

A few minutes before, when I had told her I was originally from Atlanta, she had said how much she wished to go there—"to buy some new clothes, go to Charles Jourdan for high heels." Now I imagined her stumbling toward the front lines in red fuck-me pumps, leaning on the purposeful Harry's biceps. In Jennifer, I had the sense of a woman in a state of perpetual exhilaration; like Darcy, she obviously didn't want to lead a boring life. "Lebanon's *the* place to live right now," she was enthusing. "The rents are cheap, the seashore's nearby. . . ."

"How much danger *is* there in your way of life?" I asked, beginning to see that here, *danger* was a synonym for excitement, pleasure, meaning. "Well, when Ed's gone into a war zone, separations *can* get pretty grim—I'm imagining things worse than they are," Jennifer mused. "'N' if you're the one there, you risk strap-hangin'—being caught in a dangerous situation." "With some fool who might kill you if you try to go back," Ed added. "But because you're an American, you're not supposed to carry anything in case you get killed with it and the government is held responsible."

The mention of weapons seemed to remind Jennifer of something. "Do you want to drive over to the convention center, see some of the displays?" she asked me in the girlishly chummy tone women often use to invite one another to check out dress shops. In a few minutes, we were meandering into a huge midtown convention hall. "I don't know *why* the people around here picketed the conference," she went on as we passed table after table of pistols with and without silencers, submachine guns, daggers, stilettoes, and black knives. (I knew what the last was because Zane had brought one home, pulling it triumphantly from a sack with the name of the shopping center where he had purchased it as a going-away gift for an army buddy. "I got it engraved the way I wanted, with his name," he had said, waving the ominous dull-black blade in the air as I cringed. Then, drawing pink ribbon and paper from another sack, had added, puzzled: "But for some reason, I couldn't get anybody to gift-wrap it!")

At a stall full of books on such subjects as *How to Kill*, volumes one to five, we stopped to chat with the person manning it. Jennifer had greeted the frizzy-haired woman with a delighted hug. Now she explained—in the tone of one speaking of a near-inconceivable past delusion—that they had both once been antiwar protesters, in fact, had marched in Washington together.

"And now you're publishing these—uh—*books!*" I marveled to the frizzy-haired friend, my eyes leaping nervously over cover illustrations of one man garrotting another, a machine-gunner squatting in position to fire. "Yeah—'n' I sure am glad!" she said. "For one thing, I like the *men* better." Indeed, milling around us were some of the best-looking men I had seen off a movie screen. Yet watching them pore over sheath knives and phone-tapping devices was disconcerting, to say the least. "They're a *lot* less sexist than those 'deep, sensitive, liberated' types I used to date—'n' type 'n' cook 'n' pick up laundry for!" she asserted, as though reading my mind. I had to nod in agreement to *that*.

"Yeah, when I was a liberal, there was a *lot* more perversity,"

Jennifer joined in. "Drugs, group sex, orgies. And my second husband couldn't even get it up without the kinky stuff—crotchless panties, stockings 'n' garter belts. Yet he was so jealous, so unsure of himself as a man, that if I went *outside* the house dressed up, he went bananas. And *he* was the one who beat me up, not Ed. Ed's too sure of himself for *that.* . . .

"Because these guys are straightforward about it," she went on in what was beginning to sound like a defense of the trained killer as lover, "they flirt without being lewd or lecherous. Most are very straight, monogamous, yet they really like the ladies, they like to fuck—and *do* have a genuinely higher sex drive, with more of their masculinity tied up in their ability to perform sexually. And the woman *has* to come out totally exhausted and satisfied, or something's wrong. . . .

"And, true, they *do* have more of that ole madonna-whore complex," she continued as Ms. Frizzy-Hair and I smiled in agreement. "They're just *dyin'* for another man to be rude to a woman or make a pass so they can deck 'em, but I *like* havin' my car door opened, or my cigarette lit for me. Also, they're more open, expressive. Ed 'n' I talk to each other at least two hours a day." Feeling suddenly exhausted, I tallied up the hours Ed spent running, doing yoga, and keeping Jennifer sexually satisfied, not to mention parachuting into Thailand, or marching on patrols in Central America, then writing about it. "Why, I've seen him tear up, cry, at a certain song, the memory of a friend who got killed. . . ."

It sounded as though all women had to do to find the Rhett Butlers of the world was what Jennifer and I had been doing, search them out in their natural habitats. I had to admit that—though he had sort of spoiled it by confessing that his father had once advised him that during any conflict with a woman, the solution was to send her flowers or to the beauty parlor—I had received more roses from Zane during the short months I had known him than from any of the more "appropriate" men in my life. And Jennifer's litany, which continued as we walked on, sounded like all the things I had learned and liked about the macho man.

Yet there was more to it than that. Jennifer may have looked like her home state of Arkansas's version of Scarlett O'Hara, but she was definitely macha to her man's macho. "One thing they do," she was saying now, "is mentally assign you a military rank—I'm sure to Ed, I'm a master sergeant; they run things—or maybe even a captain by now. They're lookin' for a woman who, if they're gone for a while, or the shit hits the fan, can take care of things. . . ." Doubtless Jennifer could. Despite her Asian-doll appearance, our shared fantasies of working as a topless dancer, or worse, I was beginning to realize she was even less fragile than I. "Were you always so risk-taking?" I asked. "Oh, sure!" she said. "I rode horses bareback growin' up, was into spelunkin', mountain climbin', rappelin'—just did what all the folks around me did. Ed says I drive like the chase scene in *To Catch a Thief*. I had a Super Sport with a three-twenty-seven V-eight engine—man, I could lay about two miles of rubber in that dude!"

She had already told me about her best friend in Bangkok: "A beautiful whore who would cut your heart out in a minute—a *lot* more interesting—and fun—than those stuffy embassy wives!" she had said, conjuring up Junior Leaguers abroad in Villager shirt-waists and closed-toe pumps, serving up proper yet boring teas while Jennifer and her friend, dressed in sexy cheongsams, sipped Singapore Slings in incense-scented bars hung with beaded curtains. "Because the men there were so bad, the women were always ahead, could get away with *any*thing. . . ."

Apparently, Jennifer and I had discovered the same secret: by surrounding ourselves with bad boys, we could be as tough as we wished without losing our femininity. And because *they* did it so much to us, we could freely objectify them.

"Oh, there's *Hiney*," she breathed with the same reverence a less macha woman would have reserved for Cary Grant, indicating a sweet-faced middle-aged man. "He *started* Air America! And Bill Brooks!"—she nodded toward the winsomely handsome man whose face I recognized from "Donahue" and Zane's books on the French Foreign Legion. "I just think he's the cutest thing. . . ." True, five years of fifty-mile road marches, sleeping on the hard ground or filthy sheets (issued once a month, according to one of Zane's books), hadn't seemed to age him. In fact, he looked remarkably young, fair for his age—a perfectly credible librarian. "Of course, the *real* mercenaries don't meet at a place like this— you should go to the convention the Special Forces vets put on each year," she went on as though describing the delicacies at Zabar's, David's chocolate chip cookies, or pesto sauce to die for. "*That's* where the *real* hard-core guys are. . . ."

I stopped to buy Zane a T-shirt that read "Death from Above" in bright blue to match his eyes—no shortage of size extra-large here—and considered a teddy bear dressed in Green Beret camouflage and insignia for thirty-five dollars. But, despite the sign that read SUPPORT YOUR RIGHT TO ARM BEARS, decided it cost too much. When I turned around, Jennifer was talking to a tall, striking blonde in a pink picture hat, whom I had seen in the coffee shop. She was now standing behind a booth for "The Committee for a Free Afghanistan," and when Jennifer introduced us, was eager to talk.

Beneath the coyly romantic hat, Karen's face was determined, androgynous. She looked like Robert John in the photograph he had given me of himself in drag. The equality of women in the armed services, their right to bear arms, it turned out, was her greatest passion, making her an unlikely ally to more left-wing feminists: "I've debated Phyllis Schlafly on TV on 'Freeman Reports,' a Communist antiwar protester on the 'Barry Lynd' show . . . am positive about women in the Army, furious about closing twenty-eight MOS's to them—just those mindless men! 'The Forward Edge of Battle Area' no longer exists. We now use Defense in Depth, therefore keeping women out of combat roles is inoperative. All women should serve in the military, even the handicapped—have six months basic training, then go active or reserve. That's why I'm not on active duty anymore—I'm too outspoken!"

Shades of Dr. P. and Dr. G.! I thought, as we drove away from the convention hall. "I came to research macho men, instead I'm finding out about macha women," I said to Jennifer. "Wait till tonight when you meet Mary, the publisher Bob Brown's girl friend. She used to be a war protester, too, but she's just as feminine as can be," Jennifer said, as though the two were contradictory, then went on to prove herself literate as well as pretty and adventurous. "After all—'Every woman loves a fascist,/The boot in the face, the brute/ Brute heart of a brute like you,'" she said gaily, laughing her tinkly laugh while quoting Sylvia Plath.

Back at the Holiday Inn, Jennifer decided to crash for some beauty sleep, and I wandered the lobby, looking for more macho men. "We're not macho, we're *moderates*," said the fat bagpipe players in kilts. "We still like to open doors 'n' thangs like that. Why, we're really just *kids*," explained their leader, who had told me they were all First Airborne Division parachutists from Shreveport. He motioned to each of his compatriots in turn: "*He's* got a train set and racing cars, I've got a train set, 'n' *he's* got the best thang—a Mickey Mouse set where Donald Duck reaches out 'n' hits Mickey 'n' all. . . ." "'N' ah just came to this here because ah lak to join up with thangs," added the one who had told me that he had formerly been a member of the Eagle motorcycle gang. "God's gift to wimmen!" they chimed in unison when I asked the traditional question about what was under the kilts. "'N' did you know that men have only been wearin' pants for nine hundred years? 'N' those Scots were *great* fighters—the only ones to defeat the Romans. . . ."

It seemed time to try to find some more *serious* soldiers of fortune. In the coffee shop, I spied Lollie, the seventeen-year-old official "seamstress" for the convention. When I first met her earlier in the day, she had explained to me that her father, a retired major, now manufactured the insignia that the conventioneers were purchasing. Her role was to stitch this insignia on their camouflage fatigues. "Sewing on buttons 'n' stuff—that's what *moms* are for, I tell them—but then they bat those big blue eyes. . . ." Lollie's baby blues were pretty big, too, and she looked, well, *adorable* in olive-drab shorts, a red beret, two long blond ponytails. She had told me that she liked "masculine guys—you know, *jocks*," and now she was sitting at a table with what looked like three of them.

"Johnathan Lee—spelled J-O-H-N," explained the one with the blond surfer's hair, the professional tan, when I introduced myself. He was a movie actor from Toronto, in fact, had performed in New York in "General Hospital" ("Isn't he good-*looking*?" Lollie moaned into my ear. "But when I went up to his room with him, he told me he *had* a girl friend . . ."). The other two—more working-class, less flashy looking—were an auto mechanic and a carpenter in "real" life. But all three were veterans: Johnathan, of skirmishes with the IRA in Belfast—"where the worst thing was fighting with people who spoke the same language you did"—the others, of Vietnam. "The worst thing to me was comin' back to this country 'n' not bein' able to buy a beer yet because I wasn't twenty-one!" said the carpenter when I asked what had bothered *him* most.

"You guys seem nice enough," I went on, employing what I knew by now to be the acceptable rhetoric, "normal, all-American men committed to killing Commies. But who are the people who come to this thing and buy books like *How to Kill*, or go to the demon-stration on 'Attack Dogs, Knives, and Machine Guns'?"

With a near-imperceptible motion, the handsome actor sud-denly drew a six-inch stiletto from somewhere on his person, wav-ing it with a theatrical flourish within a half inch of my nose. "I learned *that* in *How to Kill*—I think it was volume three," he said earnestly, ignoring my start. "'N' I've found it *useful*. For instance, the last time a guy jumped me in a bar—or when this other one jumped me in a parking lot, tried to whip me across the face with a radio antenna—"

"Yeah," the carpenter broke in enthusiastically. "This guy stole the radio outta my car three times. The third time I was waitin' for 'im 'n' hit 'im on the leg with a board, broke 'is ankle. . . ." The auto mechanic nodded vigorously, as if in agreement that this land was a dangerous one for the honest man, when the carpenter continued indignantly, "Then *I* got charged with assault 'n' battery!"

The actor looked at me seriously, leaning across the table, hold-ing my eyes with his long-lashed blue ones. "The way I see it is this: my home is my castle, and my castle is my kill zone. And I'm gonna protect myself and my lady, no matter what!" he said dra-matically.

Robert Brown's girl friend, Mary, looked so good in camouflage that had she gone to a fashion colorist, the muted greens and browns would surely have come up as her most flattering shades. A divorcée with two children, she lived in Boulder, where she had served as the magazine's art director, arranging the rag's bloody photographs, malevolent ads, and now directed art for *Survive* magazine, also published by Brown's organization. Her first hus-band, she revealed over before-dinner drinks with me, had been a carpenter in Boulder; during the late sixties, while Brown had been in Vietnam, she had been a student and anti-war protestor in Berkley.

"But what about the men *here*?" What are they *really* like?" I asked, meaning, by implication, Brown as well.

"There are so many theories," she murmured, "that military men are trained killers, wife abusers, latent homosexuals." She went on to explain that her parents, who were extremely liberal, had come to accept Brown, "because he's so good to me and the children."

She looked at me mutely, as though there was more she wanted to say but couldn't. Jennifer had mentioned Mary's arguments with Brown about his violence, his militarism. Which probably had been as effective as trying to talk a tomcat out of stalking birds, I thought as I sat down to Brown's right in a semi-fancy continental restaurant. Throughout the meal, from Veal Oscar to chocolate mousse, Mary's barely suppressed, yet barely audible, anger floated almost tangibly up the table from where she was seated on Brown's left. Her words—and his response as henpecked spouse— were as familiar as lyrics to the Baptist hymns I had grown up hearing in Georgia. Mary's was a role I had watched women play my whole life, from Mother, in her powerlessness with Daddy, to, more recently, Jack's put-upon wife and Randy's angry lover. Yet it was one, I was beginning to realize, that had little to do with region or education or intelligence—and one that the macho man was particularly adept at agitating in even the most experienced woman!

From across the oblong table, John, the man with the skeleton of the human hand around his neck, introduced his fiancée, who was seated opposite me. They had just decided to be married at the banquet Saturday night, right after Westmoreland's address, he explained, and now Pam was concerned about her dress. "I don't think the blue one is fancy enough," she was saying, looking anxiously toward editors Donna DuVall and Jim Graves, seated at the other end of the table, her small voice matching her petite stature. "Do you think somebody can take me into town tomorrow . . . ?" Ignoring her question, John took her tiny hand in his. "See this girl?" he asked, looking at me. "She's changed my whole life. I was miserable, depressed all the time, then she came to the office, answerin' the phone, a temporary"—Pam looked demurely down at her hearts-of-palm salad, her tinted nails, then flicked her long blond hair—"'n' now I'm the happiest man alive! Why, when I'm outta town—no matter what country I'm in—I call 'er at least three times a day. . . ."

Back at the Holiday Inn, John went upstairs for more money, Mary and Brown for a more private conversation, and Pam and I wandered into the motel bar, which was now crowded with drunken soldiers of fortune. "He'll be mad when he realizes I came on in here without 'im," she said as we perched on the edge of a couch waiting for the drinks we had ordered. "He doesn't like me to go into bars alone—'n' especially wouldn't like this, with all these guys here!

"Well, it's sort of a drag when he calls three times a day, when he doesn't want me to *do* anything," she confessed when I asked how she liked having such an attentive lover, "but he takes good care of me, treats me like a lady—a *lot* better than my first husband. . . ."

It occurred to me, looking out through the dimly lit forest of camouflage-clad thighs, that the macho man in his pure form was dominant *and* dependent—an attitude that left the woman to whom he related with the choice of submission (Pam's), rebellion (Mary's), or collusion (Jennifer's)—with submission as the traditional route. Or, as a therapist friend had said, describing possible relationships, "You are me," "You or me," or "You and me." I didn't yet know about the last, the way of the New Woman; nor that I still could—and soon, like Mary, would—be driven inexorably toward the unpleasant middle route.

But we weren't in the place for such serious thoughts. Ed the Munitions Dealer, in his V-necked sweater still the only preppy in the place, came over, and we sat down at a table with many drunk people. The bagpipe players, followed by a drunken conga line of camouflage-clad bodies, tramped through, playing military music. As shouts filled the smoky air, I felt myself getting into the belligerent mood of things, helped along by that dark feeling that comes on with too much drinking and fatigue. Suddenly one of the men across the narrow table—an especially large, darkly bearded one who, ironically, resembled Fidel Castro—leaned over, looking intently at me, the press badge on my pink sweater. "Whut 'er you doin' settin' at my table?!" he growled, some paranoia tripped behind his guarded eyes. "I didn't know it was *your* table!" I retorted angrily, the aggression of the scene rubbing off on me. Ed, the Munitions Dealer—plump, well-dressed ("I wasn't fat like this when I was in the military," he had said to me, holding my hand, looking earnestly into my eyes), looked around uneasily. As I caressed the biceps of a well-muscled blond to my left, the bearded man looked even murkier. "Are you a *real* macho man?" I asked the blond provocatively. "We better get outta here," Ed said to me from under his breath, then more loudly: "Can I walk you back to your motel?"

"Those guys were the bodyguards, the motorcycle-gang types Brown hired to police things," he explained as I reluctantly followed him through the swinging door and into the parking lot. "I just thought we'd better get out of there before something happened. . . ." He looked at me sadly, probably wishing he was harder, that he had worn camouflage—then even more sadly when I said I was going home the next day to my own soldier.

In the morning, at the Days Inn checkout desk, a Clairol-blonde took my MasterCard between her own long vermilion nails, and looked at mine: "I luv-v-v yore color! What is it? L'Oréal?" Then she motioned toward the far end of the counter where three conventioneers, in identical T-shirts reading "Kill 'Em All and Let God Sort 'Em Out," awaited her services. "Aren't they the *sweetest* thangs?" she whispered to me under her breath, "protectin' us 'n' our country 'n' all?"

About as sweet as John and Pam's wedding, I thought cynically when Jennifer called to describe the event: The cake had been tiered, with camouflage-colored frosting and black and green roses that had later been thrown in a cake fight. The ceremony had been performed by the only minister in the Charlotte area who was willing—Cowboy Bob, whose mission was "to take Christ to the cowboys," apparently had felt the Soldiers of Fortune could use his influence as well.

ACROSS COUNTRY TO THE ROCKIES,
WHERE I RECEIVE FURTHER
LESSONS IN COURAGE,
TRUE AND FALSE.

Five days later, after a brief trip home to Savannah, I was in Colorado Springs to give the keynote address at a three-day conference on "Women and Violence" at Colorado College.

I had just driven into town in a rental Rabbit, checked into my motel, and now, at the dinner prior to my lecture, was being offered not the bourbon-and-steak dinner I had fantasized having during the flight to Denver on my first night out West, but a tumbler of cranberry juice mixed with Perrier, and a plateful of steamed, faintly seasoned vegetables. My hosts, it turned out, were serious scholars, Marxists, teetotalers, and vegetarians, who had invited the head of the philosophy department and several graduate students to dinner on my behalf. Depressed by the cranberry juice, the bloodless fare, phrases like "according to empirical rather than interpretive reasoning" and "the system versus individual oppressions," I yearned for my fun-loving, hard-drinking, storytelling—if not war-mongering—companions of the week before.

My hostess, Ann, delicately lovely in the pale style of totally unmade-up vegetarians, looked—as she dished up more celery-and-carrot compote—as though she might burst into tears at any moment. Later, in the privacy of my rental car, she would confide—real tears streaming down her cheeks this time—that she had been born into a wealthy Wyoming mining family, had been unhappily married to a macho—and abusive—man, but now was married to James, a Marxist Ph.D. candidate in philosophy. While her family had cut off her funds—"They don't believe in what we're doing"—and she and James had to live on her $8,000-a-year salary as a reading teacher, at least James was *brilliant*—why, he had applied for a Mellon foundation fellowship, had wanted to go to El Salvador, but had been denied a visa. Wisely, I thought as she spoke, thinking that the dour-faced James would be the first executed in almost any situation; in fact, I could imagine him being "disappeared" on the basis of personality alone. Whereas Ann looked like a woman made for flowers, for satin cushions, for *love*; indeed, before my arrival, she had gone to my motel room to place a vase of small pink blossoms beside my bed.

She would have made a good Junior Leaguer or hostess for Savannah's Tour of Homes. But instead she was here with the humorless James and her best friend, Shawna, a graduate student in sociology. After my address, we three women went to a student bar near the campus. As I quaffed margaritas and munched nachos to fill the space left by the vegetables, they sipped herb tea and discussed the problems of women and abusive men. Ann had been raped on a trip to Hawaii with an elderly aunt by a Hawaiian who had come to her hotel to pick her up in his jeep to take her to visit her sister, a man with whom she had made friends—here, her blue eyes filled with tears again. The experience was something she had long been unable to tell anyone about, especially the aunt. Shawna, her black eyes glittering angrily, talked of how she had been married to a man who regularly battered her, even when they were living in a commune. "The others simply ignored it—and now he's a prominent Denver psychotherapist!" she said bitterly. "But the worst thing to me was the rage *I* felt in response to his rage!" I looked at her, interested. I understood the fear of tapping into one's own aggression. But as she went on to explain that she now worked in a battered-women's shelter and led a *serious* life, she looked down at my Revloned nails with disapproval, and I realized I was not the militant, angry feminist—the razor-carrying protagonist of my poems—they had hoped for in hiring me to speak at the conference. "There's *no* man I would trust now," she said accusingly as my eyes drifted toward the hunks standing at the bar. As Ann looked anxious, a hostess worried that her guests aren't having a good time, and I stood reluctantly to leave, Shawna wrote a check to the waitress for one dollar in payment for her cup of tea. It was something she would do almost everywhere we went for the next few days—the true socialist way, I guessed, trying to rouse some of the empathy I knew I should be feeling. It was not as if I had not had my own experiences with abusive men. But the only thing Shawna had said that I could identify with was her reaction to her own aggressive feelings.

The next day, Ann mentioned a local woman, a Polish death-camp survivor, who ran a real burlesque theater, complete with extravagant, hand-sewn costumes, intricate choreography, at a motel on the outskirts of town. "She's so tough she's said to have broken a little motor—placed there because of bone cancer—in her wrist when she threw a man out while acting as her own bouncer." Ann didn't think she'd like to see the show, though; it would upset her too much to see women sexually objectified, she told me when I said I would enjoy a visit. But Shawna said that she would go with me in the name of objective research, sociological scholarship. That night, I picked her up in the Rabbit, and we drove to "The Mustang," which was, indeed, on the sleazy side of town.

As we walked in the door, a large, sixtyish woman in sweater and slacks, with a dark, mannish haircut, greeted us. I had called Clara in advance to say that I wanted to talk with her, that I was a writer, and now she pulled out chairs at a table, instructed a silent, gray-haired woman about her age to take our orders for drinks, and sat down to chat. She had gone into the death camp at eight, she said, and was there for four years and sixteen days. "My job was to crawl into the pits, get the gold and silver out of the mouths of the dead.

One morning, they came to take my mother to the chambers. I still had to go down to the pits, where my mother's body was. That day, I crawled on my hands and knees, I was shaking so. . . . I saw every kind of cruelty, every kind of degradation, perversion. I ate rats. You learn to see the fat on rocks. . . . When we were liberated, I was five feet seven, weighed eighty-one pounds; had two crushed hips, a swastika branded on my face. . . ."

It was easy to see why throwing a belligerent man out of her bar would be all in a day's work for Clara. "In Israel, I had plastic surgery, medical care. I married, but my husband died. When I arrived at Ellis Island, I had a two-year-old son, a one-year-old daughter, a three-month-old baby—and my friend, Hertha, who had been in the death camp with me, too—she had two babies, but had never been able to speak again. . . .

"When the boat docked, and we saw the black people, we both started screaming. We thought we'd been taken to Africa by mistake. I couldn't speak English, and she couldn't speak at all. I had one dollar and forty-seven cents in my pocketbook. Some synagogue people helped us get an apartment in the Bronx, two rooms on the fourteenth floor. I worked nineteen hours a day, as a chambermaid at the Waldorf, a waitress for a dollar and seventy-five cents a day . . . supported all of us: Hertha, her children, mine. . . .

"Then one day a man came into the restaurant where I worked, asked if I wanted to audition for the Rockettes. I did, and started making one hundred twenty-five dollars a week—we were rich! Later I danced at the Moulin Rouge in Paris, took Hertha and our children with me wherever I went, traveled all over the country— Vegas, L.A., Atlantic City—by train, finally saw Colorado, the mountains—so peaceful!—and fell in love with them. . . ."

"What about men, marriage?" I asked, as Clara lit a Salem Long, and Hertha mutely refreshed our straight bourbons, Shawna's club soda. "There's nothing I like more than a man—unless it's a whole bunch of 'em!" Clara laughed, giving an entertainer's ready answer, then said more seriously: "Hertha 'n' me both got married again once, but now we're back together—*I've never* taken a backseat to a man in my life. 'N' I don't want these girls to, either," she said, motioning toward the ostrich-feather-and-negligee-clad women who were now floating around us like ethereal virgins despite the fact that they were probably prostitutes. "I take 'em under my wing, get 'em straightened out, design their costumes, choreograph their dances, teach 'em self-respect. A lot of 'em have boyfriend problems—they got to have that man hangin' onto 'em, even if he pushes them around. Take her, for instance." She indicated a skinny, intense-looking girl, now dancing across the stage in baby-doll pajamas, black patent Mary Janes, lip-synching the words to Shirley Temple's voice singing "The Good Ship Lollypop." "She had a little heroin problem. I put 'er in the hospital, helped 'er take care of her little babies—a *lot* of 'em have little babies to support," she added seriously, as though it was something with which she could especially identify.

"But what about *you*?" she asked, the con artist picking up on a favorite fantasy. "You said you're over forty, but I can't believe it! Why, we could get you out there, choreograph a dance for you, you could stay around town for a while. . . . Oh, don't worry about *those*—we can light *those* out," she went on when I demurred, murmuring something about stretch marks. I was enjoying the image of myself, naked but for a few sequins, a bit of satin, some flattering veiling, dancing with a talent heretofore unevidenced across the stage to a chorus of ego-enhancing catcalls, even offers of diamond bracelets and trips to Paris on the Concorde. But I could see that Shawna the Sociologist, livened only by as much club soda as she could drink, was growing restless. "I'm sorry—I'm having such a good time—but I guess we'll have to go soon," I said to Clara.

"Just one more thing," she said, taking the hand of a tawny blonde who had just materialized before us in pasties, transparent harem pants. "This is Cimarron. And you've *got* to see her fire dance—it's the specialty of the house!"

"Clara's so into self-esteem, treatin' oneself like pure gold—a real Jewish mama," Cimarron confided as Clara left to attend to something backstage. "When I first started dancin'—to put myself through college—I hated myself, thinkin' about dancin' topless in a bar 'n' all. But now I think of it professionally—Clara makes us practice *hours* every day—just like we were in a Broadway musical or somethin'." She was twenty-nine, she told us, had a six-year-old daughter, a car, a house. For three years she had been featured as the club's star.

"But my daughter is my *real* career," she said. "This kind of job can make it hard to have a relationship—a man here tells you you're the most beautiful woman he's ever seen on the same day you've had an argument with your boyfriend. Most of the dancers are either in long-term relationships, or else very independent. And Clara's always here to keep your head on straight!"

As she disappeared backstage, I looked around at the "girls" in their peignoirs, sitting with their customers as chummily as housewives at dinette sets with their husbands. "The next number is for the lovely Miss Rose!" Clara announced from the microphone, motioning in my direction as Cimarron came on stage, wielding torches that she flicked up and down her body, over her breasts, between her thighs, as I sat mesmerized.

When Shawna and I finally walked into the parking lot, she suggested we stop by the campus bar to "analyze our findings." "I'm not sure I really *believe* all her story," she said sourly over herb tea again, "whether, *empirically*, the evidence adds up. Also, I heard that she used to *hook*—which probably means that her girls do, too. . . ." Marxists might be right, but they sure weren't much fun, I thought. "Haven't you ever heard of *survival*?" I asked, exasperated.

I was looking at a handsome man across the bar, but then Shawna burst that bubble, too. "*He's* one of the worst batterers in Colorado Springs," she said. "Why, last year he broke his girl friend's *arm*. . . ." As she wrote another check for one dollar, my good humor evaporated.

The next day, when Ann handed me my check for my part in the conference, it was a hundred short of what she had promised me on the phone. "You don't mind, do you?" she said anxiously, obviously hopeful that I shared her attitude toward money-as-filthy-lucre. "I needed it to pay one of the other speakers." "No, it's okay," I said, eager to be on the road to Denver, capitalistic pleasures, and macho men.

But not *that* macho, I thought, as I wandered through the Air Force Academy museum.

Before leaving Colorado Springs, I had phoned ahead, but a public information officer had told me that it would be impossible to talk to a cadet on such short notice. But after passing Pikes Peak to my left, I had pulled off U.S. Highway 25 North to enter the Academy grounds, following arrows along the sanctioned route for visitors through a barren, if hilly, terrain. Parking the Rabbit on a high slope above the campus, I had stepped out to hear nothing but the drone of crickets and other insects and what sounded like the rattle of a snake. The only human life visible was the occasional distant black speck, moving rapidly from building to distant building; in the cockpits of gliders being pulled by other planes; or beneath brightly colored parachutes dropping from the sky toward the ground.

In the museum, I read the Academy's motto—Bring Me Men— and stood beneath the illustrated story of "one of the institute's five Rhodes scholars, Capt. Lance Peter Sijon, in 1965 the first Air Force Academy graduate to receive the Congressional Medal of Honor." Under a drawing of a man fittingly handsome was a matter-of-fact description of his valorous resistance:

Ejected from his disabled aircraft over North Viet Nam on 9 November 1967 and evaded capture for more than six weeks. Seriously injured, suffering from shock and extreme weight loss, he was finally captured and taken to a holding point. In his emaciated and crippled condition, he overpowered his guard and escaped, but was recaptured. Imprisoned, kept in solitary confinement, interrogated and severely tortured, he divulged no information. Captain Sijon lapsed into delirium and was put in the care of another prisoner. During periods of consciousness, until his death, he never complained of his physical condition and on several occasions spoke of future attempts [to escape]. Born Milwaukee Wisconsin 13 April 1942.

As I drove back onto U.S. 25, I thought of the twenty-five-year-old Sijon, faithful to the death to an unpopular conflict, and of Clara, her survival of the death camp, her rugged remaking of her life. When I began my travels, I had expected to feel critical of the Soldiers of Fortune, to feel philosophically at one with my hosts at the symposium on "Women and Violence." Instead, I had enjoyed many of the conventioneers despite their ostensible commitment to mayhem—in fact, was looking forward to having dinner with Jennifer and Ed that evening in Denver—and had felt alienated among the left-wing Marxist intellectuals with whom I would have imagined myself to be sympathetic. I could even understand—at least, emotionally—how Jennifer and Mary had once been antiwar protesters but now were intimately connected to "warmongers," and how Captain Sijon had courageously upheld his country's part in a war I found contemptible. I had long since realized that one reason for my attraction to the macho man, my interest in researching him, was the macha inside myself. But had the faces of the hysterical, teary housewife, the bleeding-heart liberal, the determined antimaterialist, simply been masks for my own aggression and greed? Did I really have more in common with adventurers, risk-takers, survivors—whatever form that might take—than the tender liberals I had always automatically considered myself akin to?

In need of some diversion, I took an exit ramp off the highway toward the "Pro Rodeo Hall of Champions & Museum of the American Cowboy." At the entrance, I paid a two-dollar fee, but was told I could enter the museum only through the mixed-media slide show, which would begin in fifteen minutes. I had already seen one Madison Avenue–slick slide show at the Air Force Academy. Was that becoming the only way available to experience America, I wondered as I wandered through a lobby filled with bad paintings and huge, cold sculptures of cowboys, cows, and broncos. Around me milled a few other men and women in determinedly Western dress—fancied-up Stetsons and turquoise-and-silver belt buckles—who stared at the "art" as though they might experience something if only they looked long enough.

At last, a blonde girl in a short, fringed cowgirl skirt announced the "show." A metal door slid open and I climbed to the top of the bleachers, watched a dummy cowpoke on a high wall suddenly light up and begin to speak, then walked out the back door into a museum filled with boots, spurs, lariats, and life-size models of bucking broncos or bulls, held tight between the thighs of Real Men. "Black cowboy Bill Pickett," I read beneath one display, "originator of steer wrestling . . . developer of bulldogging by wrestling steer to the ground, then pinning it down with his teeth. . . ." I left the museum through a back door that led to an area where a senile-looking Brahma bull, an elderly horse—eyes half-closed, hides scarred—lounged behind fences. For a while, I futilely teased the bull, then stroked an orange cat—the liveliest animal in sight—as it stretched in the sun at my feet.

"Ask him, he knows all about it," said the blonde teenager behind the cash register in the gift shop when I asked where I might find out more about the rodeo, and whether the animals were abused to make them buck. From behind the counter, a skinny, weathered-looking man handed me a pamphlet entitled "What Is Rodeo?" "This'll answer all yore questions, ma'am," he said, smiling reassuringly.

"Hey, I like those purple boots!" the girl exclaimed, looking down at the lavender cowboy boots I had bought on Bleecker Street in Greenwich Village. "What're you doin', anyway?" she asked as I made notes while perusing a rotating rack of bumper stickers reading *My best friends are the Daniels Brothers—Charlie and Jack*, or *I'm a lover. I'm a fighter/ I'm a wild bull rider*. I was looking for macho men, I said, and wondered whether any ever came here. "Some of 'em *think* they are," she giggled. "At least they try to *act* like it!"

Out in the parking lot, I saw a hot-pink pickup decorated with circus-y gold curlicues, and in gold-swirled letters, "MISS RODEO." Back in my car, I flipped through the pamphlet; there was nothing in it about the treatment of animals.

That night in Denver, I greeted Jennifer and Ed like long-lost friends. "I don't see *how* you resisted stayin' over 'n' workin' as a stripper for a while," Jennifer laughed over eggplant parmigiana— even meatless meals tasted better with them, I thought—at the little restaurant to which they had whisked me.

"And you just had to tease that bull, didn't you?" she said later as we sat curled on the couch over bourbon and water at their midtown apartment—chosen, Jennifer had jokingly explained, because they could so often hear gunshots there. "You're just like me—if there's not trouble already, you'll go out of your way to start some!"

MAGNOLIA AMONG THE MESAS,
OR A SOUTHERN WOMAN OUT WEST.

When I drove into Rock Springs, near the southwestern corner of Wyoming, I felt as though I were landing on the moon.

I had spent the night with friends in Casper, driven the six barren hours past Goose Egg, Independence Rock, Muddy Gap, Whiskey Gap, Red Desert, Point of Rocks, and Reliance, stopping only for lunch at the Holiday Inn in Rawlins, a cup of coffee at some nowhere café, where the two male customers and the waitress looked at me as though a lone woman was a distinct curiosity. The other human beings I had seen en route—two real cowboys herding sheep, two more men repairing a fence beside a single grave—had looked, against the mesas and buttes, the distances of a hundred or more easily visible miles, exotic, out of context. What had appeared more natural were the animals—the sheep and deer grazing, often together, near the highway; the buck who stepped out into the road, then turned back, startled; the elegant antelope and an occasional elk; low-flying hawks, even an eagle. I had felt a seductive pull, a desire to park the rented Rabbit and walk out into what looked like endless space. It seemed as though the hills would embrace me, holding me tenderly against the pale green blanket that was really—I had to keep reminding myself—cold prickly sagebrush.

When the dirty-looking, blackened slopes outside Rock Springs finally appeared, then a steadily increasing number of billboards, four-wheel-drive vehicles, even a neon sign indicating "The Outlaw Inn," I felt comforted, kept safe by impending semicivilization.

"That's the first time I've ever heard anybody call Rock Springs *pretty*!" laughed the hearty feminine voice over the phone. I had just checked into my room at the Motel 8, which, like everything else in town, was visible from the freeway exit, and had just called Barbara, the English-department head who had arranged the two-day reading-and-teaching gig at Western Wyoming College that was the ostensible reason for my visit. The real reason was that I had learned that, thanks to recently developed oil rigs and coal mines, the community was a genuine boomtown—thus the natural place to research the macho man.

At her office at the college, I found that Barbara matched her voice: white-white of complexion, she wore a shirt, a soft halo of the kind of fine, white-blond hair that, in the Deep South—though it was rarely seen there on anyone but children—would have labeled her "cotton-headed." Her generous body was covered, rather than enhanced, by a nondescript polyester print skirt and blouse. "I came down here *before* the boom," she explained in her flat, Scandinavian-edged accent, "as a young teacher just out of college in Minnesota—this town was sure a lot quieter then! And people thought I was strange—a woman livin' alone." She had taken me out in her jeep to see the town, and now she pointed to a small frame house she had once shared with another woman. "There wasn't much to do in the evenings 'cept go out to bars, 'n' schoolteachers weren't supposed to do *that.*" As she talked, I imagined her as a dance-hall girl, her voluptuous curves crammed into something a little more provocative—maybe a waist-cincher, an off-the-shoulder dress of ruby satin—during a time when avoirdupois had been more popular. Yet her boneless pragmatism—she had mentioned that beside her college-teaching job, she had two-year-old twins and a third child at home—also recalled the hausfrau calm of my oil-rig pal, Madge. And apparently Western men—like the riggers—still like Renoiresque women—yet another reason for me to feel comfortable here!

"Then the boom came, 'n' people from all over were campin' out in Tent City over on the hill by the college, 'n' the whores came from Denver. . . . And oh, yes," she went on as we joggled along muddy unpaved streets, passing rows and rows of house trailers differentiated only by small, futile efforts—different mailboxes or curtains, a windowful of potted cactus—at distinction, "years before that, this was the scene of the Chinese Massacre. When the locals who were workin' the Union Pacific struck, the railroad brought in the Chinese, who would work for practically nothing. The strikers massacred them—or at the very least, cut off their pigtails! People still occasionally find the opium pipes.

"In fact, the whole town's pretty ethnic," she continued as we drove down a narrow winding street of tiny frame houses on which every front door was painted a different bright color. "The Italian women on this street painted their front doors differently so that when the men staggered home from the bars at night, they could tell which house was theirs by the color. In fact, there's a group of men in town who dress up like the Mafia, clothes right out of *The Godfather*, who occasionally go out and pretend to shoot things up with machine guns."

I was beginning to feel I had been dropped into some particularly outlandish outpost, a town as weird as the landscape that surrounded it. At the Country Kitchen, where we had stopped for a cup of coffee, our waitress wore, despite the daylight hour, extra-long fake black eyelashes, further thickened by Maybelline, an orange feather drooping through her long teased jet hair. "Just a fad, all the girls are wearin' 'em," Barbara explained, then went on to say that she had met her husband—"he's a carpenter"—at a local bar, the Kasbah. "Maybe we'll go there tonight after class."

As she spoke, her friend, Lisa, from Massachusetts, joined us as planned in our booth. She had originally come west to work in the oil fields, "because I heard I could make such good money here," and had met her boyfriend, Rick, an oil rigger, at the Kasbah, too: "I saw him there one night, and chased him outside into the parking lot, I liked him so much!"

With her clipped, upper-middle-class Boston accent, Lisa seemed an unlikely pipe inspector, despite the old blue pickup she had driven up in, the cotton blouse tucked into worn Levis. Her long, jet-brown braids, the soft-soled deerhide boots laced up around her slender calves made her look like a storybook Indian maiden. And it turned out that her Northeastern social conscience was still as much with her as her brunette good looks. For her present passion—aside from Rick, "and traveling whenever we can get some money together; the only thing I like to spend money on is airline tickets"—was the problem of battered women.

"This county—Sweetwater—has one of the highest rates of spouse and child abuse in Wyoming," she told me indignantly, "and Wyoming has the third highest rate in the United States! The wind blows"—I could see its movement through the restaurant window; it had been the first thing I thought of when I noticed her bralessness beneath her thin blouse—"and the more the wind blows, the more abuse and suicide there is. You can feel crazy in a trailer, the wind blowing constantly—there's no escape. It's freezing or below outside; vegetation is sparse. And some women don't reach out, try to survive. . . ."

Lisa had helped start Sweetwater County's first safe house, and had traveled throughout the state conducting workshops for battered women, including one at the state prison for women—where I would be leading writing workshops the following week—and where, she believes, virtually every woman there has been incarcerated because of her relationship with a man. Like the isolated ranch wife whose abusive husband had rarely bathed, but who had once seen the film *Deep Throat* and thereafter had forced her for years—despite her revulsion at his nonexistent hygiene—to fellate him, till at last one day she had shot him. It was for that reason, Lisa said, that she became upset when she heard people say pornography was harmless.

"The women here are strong," she continued, "but lack confidence. For the men, this is the last frontier, the place where 'I'll be able to be a man, have my family the way I want it.' People who left the East left for a reason—sometimes adventure, sometimes family problems, sometimes trouble with the law. Out here, people don't ask about your past. And isolation equals alienation equals paranoia. Then there's no one to turn to when abuse takes place—you should see the hospital emergency room on a Friday night!"

In a culture where sexism was the norm, Lisa rejected every sign of it, even refusing to attend a poetry reading given by Allen Ginsberg because of the woman-hate in his work. That she was difficult, too hard-nosed a feminist, in a place where live-and-let-live was the motto, was a comment I would hear repeated of her several times during my stay. But to me she seemed like a breath of unpolluted air. However different their politics, she reminded me of Jennifer—risk-taking, high-energy, intelligent. And she had her frivolous side, too. "Hey," she grinned, pulling on a faded down jacket, "you want to go to the Kasbah?"

That night—fortunately, a Thursday—Lisa, Barbara, their friend Rhonda, and I bounced along in Barbara's jeep on our way to the Kasbah.

"I came out to work on the rigs, like the high-risk stuff. I like to fish, to hunt big game, to shoot, to go to Vegas, play the slots, gamble, sometimes hitch a plane to Alaska," Rhonda was telling me. Riding with my eyes closed against the evening chill, I felt a curious jab of gender disorientation. I knew that the person jammed into the seat beside me was small, round-faced, with long, dirty-blond hair, and I heard, as she spoke, the soprano in her voice. Yet her words hung in the air like the misplaced monologue of a burly roughneck.

"My old man, the one I'm livin' with in the trailer, wants us to get married, but I don't want to, don't wanna be tied down. I *had* a little son"—here I heard tears in her voice, and when I looked at her, saw them in her brown-flecked green eyes as well and took her small, rough hand in mine—"just seven, from my other marriage, but he got killed last month in a car crash—I know I hadn't been a good mother, leavin' 'im 'n' all. But I was just waitin' till he grew up, so we could go huntin' 'n' fishin' together. . . ."

Ahead, I saw a neon sign flickering the club's unlikely name, and when we pulled off the main road, a one-story concrete-block building surrounded by what looked like thousands of four-wheel-drive vehicles. As we walked across the parking lot, passing two men who were drunkenly squaring off, fists raised, I tugged at Lisa's arm, but she only laughed. "Just some macho *machadas!*" "Yeah, I call 'em Nacho Men," Rhonda giggled, her mood revived. "You'll see plenty of 'em in here!"

As we stumbled over male feet, bumped into musky male bodies, making our way toward a table, the voices I heard around me were mostly drawls like mine, belonging to Southerners, who, it seemed, went west in droves to make oil-rig money. The band, who stood in front of an oversized Rebel flag, was playing a Mickey Gilley song; the dance in progress was a Texas two-step. I had come all this way to research the macho man and his women, but I might as well have stayed home in Georgia.

Except that there were so *many* of them. As I looked around the room through the dim, smoky light, I realized we women were a distinctly small minority. "No, thank you," I said when the first man stopped by our table to ask me to dance; he smiled in amazement. "Most of the women around here just say 'Get lost!' or 'No way!' or somethin' like that," Rhonda explained. "There're so many men, and so few women, that they don't even *bother* bein' polite—they just brush 'em off like flies." I couldn't help but think that for certain women in certain cities—say, those confronted with the arrogant New Yorker or the spoiled Californian—this would be a refreshing change, if not revenge. Susan Brownmiller, author of *Femininity*, claims that women cling to feminine wiles because they are desperately competing for men. Yet all a woman need do is come West, I thought, toying with the idea of reviving shipments of "brides" from the East.

"Yes, I'd like to," I said when the band played "Cotton-Eyed Joe." The offers were now coming as persistently and almost as annoyingly as mosquito bites, so I could be sure without even looking that there was someone at my elbow. "You *would?*" my partner asked as though stunned, leading me through the crowds to the dance floor. A handsome, if rough-hewn, blond in his twenties, dressed in de rigueur cowboy hat, plaid flannel shirt, worn Levis, and cowboy boots, he looked like a man who wouldn't have much trouble finding a partner elsewhere. After several of his expert turns at the two-step, I sat down, out of breath, declining his subsequent offers. In a few minutes, when I looked up from my conversation with Barbara, I saw that the man at my elbow now was the buddy I had seen sitting at my partner's table. "No," I said patiently, "I just turned your friend down."

"You mean you *care* whether you hurt his feelings or not?" he said in what sounded like bitter astonishment.

I was beginning to sense something in the air, an epidemic of what Gloria Steinem calls testosterone poisoning. A man sprawled drunkenly in a chair a few yards away tripped another one as he made his way toward our table; the latter responded with a scowl, raised fists, biceps visibly clinched, then slowly relaxed as he was pulled back into his seat by his mates. No, I wouldn't recommend that a woman from a more civilized environment come here unless she were able to deal with *excessive* male attention, I thought as I made my way to the ladies' room. By now, I wasn't even surprised at the angry words, the stances, of the two men outside the door labeled "Bulls."

"Wall, if yuh wanna do sumpthin' about it, let's jes' step on outside, how 'bout it?" one said, raising his fist. Yet in mid-sentence he caught my eye, grinned apologetically, as though to say, "It don't mean anythang, lady—we jes' gotta do sumpthin' with all these fuckin' hormones!"

If this was the Real West on a Thursday night, what was it like on a Saturday, I wondered as I ordered a Coors Light. The man standing beside me, I noticed, was large, a bit more expensively dressed than most, and well hung with silver-and-turquoise jewelry. "I make it 'n' come to Rock Springs from Colorado to sell it," he said when I asked about the jewelry. "'N' no matter how many times I get turned down, I end up standin' here in this bar night after night"—he sounded as though he might burst into tears—"'cause if I didn't, I'd just end up stayin' in my motel room, dyin' of loneliness.

"'N' what women there are," he went on sadly, his words like the lyrics to a country-western song, "at least, the ones who've been out here for a while, 're too much like the men. It's like they start workin' at the same jobs the men do, then competin' with 'em huntin', fishin', gamblin', all the rest"—here, his voice turned bitter. "The men are confused—'n' the women've made 'em that way! Hell, they've *got* the upper hand—ev'ry one of 'em's sittin' on a gold mine! No woman has to work out here—there's men just jumpin' at the chance to support ev'ry one of 'em!"

"But for a *price*!" said Lisa, suddenly materializing at my elbow.

"Hey, are you ready to go?" she asked me, abruptly tuning out the man in the silver. "We're all danced out, drunk, have to go to work tomorrow. . . ."

"See what I mean?" he asked me resignedly. I nodded. During my sleep-around period, I had felt the power of being predatory, making the choices—and it would be even easier to say no if you knew you would have fresh chances the next night. And the next.

"Mama always said, 'Be sure to wear a few ruffles so you'll look feminine,'" Ann Strand confided, belting double bourbons to my singles. We were sitting in the Silver Dollar Bar adjacent to the Outlaw Inn. She had just told me, in the tone of one proudly mentioning a particularly scenic spot, that the parking lot outside had been the scene in 1979 of the controversial shooting of undercover narcotics agent Mike Rose by Sheriff Ed Cantrell.

Ann, from Georgia like me, had been sent to college at Tift College, a prim and proper establishment for young ladies outside Macon. "But that damned finishin' school near 'bout finished *me!*" On a vacation in the Wild West, she had met her first husband in Laramie—like her second, and all seven of her children, a Wyoming native—and had never gone back to Georgia, except to visit. Now she was running for her third term as state representative, but despite our shared origins, the perfume—"Jungle Gardenia?"— that wafted across the table toward me, the ruffled pink polyester blouse, the gray suit with its softly gathered skirt that Mama would have approved of, her slenderness seemed tensile rather than fragile. The dry winds of Wyoming had long since taken their toll on her skin, and while her face was decorated by an abrupt slash of hot-pink lipstick, her short, gray, permanent-waved hair was not that of a woman overly concerned with Loving Caring the gray away.

"The rest of my people all live within a hundred fifty miles from where they started out," she continued, revealing her latent Southern romance with family, roots. "My maiden name was Scott— originally from South Car'lina. Why, Strom Thurmond is my second cousin! And, hell, I'd love to sit down there 'n' have somebody feed me peaches 'n' cream. But I wasn't meant for that pink-satin-tuffet syndrome—I'd just fall off, have to claw my way back up. . . ."

She paused for a few minutes to listen with interest when a rough-faced woman who had worked in the mines came by our table and sat down to complain about how "They wouldn't give me a chance to go to the bathroom down there—I got a kidney infection from holdin' piss. 'N' they don't even call it discrimination!"

As the woman walked away, apparently satisfied, I could see why Ann Strand was affectionately called "Lady Ann" by her constituents. "This is the 'Equality State,'" she said. "We had the first woman governor in the U.S.—Nellie Tayloe Ross in 1925—'n' this was the first state to give women the vote. Ole Leslie Petersen is runnin' for secretary of state—'n' she's a rodeo rider, dips snuff. But now that she's runnin' for office, she's tryin' to act dainty, not drink too much.

"Hell, yeah," Ann went on, warming to her subject. "I'm happier out here than a dead pig in the sunshine! There're opportunities I *never* would have had in the East or the South. And, besides, I like to be where I can see as far as I can look, and look as far as I can see. I took my son for a visit to Georgia, 'n' he said: 'When're we gettin' outta the trees, Mama?' I said, 'In the South, you *never* get outta the trees.' 'Well, couldn't sumpthin' sneak up on you?' he said."

An older son was running for county attorney, she told me. "Yep, I'm raisin' my own dynasty right out here in Sweetwater County, where not all of the people are good, but none of 'em are bad," she laughed, paraphrasing comedian Brother Dave Gardner's statement that while Southerners might not always be right, they're never wrong. "'N' sometimes I get my foot in my mouth clear up to my elbow. But maybe, just maybe, I'll gain a quarter of an inch, a half inch, maybe even an inch of equality for my daughters, my daughter's daughters. . . ."

I didn't doubt it for a minute, I thought tipsily, my boozed-up brain jumping in sync with the screech of the country-western band tuning up a few yards away. And I hadn't even had a chance yet to ask her about macho men, I realized as she smiled encouragingly at the two silver-haired gentlemen in Western dress who had just bent over our table to ask our hands in the dance.

"But the women here are so *large!*" the Radcliffe-educated screenwriter who wanted a man just like Jack had exclaimed when I took her to a Savannah country-western bar. Yet if rural Southerners often come in size large, then Western women frequently come in extra-large—not necessarily fat, but firm, muscular—I thought as Bunny walked toward me across the coffee shop in the Ramada Inn the next morning. Polyester, I was quickly learning, was *real* Western dress. Wearing—at ten a.m.—extravagant eye makeup, a low-cut, purple-flowered dress, stockings, and high heels, Bunny was a well-shaped Valkyrie costumed by Frederick's of Hollywood. But her childish face, surmounted by ash-blond curls, and overlaid by what looked like permanent sadness, was also open, eager to please. Which was the reason Lisa had given me her number when I had said I would like to meet more women of the New West.

Now in her early twenties, Bunny had met Lisa at a battered-women's workshop. She had been married at fifteen, in fact, had deliberately become pregnant to do so. As she spoke, her sadness seemed to deepen, and I recalled my own teenage dreams of a baby to fill my arms, the endless chasm of my own loneliness. But the infant had died at seven weeks of crib death, and her young husband had begun to beat her, finally bashing in one violet eye, which, tilted at the corner by scar tissue, was felinely and ironically emphasized by her jet eyeliner, her purple eye shadow.

She had grown up in spaces so wide open, so isolated, she told me, that she had had to wear snowshoes much of the year to go out of doors. Her father was a wilderness guide. Her mother she described by saying, "Her skin is real wrinkled—she never used any moisturizer." But Bunny wanted to take good care of herself. "After the divorce, I worked as a pipe inspector out on the rigs. But one time, when I had to work forty-three straight hours out in the open at seventy degrees below zero [a temperature created by a −40-degree wind-chill factor] I decided enough was enough—despite that I was makin' five to six hundred dollars a week, plus a six-hundred-to-a-thousand-dollar incentive check ev'ry month." At that time, she was still a teenager, but Bunny was only one of the very young people I had met who made, or had made, good salaries, yet whose life-styles didn't seem to reflect it.

"What did you do with your money?" I asked, curious.

"Oh, buy drugs. And snowmobiles, four-wheel-drive vehicles, cars, stuff like that—I used to go into a bar, 'n' buy ev'rybody there a drink, then another round. That could take a couple of hundred a night."

Now she lived with her boyfriend—one of the few blacks in the town—who, at twenty-four, had a good job in the mines and didn't want her to work. "That's why I bought this car," she explained as we stepped into a silver Cadillac in the parking lot. "The payments are three-fifty a month, but I figured since everybody thought he was a pimp just 'cause he was black, I'd play it up. So he puts up with this part-time job I have drivin' a school bus, 'cause I wanted to make the payments myself."

We were to come back to the Ramada at one to meet two other women for lunch, but had decided to go to the mall to shop during the interim. "Yeah, you can get one for yourself there," she said after I had commented on the beribboned pink feather, like that worn by the Country Kitchen waitress, dangling from her rearview mirror. "And they even have a *bookstore*," she enthused as we approached what looked like a raw scar where one-story buildings had touched down on the mud-slicked horizon. "I brought you all my old *Hustler* magazines," she said, nodding toward the backseat. "It's my favorite book, 'n' I thought since you're a writer 'n' all, you might wanna read 'em."

At the mall, I bought a polyester blouse, a pink feather, and two photography books. Bunny bought the latest issue of *Hustler*. As we headed back toward the Ramada, I told her that I had met the two women who were to lunch with us the night before with Ann Strand at Gio's, the Italian bar. Just as Barbara had described, the owner, Giovaldi, and some of his cohorts, had been standing around in black, wide-lapel suits, dark shirts, and black hats, *Godfather*-style. I had mentioned to them that while I had come West to look for macho men, I was finding the women so interesting that I wanted to meet more of them.

"I've got two for you," said a man with a fat cigar clenched between his teeth who had just opened his jacket to reveal suspenders and a side holster with submachine gun. "They're typical Western girls—hard as nails!" When he brought the short muscular blonde, the tall muscular brunette, both in jeans, by my table, I told them I wanted to talk about Western women and macho men. The shorter one hooted, and we made a date for the next day.

When Bunny and I walked into the coffee shop, La Rue and Janna were already sipping huge frozen margaritas. As they made room for us in the booth, I introduced Bunny, and we fell into the kind of girl talk I was used to down South, but which I was finding was ubiquitous even among the most macha women. "I can't *believe* you weigh one hundred and fifty pounds!" Bunny, her violet eyes widening dramatically, was exclaiming to Janna, the tall brunette, who did, indeed, look fine in her Levis and hand-knit burgundy sweater. "That's what *I* weigh, too, but I sure don't look that good in pants!"

"Oh, it's just because I get so much exercise out in the field," Janna said, referring to her job as an oil-field mechanic. "You can carry a *lot* of weight when you're hard. But I wish I was a little more feminine-lookin' like *you*," she added flirtatiously, looking down the front of Bunny's dress.

"I don't have a problem with *that*," La Rue, the short, short-haired blonde, said. "What I'm concerned about is my *complexion*. Janna has that near-perfect kind of skin, almost as good as yours"— she nodded jealously toward my Southern-steamed epidermis— "but I'm gettin' these little lines around my eyes." We all obediently squinted at her squint, as though finding the deep grooves beside her eyes nearly invisible. "'N' I guess workin' outside all day drivin' a Caterpillar doesn't help!" From long practice, I knew the rules of the game, that now it was *my* turn to protest. "Oh, it's just because it's so hot 'n' wet down there!" I said. But when they launched into a discussion of the virtues of Oil of Olay versus Charles of the Ritz, I became restless. Everywhere I turned, it seemed, macha women preferred discussing moisturizers to the men they were involved with. In fact, it was as though—except to the economically dependent women captive in the house trailers with 3.5 kids and the blowing wind—the men were as ubiquitous as the sagebrush, too profuse to be worth bothering with, much less being bothered *by*.

"Oh, him?" La Rue replied disparagingly when I asked about her husband, the good-looking man I had seen standing solicitously at her elbow with a drink the night before. "I had so many boyfriends out here, but it's *easier* to have one, so we got married, 'n' now we live in this house with three other guys. They do all the cleanin', ev'rything."

"Yeah, she's got it made!" Janna interjected cynically.

"It's an open marriage—*my* choice. If he wanted to get married, he had to go along with it," La Rue went on, as Janna looked as though she might snort with laughter at any moment. "For instance, I love Janna, 'n' I hug her—why should I stop there?"

Janna had once been married to a rock musician, but didn't see herself marrying again. She loved her job, she said, and planned to go to engineering school in Houston sometime in the future, so she could go even further in the oil industry. She obviously had another little business on the side. "I'll *bet* you would," she was saying teasingly to Bunny, as she held a handful of capsules in her palm beneath the table's edge.

"We *both* did *other* things," La Rue said slyly over a third margarita, searching my face for signs of possible disapproval before continuing. "I was a bartender in Denver, ran strippers on the side. . . ." It was during that time that she had been battered, her nose broken, by her first husband, whom she finally left after several—"too many!"—years.

"And I ran an escort service—well, a high-class call-girl ring, really—in Washington, D.C., just six blocks from the Capitol," Janna said casually.

So it wasn't just men who came West to start life afresh no questions asked, I thought. Despite her look of health, her makeup-free face, it was easy to imagine Janna, with her demeanor, as either stern madame or dominatrix. She had casually mentioned the callousness, the infidelities, of her musician-husband. Now I recalled something Shawna had said, that what finally made her leave her abusive spouse had been her realization of a potential for violence growing inside her in response to his, that she didn't want to become that kind of person. Was becoming equally harsh themselves one of the ways women dealt with the insensitivities of some men? Or had these women sought an environment to fit an already established temperament?

If the latter, their toughness didn't necessarily include physical fearlessness. "I wouldn't drive up there *today*," La Rue said when I mentioned my intention of driving north five hours to Jackson Hole, the resort town at the edge of the Grand Teton mountains and Yellowstone National Park. I planned to stop there before traveling on to my final Wyoming destination, Evanston, another boomtown, and site of the state prison for women, where I was to teach for three days. Wyomingites like to talk about weather, the dangers of white-out (in which the horizon cannot be seen at all), black ice (an invisible yet treacherous film sometimes coating a highway), and how far one can walk from one's car in certain temperatures without freezing to death, and La Rue was no exception. By the time she had cited all the fearful possibilities, given the state patrol's weather predictions for that day, and assessed my potential for survival in the rental Rabbit—"Why, that car doesn't even have four-wheel drive!"—I had tremulously acceded, feeling that—no matter how strong my desire to hit Jackson's famous "Cowboy" bar on a Saturday night—I had barely been saved from certain death.

In particularly bad weather, La Rue told me, the state patrol closed off some highways with huge gates. That night back in Motel 8, after Chinese food so bad it made me wonder whether the Chinese Massacre had included tastebuds as well as pigtails, I dreamed first of a disco in the bottom of a mine shaft, lit by a huge neon sign that read HAMMERERS, its walls studded by huge, glowing purple-penis stalactites, filled with milling cowboys, miners, and oil riggers; then, of being alone in a white-out in the middle of the night in the Grand Tetons—caught like a rabbit in my own headlights, the state-patrol gate inexorably descending before me like the spikes of a dungeon, the teeth of a trap.

The next morning, I awoke thinking of the unhappy woman who had come to speak to me after I repeated my lecture on "Women and Violence"—first given at Colorado College—at Western Wyoming College in Rock Springs. The wife of an abusive oil rigger and the mother of two toddlers, she was holding down two jobs to save money to free herself.

"I married him partly 'cause he was so good-lookin'," she said grimly. "But after three weeks of marriage, he stopped wantin' sex altogether. Then I realized he had really just wanted a mother. Which was hard on me, because livin' in Rock Springs, I had been *very* sexually active." During hunting season—then under way— her husband's moods, and whether he would beat her or not when he got home, depended on how well his hunting had gone. "He goes out there to track elk, takes a lot of booze with 'im, dehydrated food, orange tape to mark his way. Even when it's snowin' or rainin', he might stay two or three weeks at a time."

Which would have to make him more animal than human, I marveled as I drove toward Jackson Hole, observing the majestic scenery around me. The state patrol had reported fair weather—only occasional light snow and rain—between Pinedale and Jackson today, but, still, the landscape was overpowering, the distant mountains as unreal as white paper cutouts. And though I knew hunters really did it—I had already passed a number of the fluorescent-orange-slickered men, hanging elk or deer from trees beside the road to slit their bellies—I couldn't imagine wandering off the narrow track into those hairy forests, those raw rock chasms, alone.

In Pinedale, I stopped at the 7-11 for coffee, and on the newsstand I spied the December issue of *Playgirl* magazine with my name—followed by "The World of Whiskey, Sex, Tattoos, Sex, Muscles, Sex" on the cover, advertising a story I had written about my weeks on the oil rig. As I handed the large-boned blonde clerk my money for coffee and the magazine, I momentarily wondered what she would think had she known I was the author of the piece; but, in fact, the Western women I had met so far were far less sexually repressed—at least, verbally—than my Southern sisters.

And they were at least as hospitable, I thought, as I checked into the Antler Motel in Jackson Hole. Clarene, the proprietor and Ann Strand's friend, had given me a huge, pine-paneled room with king-size bed, sitting area, stone fireplace, and had insisted that if I needed anything—anything at all—that I please call.

I wandered through the Sunday-quiet town, looking into the windows of continental restaurants, expensive ski or dress shops, strangely juxtaposed with genuine Western stores and businesses along the raw sidewalks, then went inside the Silver Dollar Saloon at the Wort Hotel, where I sat at the bar and ordered a bourbon. Entering a bar alone was something I had made myself learn to do, and while it was still hard, it was a skill I felt I had to practice regularly, like flexing a muscle to keep it in shape. And sitting at the bar, I had found, at least ensured that I would have the bartender to talk to. "Sure do!" he replied when I asked whether anyone ever tried to scoop up the silver dollars, embedded in plastic by the hundreds just beneath the long circular bar's surface. "Especially when they're loaded."

Having done maintenance on my independence, I ordered fresh mountain trout and a couple of glasses of wine at the restaurant next door. As I ate, three weathered men in worn Western garb and black cowboy hats looked my way on and off, grinning sheepishly. When they rose with their checks, one shuffled toward me like an eleven-year-old on a dare. "I shore do lak them purple boots, ma'am!" he said, moving his hat from one hand to the other as his buddies looked on delightedly. "Wanna swap 'em fur mine?" "Thanks, but no thanks," I smiled back, playing into their game. When I looked down at his big work boots, I saw they were completely covered with blood-black stains.

"Yeah, a lot of these boys are just not around women that much," Clarene said the next morning as I checked out. "One of them city gals dances with 'im *once* over at the Cowboy, 'n' he thinks she wants to go to bed with 'im. Then, if she makes the mistake of lettin' 'im know her room number, he'll be over here in the middle of the night, bangin' her door down, 'n' my husband Creed or I have to go save 'er."

"This is Pete," she said, introducing a man who had just stepped into the motel offices. If his clothes had looked a little cleaner, his face not so closely resembling crumpled tan leather, he would have been handsome. "He's a guide, just finishin' up huntin' season," she went on in a motherly tone, as though he might be unable to speak for himself. "What will you do next?" I asked.

"Heck, ma'am"—he shuffled his feet, looking down at the floor like the man from the night before—"thar's at least a hunnert ranches around here whar I could git a job—that's whut I us'ally do, cowpikin'. But this year, I thank I'll go out to Utah, git me a li'l cabin, trap ky-otes—they use them li'l bellies on ladies' fur coats. . . ."

"But doesn't all that moving around interfere with your *personal* life?" I asked.

He stopped shuffling and looked up at me, genuinely puzzled: "Pers'nal life? Whut's thet, ma'am?"

All I knew about Chilton Williamson, Jr., whom I planned to stop en route to meet in Kemmerer, was that he was the author of a recently published book on the oil-rig life, *Roughnecking It*. When I finally—after a road that stretched out and stretched out—arrived at a town that looked even more of a muddy scar, a trailer-swollen boomtown, than the others I had seen, I quickly found Chilton's—or Chip's—apartment, which, like everything else on the horizon, was only feet from the main road. Over our first drinks—his Scotch, my bourbon—in his spacious living room, I learned he had grown up in New York and Vermont. In fact, he still flew east each month to edit the "Books, Arts & Manners" section of the *National Review* for William F. Buckley, Jr.

I experienced again that small shock of finding myself liking someone with whom I would have thought I would have nothing in common, at least politically or philosophically. It was as though the very harshness of the landscape reduced other stratifications to insignificance, producing a genuinely classless society. From this perspective, the lush decadence of the deep South, the cynical hedonism of the West Coast, the hyperintellectuality of the Northeast, all appeared effete, indulgent.

When Chip came to Kemmerer to research his book, he made himself part of the community, spending weeks hunting, hanging out, and visiting the rigs. His book describes the way of life of men who carry male bonding to the point of self-destruction, who use "motherfucker" in almost every sentence, who apparently think of nothing but booze, guns, four-wheel-drive vehicles, hunting and oil rigging, occasionally throwing Mother—as the wife is called—the bone of a new house trailer, the promise of a trip back East.

But Chip had fallen in love with the life-style, as well as with Norma, a soft-spoken former Tennessean whom he had met at the Methodist church. She had been married at the time, was already the mother of three, and now her former spouse lived about a mile down the road, her children spending half their time with each family. A brave—or foolhardy—thing to do, taking another man's wife in a town where men still carried guns, I commented. Chip chuckled. "Well, what do you think, Mother?"

"I don't know—I think it worked out real well," Norma said in an accent that was balm to my ears after days of flat Western speech. "Anyway, *you've* got as many guns as anybody else!"

I had already noticed the gun case and gun rack on the wall, and when we went outside to drive to a local bar and steak house, I saw that Chip owned not one, but two, four-wheel-drive vehicles, and dressed just like all the other men in town. He may have been a former New York preppy who had written a book on Block Island, but he now appeared—except for the undeniable intelligence in his blue eyes, his occasional lapses into upper-middle-class mannerisms—completely assimilated.

"What'll you have, hon?" he asked Norma, using a diminutive scorned as redneck in the deep South, yet apparently popular in the new West. We had just taken off down jackets and slid into a booth. We ordered more bourbon and Scotch straight up, and, from looking around me at the diners who were in turn looking back at me with frank curiosity, I suspected that the entree was not a celery-and-carrot sauté. Anticipating the bloody steak I had longed for since I had flown into Denver's Stapleton Airport, I suspected that vegetarianism, like teetotalism, just might be considered a felony here.

"I have to have a beer 'bout ev'ry hour when I'm doin' that!" laughed Michelle, the pretty woman who had shot her husband because of abusive oral sex influenced by the film *Deep Throat*. She had been talking about castrating sheep back on the ranch with her teeth, then spitting the results aside till the corners of her mouth, her shirt front, had been sticky with blood.

"Your life certainly has been *oral*," I joked, and she and the other women in the class—at last safe from men inside the prison— laughed, too. But beneath the levity, there was a pervasive melancholy. We were inside the Wyoming Women's Center, the one state prison for women, housing about thirty-four inmates, and though I had been teaching there for only two days, the constant presence of the "security officers," the random interruption of our classes for "freeze counts," and my knowledge that every time these women went to the canteen for cigarettes or a Coke, they were strip-searched, had kept waking me throughout the night with fantasies of what it must be like never to eat, sleep, or go to the bathroom alone for years, or for the rest of your life.

My realization of the truth of Lisa's theory that almost all of the women were here because of some distortion in their relationship with a man had kept me tossing on the teeth of my awareness that I, too, had shared their crazy-house vision, their magnification of the importance of the men in their lives.

There was a recurrent rationale in all their stories, from the stout and pleasant-looking grandmother who had, in a burst of rebellion, embezzled funds ("I had never done anything my whole life but wait on men!") to the pretty young woman who had continued dealing drugs with her boyfriend, despite the fact that he had once broken her jaw, another time shot her; to the mother of six, who, along with her husband, had set fire, during her last pregnancy, to their house trailer with several of their children inside. "If only we had had one of those fire extinguishers," she said to me wistfully, weaving invisible cat's cradles in the air with her fingertips. It was as though all the mad extremes of the West, the forces that demanded that women either placate the most macho of men, or surpass them in insensitivity, had surfaced in these women.

"It really gets to you, being there year after year," said Nancy, educational director of the center and my hostess. "Especially when you know some of them are there for multiple life—that they will literally spend the rest of their lives together." Again I tried to imagine their situation, realizing that the prison was so small, security so tight, that the women were undoubtedly denied even the comforts of lesbianism.

"Then there's the energy I use fending off their cons, tryin' to remember that most of 'em *are* real criminals, whatever the reasons."

That would be hard for her, I thought, noting her look of gentle sadness as she described the young blonde woman who still denied that she had placed the plastic bag over her baby's head, who was so unresponsive that she hadn't even noticed when a male security officer had left his wife, and been fired over her.

Nancy had recently gone to a concert given by feminist performer Margie Adams in Salt Lake City and had marveled at the singer's empathy. Now I noticed that Nancy's own blond frizz gave Nancy the same post-hippie look Margie wore on her album cover.

But if Nancy had rejected Western severity, she had retained the pragmatism, I thought, as she plopped the one-dish casserole on the kitchen table in its baking pan, tore off paper towels for napkins, and distributed them as we sat down to eat. We were sharing the taco casserole with her husband, Bud, a quiet, retired high school principal, and the only nonmacho man I had met out West to date, and her husky twenty-one-year-old son, Buddy, who worked at the trona—or soda ash—mines.

"The only part of the world besides Ireland where it's produced," he explained proudly. "You know—it's that stuff in bakin' soda."

"It scares me for him to work there because the fumes are so deadly," Nancy said. "But it's gettin' hard to even find jobs out here now."

Driving into town, I had noticed that, though I knew Evanston had once been, it was not now, the most booming boomtown I had ever seen.

"Still, you *do* make good money—twenty-one thousand dollars a year," she teased Buddy, "even if all you have to spend it on is Coors 'n' that four-wheel-drive thing of yours!"

"Yeah, plenty of money—'n' no wimmen to spend it on!" he complained, echoing what I had heard in Rock Springs.

Nancy described the entertainment she had planned for my visit. That night, she and Bud would drop me off at a reelection party for the incumbent sheriff. "You're *sure* to meet a lot of macho men *there*," she said in a tone that implied that while I might be interested in researching them, that was something she would rather avoid. The following night we would go with the security officers and other women employees at the prison to see a male stripper. I didn't want to tell her that I had had quite enough of the macho Western man, or that I wasn't particularly interested—since I lived year-round in one of the gay capitals of the United States— in watching a fag gyrate in a G-string.

And as I walked past a driveway full of four-wheel-drive vehicles, up the stairs of the sheriff's constituent's split-level house, the scene was, indeed, predictable. If, in fact, my host owned more guns—not just a caseful, but a wall totally lined with rifles, shot-guns, pistols—than any one person I had ever met, the men were still dressed the same way, the talk was still of the same things, the same admiring things were said by everyone who saw the deer, its belly slit, hanging in the carport.

But in the kitchen, a woman was telling a joke in an exuberant yet raspy voice. "Do you know why a man is like snow?" she was asking as I rounded the corner into the room where the other women were setting out platters of nachos, bowls of chili, frosted bottles of Coors. "Because you don't know how many inches you'll get or how long it'll last!" she said, hooting at her own joke while waving a pink plastic pacifier shaped like a penis. Despite her per-manented bright-blond hair, I could tell she was old enough to be my mother, maybe even my grandmother, but before I could stop her for a chat, she had grabbed a muscular young man as he walked into the room, bending him backward in a French kiss that almost knocked off his Stetson.

I experienced the same shock of surprise the next night when the muscular prison guards, now dressed in "street" clothes—polyester pants and shirts, beehives teased higher than usual—bumped and ground themselves into the male stripper, surrounding him, plucking at his G-string till he fled the dance floor in barely concealed terror. And again, when a—"usually so shy," Nancy said— file clerk stood on a table and unbuttoned her blouse to dance topless. And again when a seventyish grandmother who worked in the kitchen outdrank everyone, and—refusing the offer of a ride home with her daughter, also a prison employee—stayed at the bar dancing with cowboys until three, when it closed, then drove the fifty desolate miles to her ranch alone.

"Aren't you tired?" I asked her the next day. "Naw, it was fun," she giggled, confirming my impression that the Western women who survived were at least as macho as their men—leaving the latter still fantasizing about gentler, more airbrushed mates.

"I think I'll come down South, get me a Southern girl to marry," Buddy told me that afternoon in the kitchen, his biceps flexing as he pulled a just-seared hunk of bloody beef from the broiler for a snack. "Maybe she'll have a pretty complexion like you—how old are you, anyway?"

When I told him, he whistled. There was something in the air that—had I not had Zane at home, had I not grown to like men though not to need to seduce them, had I not O.D.'d on Zipless Fucks with men young enough to be my children—just might have been worth pursuing.

"The wimmen must really be somethin' down there," he mused, "that soft way of talkin', never gettin' out in the wind 'n' cold 'n' gettin' all wrinkled. . . ."

And then, managing to turn me off in the nick of time, adding the most important part of his fantasy: "Bet they'll do whatever you tell 'em to do, too!"

THE SISTERHOOD OF SICK LOVE.

As I drove toward the clean white Mormon light of Salt Lake City, where I would turn in the Rabbit and fly south to Austin where Laura was in graduate school, I considered my trip West. The first time I had visited Wyoming several years before, my primary interest—aside from my work teaching poetry in the schools—had been finding and fucking the macho man. This time, too, I had been in search of him, if only for objective research. And while I had found him in abundance, I had also found my interest almost forcibly turned toward the women who gravitated in his field.

"Rhonda and I were just talking," Lisa had said when she called me at the Motel 8 to say good-bye. "The trouble with you is that you really *like* macho men." She had found my lecture on "Women and Violence," my interest in her work with battered women contradictory to my attraction to the very kind of brutes she considered most likely to do the abusing. Yet in the next breath, she told me that the night after we had gone to the Kasbah together, she had had to go to the hospital emergency room to pick up her boyfriend, Rick, who had been "jumped by some guys outside the Silver Dollar." It reminded me of the story a friend had told me of a Wyoming rape trial. The woman who filed charges had been working at the desk at a local motel; she claimed the man had taken her through a door to an office and raped her. But during the trial, the defendant testified that he had been beneath the desk performing cunnilingus on her for at least two hours prior to the "rape." The woman's claim seemed to me to be symbolic of the paradox that was the Western woman.

A Wyoming judge's wife I had known shot herself through the mouth when she learned that the young prison parolee who had been boarding at her house and sleeping with her had been sleeping with her fourteen-year-old daughter as well. She pulled the trigger in front of her daughter and their mutual lover, but dental work had stopped the bullet, leaving her with a bitter smile permanently lifting one side of her mouth. When I last saw her, she had been severely dressed in jeans and turtleneck, her distorted, once-pretty face free of makeup, her silver hair skinned back in a tight chignon, and said she had begun writing poetry. During my more recent trip, I had heard that after her divorce, she had gone south to New Mexico to live near her daughter in a commune and had been killed—accidentally?—in a motorcycle wreck.

And in the Wyoming Women's Center, I had heard of the two sisters, eleven and twelve, who were promised help with car trouble if they would get into a pickup driven by two men who had stopped for them. Instead, the men had raped them and had thrown them over a dam. One of the sisters died; the other had inched her way up the embankment the next morning despite a fractured thigh, to be found the next morning on the side of the highway. Had Lisa been right in implying a connection between an attraction to the macho man and such terrible events? Were women who failed to acknowledge their own impulses toward sex and aggression more likely to seek out a man to act out those impulses for them, thus inadvertently contributing to male sociopathy?

In Casper, I had dined with the unofficial state poet laureate, a woman in her sixties who drank her bourbon neat and who still bore on her cheeks the broken capillaries that were the marks of the time she was trapped in a wagon in a blizzard as a child. She had told me of the ranch women who spent six months of each year a hundred miles from a drugstore or doctor, with only a shortwave radio for communication with the outside world, and of the ones who simply rode off into the snow (or, less destructively, with a ranch hand). This happened so often that she felt she could predict the phenomenon. "But there's nothing you can do—you can't tell them," she said, indicating a taut, weathered-looking woman in denim ranch clothes across the room whose eyes did, indeed, hold the desperate vacancy, the unfocused quality, that I recalled from the weeks before my mother's first breakdown.

Her comment reminded me of the Western miners' and riggers' wives who had turned out to be engaged in a merry-go-round of shift-change love affairs, with frequent divorces and remarriages, activities designed to break the monotony of their trailer- and-childbound existences. "My daddy used to be your daddy," I heard a fourth grader say conversationally in one of the boomtowns I visited. Apparently, stimulation for one of these women could rarely be found beyond a lover with a shift different from her (present) husband's.

The day before my dinner with the poet, I had met Morgan, an elegantly slender ranch wife—I later saw the pantsuit she wore listed as one of the more expensive items in the Sears Roebuck catalog—who was the mother of four and mistress of both a town and ranch house. She no longer loved her rancher husband, but would remain married to him in order to ensure her children's inheritance of the ranch, she confessed, then laughed when I gasped at her revelation that she, like Michelle in prison, had once castrated sheep with her pretty teeth.

In a bar in Gillette I had talked with Roberta, a jolly, waitressy-looking blonde, thirty pounds overweight, who had been widowed three times and made wealthy in the process. "Gillette men work themselves to death so they can leave their widows rich," she had explained proudly. And everywhere there were the ubiquitous women, heavy of thigh, with teased yellow hair, who appeared to have embraced totally the Western and Southern male's notion of women as either on the pedestal or off it. That prostitution recently was legalized in the West again (in Nevada) reflects a hard-bitten practicality about the use of sexuality that is the resource of women to whom gentler avenues to security seem blocked.

Such pragmatism was logical in a culture in which a woman's survival depended, like her man's, on toughness. Just as in the deep South, where certain crazily overdeveloped defenses—manipulativeness and almost caricatured femininity—seem perfectly reasonable and necessary to the women who have been brought up with them, those born to ruggedness, like Morgan or Barbara, seemed to fare best out West. And women like Claire, Jennifer, Ann Strand, even Lisa—who, Scarlett-like, refused the mother role, yet embraced the femme fatale, the adventuress—appeared to thrive here, too. Undoubtedly, part of my own attraction to the place stemmed from my upbringing, my training in sexual dissembling, in that other, most sexist region of the country. From growing up Southern, I knew that just because Southern women often behaved passively didn't mean that they felt that way; and I suspected that Western women weren't always as tough as they appeared; that, in fact, their feistiness was a necessary survival mechanism for facing life in a harsh culture with harsh men.

At least Texas would be *soft*, I thought, boarding the plane for Austin. I recalled the stewardess in miniskirted cowgirl outfit on a plane between Dallas and Houston who had begun the flight by saying, "Now, y'all have nice day, 'n' don't spoil it by workin' too hard!" Definitely not the kind of thing one would hear on, say, the shuttle between Washington and New York.

For the next two weeks, Laura and I gluttonized ourselves on Tex-Mex food and frozen margaritas, visiting the state house, to read monuments dedicated to machismo, Southern style. ("The people of the South, animated by the spirit of 1776, to preserve their rights, withdrew from the Federal Compact in 1861. The North resorted to coercion: The South, against overwhelming numbers and resources, fought until exhausted. . . ." Or, "God and

Texas, Victory or Death," and "I shall never surrender or retreat.") We looked at the University of Texas tower from which Charles Whitman had gunned down so many people and discussed the fact that he had suffered from a tumor of the amygdala, the part of the brain that controls sex and aggression. "I wonder if macho men drink so much as a way of keeping the amygdala down," I mused unscientifically to Laura, now a Ph.D. candidate in pharmacology, specializing in the effects of chemicals on the brain.

"It's Christmas Eve," I said to Laura a few nights later. "What are all these men doing here—don't they have wives, mothers, girl friends?" We were sitting in "Dallas," an Austin country-western disco—belting tequila shots, chasing them with Lone Star, and I knew what *we* were doing there. We had just had yet another meal of flautas and enchiladas, having put off basting the turkey and wrapping our gifts till the next day. But the whole place was crowded with men in Stetsons, Levis, cowboy boots, leaning against the bar on their elbows in that stance of single men surveying the scene. It was hard to believe, looking at their hairy faces, aggressive postures, that every cowboy had once been somebody's baby—held, cuddled, and diapered. The thought made me giggle, especially since I knew that one of the reasons men came to barrooms was to escape mother figures (Billy Bob's in Fort Worth features, besides an arena stocked with live bulls, excuse phone booths, where, for $1.25, a man can get just the right background noise—airport, gas station, office—for that call home); or to find new ones, even if only in the person of cocktail waitress or woman bartender—indeed, that the dream of every macho man was a mother who was also a topless dancer. Yet didn't they seem marvelously exempt from the family shit that had held me in thrall for most of a lifetime? Was that freedom from the acculturated female need to keep up the home front one of the things I envied in such men, I wondered, thinking at the same time how lucky I was to have a daughter who shared my predilections for Chinese restaurants at Easter, Mexican cantinas on Christmas Eve!

After a while, a sweet-faced young man in a black Stetson came up to me and took my elbow. "The Ruhl Ranch—Gentle Brahmas" read the card he handed me. "Excuse me fur bein' forward, ma'am," he said politely, "but I'm drivin' a load a lambs up to Kansas, just passin' through town, 'n' wondered if you'd spend the night with me." The larger Chicano with whom I had just been two-stepping gripped my forearm possessively. "No thank you," I said to each of them, extricating my arms, "but when you go out to your truck, pet those lambs for me."

Back at Laura's apartment, I stayed up till dawn reading *Everything We Had*, Al Santoli's oral history of the Vietnam war. When I finally fell asleep, it was first to nightmares of conflagration, then a dream of Jack: "I wouldn't be surprised if he drove up right now with a truckload of bull elephants!" Laura was saying.

The Pirate was out of the picture now, I remembered as I awakened, and back home in Savannah, my new lover was awaiting me.

PART SEVEN

SLEEPING

WITH

SOLDIERS

SLEEPING WITH SOLDIERS, OR JUST ANOTHER VICTORIAN ROMANCE.

When Zane and I first speak, he tells me he is a skydiver and a paratrooper, is in therapy and in the process of being divorced, and—pointing out a large woman, dressed in men's Levis and button-down shirt, drinking across the bar with equally husky-looking female friends—has a woman roommate.

Despite his rubber flip-flops, ragged T-shirt, and cutoffs, he is handsome—large, red-blond, dimpled. Each time he raises his Pabst can, an attractively freckled biceps moves beneath a red-and-blue tattoo of a parachute, the word "PARATROOPER"; the bright blue letters match his azure eyes.

As we talk, I take his big hand, press it to the patch of white thigh, summer-bare of stockings, revealed by my slit skirt. When we slow-dance to the jukebox, he tugs me close and, pressing the same hand to the rise of my ass, suggests we walk the three blocks to his apartment. . . .

Though I mean to leave as he still lies sprawled asleep—a huge red tomcat—on the dyke's water bed, I don't; and two weeks later, he has left her apartment for mine. For the first time in five years, I am living again with a man; and—free (I think) from the Pendulum Phenomenon, have at last chosen the kind of mate I have learned from my time of loose living that I prefer as a lover, if not a husband.

Then, too, I hope to realize a long-held fantasy: that of living an autonomous life *with* a man—one in which we would exist side by side as friends and companions, rather than as oppressive spouses. And since Zane appeared as in need of his own freedom as the tomcat he resembled—requiring for his happiness late nights at his favorite bars, skydiving weekends at Free Fall Farm, and months in the field on army maneuvers—he seemed the perfect candidate. Though I now lived with a lover, I was free to travel alone, to have dinner or go out dancing with male friends, or to my favorite bars alone or with other women—all the things I had felt unable to do as a properly married woman. At the same time, I at last had a sexually responsive man in bed with me every night, one as given to the pursuit of pleasure as I was. Zane had a woman who willingly joined in that pursuit with him, who even said she enjoyed his wildness, and would never try to tame him.

Before long, almost without our knowing it, sleeping together every night had turned into being "in love." Coming home to each other each night, we fell into a natural and inevitable monogamy. Since Darcy had decided—to my relief—to leave her tempestuous life in New York and spend some time in Savannah, my attention was further focused on family. Jack, Sean, Randy, and the rest slid easily, if reluctantly, from the picture.

"The well-fed don't steal," Wilhelm Reich wrote in *The Sexual Revolution*, first published in 1962. It was the kind of sentiment that appealed to my interest in a companionate relationship, and my recently acknowledged preference for the Noble Savage. But really, I was more like the commuter in the *Playboy* cartoon who tells his seatmate that "Ever in search of the new experience, I'm now being faithful to my wife." (I had forgotten that Reich had also written: "The sexually undemanding, not very independent, sex-negating woman who merely tolerates eroticism is the most faithful wife"—and didn't know that, before long, even a big orange tomcat like Zane would inevitably show his traditional stripes, worrying that I "liked sex too much," and would push for marriage, mothering [of him, naturally], and all the rest.)

At nine, I had had a boxer puppy so large and rambunctious that Mother had insisted he be kept at my grandparents' farm. When the dog, half as large as I, had literally torn off my best Sunday School dress in a fit of playfulness, I had been terrified and my parents had given him away. But though I hadn't even been able to calm—in fact, had feared—a big puppy, I persisted in my delusion that had I been confronted by a lion or tiger, I would have been able to tame him by the force of my love.

After our first night together, Zane had roamed the rooms of my apartment, examining books, art objects, then had looked at the fresh page stuck in my old Hermes manual: *Sleeping with Soldiers* read the title I had typed just a few days before meeting him. Now he had become my flesh-and-blood warrior, my wild animal, and in line with my fantasies of adventure, my African jungle as well. At home, I had my own live-in research subject, my own exemplar of the genre, complete with *Sky Diver* and *Soldier of Fortune* magazines on his side of my four-poster bed, the camouflage fatigues in which he looked so sexy carelessly shucked and rumpled over my pink wicker chair, hard rock at top decibel on my usually silent stereo, Camels ashes filling my previously unused ashtrays, and Pabst cans everywhere—the perfect situation, I told myself, in which to gluttonize myself on the macho man.

But I was learning that fucking such a man was one thing, and living with him was another—that he was more complex, less easily tamed, than I had imagined. And while I had almost lost interest in the genre, my new lover still shared his natural habitats. Thus, between him and Darcy—newly arrived from New York, as much a female adventuress as I had ever been and intrigued by a species as yet unknown to her, at least in the Southern variety—I found myself, if I wished to spend time with either of them at all, continuing my research on an involuntary basis.

·   ·   ·

"Then I asked 'im—Lord, he wuz little!—'You got it in yet?' . . . Yeah, an Indian *Indian—Lord, don't ever fuck one a them!"*

"That's nothin'! You know what I said to this guy once? 'Is that all!' I said. He wuz already finished, 'n' I didn't even know he'd put it in!"

I'm listening to Marlene and Jan, bartenders at one of Zane's favorite dives, the Knight's Inn. It has the kind of dark, low-ceilinged, red-velour atmosphere that takes my eyes ten minutes to acclimate to, whatever the time of day. Over the bar behind the two women a wooden plaque commemorates the most recent Snakebite Champion, who—although he had had to be resuscitated and had spent two days in the hospital recuperating—had downed thirty-nine shots of Yukon Jack and lime juice in twenty-four minutes. A few months before, someone had been shot in the parking lot, but Zane was offended when I referred to the place as sleazy.

Tonight, he has agreed to a new foreign film and dinner out somewhere other than Shoney's, if only we would stop here for a few minutes—the least I can do, I think, considering his occasional forays with me to art exhibitions and cocktail parties featuring stockbrokers. Yet now, as I down my third schnapps and he calls for another round—as the jukebox begins "Baby, Let Me Bang Your Box," by Doug Clark and the Hot Nuts, again—I suspect this might be yet another of those evenings when we suspend our original plans.

When she brings our shots, Marlene punches out the holes in the little cards that come with each drink, designating its price. She always seems to know which holes will say ten cents. In return, Zane buys her a drink. Jimmy, who owns the bar, encourages the "girls" to drink with the customers, doesn't mind if they go out back to smoke dope or down pills. "When he hired me, he asked whether I did drugs," Marlene confides. "I didn't know *what* to say—whether to say yes or no. But I guessed the right answer was yes, and I was right!" Nor does this Godfather—or is it pimp?—of bar owners mind if they take a man to the ladies' room to fuck. "But I don't do that," Marlene says, "because of my old man."

"If you bend over just a little more, I'll add another dollar to your tip!" a customer says from farther down the bar, referring to her large breasts, the décolletage of her costume, as she leans over to wash a glass. "I always wanted me a gal with big bazooms," Terry, her old man, comments jovially to Zane. As retired military, Terry hangs out here much of the time and apparently doesn't mind the way his wife earns her tips or her stories like the one about the Indian Indian. In fact, he appears pleased, linking arms with her to down Fireballs—shooters of cinnamon schnapps and other liqueurs—alternately toasting sucking pussy and blow jobs.

Jan, who has a reputation for setting fire to her long fake nails with her Bic whenever she gets drunk enough, and for being fired and rehired by Jimmy more than any other of his bartenders, is talking about a warehouse out on Highway 17 where you can get the nicest clothes and about her French poodles: "I got Coochie Coo right after I got out of Broad Oaks last time," she says, referring to the local private mental hospital as though it were a finishing school. She interrupts herself to answer the phone. "C.T., somebody wants to buy!" she yells to the bouncer, holding her hand over the receiver. "Tell 'im I'll meet 'im out back in half an hour," he calls back from the Atari game.

"Now aren't you havin' fun?" On the jukebox Jimmy Buffett is singing, "Why Don't We Get Drunk (and Screw)," and Zane has pulled me out to the tiny dance floor, pressing me close, nuzzling my neck, generally indulging in that intense, if indiscriminate, demonstrativeness for which macho men are justifiably known. "I can't wait to get you home," he whispers, nibbling my earlobe, playing his fingers up and down my spine. Yet I know from the evening's beginnings that that will be hours and hours from now, for there is no one happier—or more stubbornly insensitive—than the macho man in his natural surroundings. In fact, I may have at last met my match in self-destructiveness, if nothing else.

"Yep, Ro-zeller's mah fourth wife, but this time I've got it right, now ah really know how to treat a woman," says the man sitting next to me in the Office, a bar so named so men can call home and honestly report their whereabouts, yet another of Zane's favorite hangouts. "Fact, tonight's 'er birthday 'n'—" As he speaks, the pay phone rings, the bartender answers. "Fur you, Ray," he says, handing the receiver across the bar to the man with whom I'm talking. The happily wed Rosella's enraged queries as to why Ray is not home yet hurt even my ears.

It's Friday night, and Zane and I are here to watch the Tex Cobb–Larry Holmes fight on the oversized color TV suspended from the ceiling. I've never voluntarily watched a boxing match before, but tonight, in order to spend time with my lover, I will. I'm wearing a soft silk blouse, high heels, the stockings and garter belt that affect him like a light switch. As I join Zane and his friends at a table, the four men look up solicitously, outdoing themselves to ask what I would like to drink. The others are Dwayne, who climbs radio towers for a living, and must be drunk to do so; Colonel Cox, a fortyish playboy and remittance man who is a lieutenant colonel in the Marine Reserves; and Big Dick Donaldson, so-called because of the self-proclaimed size of his member. As I mention that I had heard on Paul Harvey that there is an increase in the number of homicides during the three days after a fight, my comment is lost amidst the drift of talk of Rocky Marciano, Rocky Graziano, Jake La Motta, yelled-out bets on how many rounds Cobb will hang in, and calls for more beer. Like subversives, Dwayne—who is surprisingly literate—and I whisper about the best books on Vietnam, even Sylvia Plath's poetry. At the same time, I realize it's his form of flirting; really, all a woman is expected to do here is sit, smile, and look pretty. Despite Zane's possessive hand on my knee, I feel like a scarlet-bottomed female inside a cage full of male orangutans.

When the match begins, I expect to feel bored, but instead find my eyes as riveted to the screen as theirs, my pulse quickening as Cobb is repeatedly battered by Holmes, as again and again he staggers around the ring, eyelids turning to slits, blood running down his forehead. As he at last walks dazed, defeated, yet grinning, through the crowd, waving to his Texas fans, I, too, involuntarily cheer.

A few days later, I find his bruised face beneath his sweaty curls and cowboy hat in the picture in *The New York Times* as appealing as any movie star's. The next week, Zane and I see Sylvester Stallone in *First Blood*, a bad movie smeared with what the title promises. Yet why am I so unfazed? Because I'm becoming one of the boys? Or because, under Zane's auspices, something is surfacing that was there all the while?

"Now, you girls can only clap for one—even if you've slept with all twelve of these here macho men," screams the MC. Despite his microphone, he still has to shout to raise his voice above the hooting and hollering of young Army Rangers, the blue-jeans-and-T-shirt-clad women, many of whom are perched on their shoulders. Though together Darcy, Zane, and I are like a tornado, a hurricane, and a tidal wave, we sometimes have family outings, and tonight, we are at a Macho Man contest. But here our craziness— as compared to that of twenty-year-olds with shaved heads, glazed, obsessive gazes and girls with spaghetti straps falling off their bare shoulders as they raise their fingers to shoot birds—is minimal, adult. At last, the band begins, at top decibel, their rendition of "Baby Makes Her Blue Jeans Talk." The contestants, in jock straps, flexed biceps, strut across the small stage. As they pass, the audience claps and yells to indicate the degree of their approval. "I like *that* one," Darcy declares of Jose, who flexes his pectorals, lifts his clasped palms above his head—who even has some hair, and indeed turns out to be first runner-up. "I'm going to get another beer," she says as soon as the winners are announced, but instead heads straight for the stage, where she retrieves her choice and brings him back to our table. "Well, what did you think of that guy you met last night?" I ask the next day. "Oh, *him*," she says disdainfully. "He wasn't macho enough!"

"He was born in the fifties, he lives in the fifties, he'll die in the fifties," Darcy whispers to me from the front seat of Bobby Cox's white '65 Pontiac Tempest convertible. Because of her interest in the subject, she has amazingly facilitated my research, ferreting out macho men and situations that before would have escaped my notice. This weekend Zane is at Free Fall farm, and she, Colonel Cox, and I are speeding toward Tybee Beach to meet Colonel Cox's best friend, Glenn, whose picture was on the front page of the sports section of the *Savannah News-Press* that morning as winner of the Demolition Derby, a stock-car race in which the participants deliberately try to wreck one another's cars.

We pass "Kim's Koner—We Buy and Sell Anything," where, as usual, the Oriental woman who runs it is standing outside in hot pants, jiggling, smoking a cigarette, looking as though junk is only one of the things she is willing to negotiate; next, "Mr. Shine's Car Wash and Seafood Parlor"; then screech into the fast lane. As we do, Darcy and I giggle subversively. What she is referring to is a local phenomenon that goes something like this: by going to the University of Georgia one hundred and fifty miles away for a few years, a man fulfills his obligation to leave home and is free to come back to Savannah to remain a boy for the rest of his life. It is a condition that reached its sickening zenith during the ascendancy, through the talents of Herschel Walker, of the University of Georgia football team. During that era, tickets to a cocktail party at the Savannah Golf Club honoring Uga, the Georgia bulldog, sold out; bumper stickers reading "Hunker Down, Hairy Dogs," and "Dawgs Do It Better in Sugah" proliferated; and men in their forties sported red-and-black-letter sweaters, carried tailgate picnics in wooden baskets hand-painted with portraits of the dog, his huge pink tongue lolling across the lid like a wet, oversized penis. That along the way, most of these men have acquired wives, ex-wives, and children deters them not at all from their true role as perpetual fraternity boys—a role that requires, as time goes on, younger and younger women, more and more booze, and, if possible, a private income.

Bobby, who wears his monogram tattooed above an ankle so that he'll still look preppy when he wears docksiders without socks, has all those things. In the tradition of wealthy Savannah families, he had been sent to a Northeastern prep school; after college, had been in the service; then, as was also traditional, he had returned home, where he worked as a stockbroker with a Savannah firm. But at night and on weekends, he had raced stock cars, and when the firm asked him to choose between stocks and stock cars, had chosen the latter. For a while, he had sold used cars, but now, in his early forties, he avoids that dirty word, *work*, by living off his investments and spends his time reading ("I'd like to write," he had told me earnestly, in a refrain I often heard from the drunks in the bars where Zane took me, "but I just couldn't stand bein' alone that much"), going out with girls Darcy's age, making himself at home at all the local dives, and occasionally attending Marine Reserve weekends in order to maintain his image as a Colonel and a Real Soldier.

"Yawl're gonna love ole Glenn," he says over the sound of the Tams singing "What Kind of Fool Do You Think I Am?" on the car stereo and the screech of the tires as he swerves into the entrance to a collection of beachside condominiums. Ole Glenn, opening the sliding glass door, holds a glass engraved, "I'm so horny that even the crack of dawn turns me on," is balding, slightly soft in his swim trunks. It's hard to see the good-ole-boy shrewdness behind his thick glasses.

"Did you hear 'bout thet nigger thet 'is employers ast 'im whut he wonnid to be called?" he said after he had handed out beers and we had put our feet up on the fake Spanish Provincial chest that served as a coffee table. "When he said, 'By mah 'nitials,' they thought he said 'Brominitious'—'n' thet's whut they called 'im fur the next forty years!" Desultory laughter: it is the traditional kind of opening for a traditional good-ole-boy conversation. "Hey, thet's a good one!" Bobby says mildly, then turns to me. "Hey, Rosemary—do you know ole Glenn's been married *five* times? Thet's a record even 'round hyah!" "How'd that happen?" I ask with the curiosity of one wed only thrice. "Ah'm jes' an alcoholic, 'n' a gambaholic, 'n' a womanizer, ah guess," Glenn chuckles as though pleased with himself. "Thet's mah last wife over there," he says, indicating the framed eight-by-ten of a Junior-League-proper blonde on a bookshelf, "the mothah a three a mah chirren—we have a wonnerful relationship!" We all sit in silence, sipping our beer, looking out through the sliding glass door at the surf. "How 'bout goin' ovah to ole Colleen's?" Bobby says after a while.

Ole Colleen, it turns out, lives down the beach in a sprawling house owned by her daughter, the teenage movie actress Diane

Lane. As we come into the living room, she is speaking in a sup-
plicating whiskey voice over the phone to Li'l Diane in L.A. "I'm
sufferin' from Post-Traumatic Stress Syndrome—ever heard of it?"
the man with whom she lives, a Vietnam vet in his thirties, now an
occasional shrimper, says to me conversationally as we sit down on
the deck, sipping fresh drinks, this time the hard stuff. "That's why
I can't work much—that Jane Fonda should've left us alone!" he
adds almost vehemently.

"If anybody knows about macho men, it's ole Colleen," Bobby
says as we gaze out over the water, and, indeed, when she's off the
phone, she comes out onto the deck carrying several scrapbooks.
Today her large breasts form a shelf beneath a loose print polyester
overblouse. But when she opens one of the albums to show us
pictures of herself as a *Playboy* centerfold, circa 1957, I see that
they were once even more pointed, that her hipbones had held out
at luscious angles the cloth of her swimsuit. She had been an actress and a singer, too, she said, turning to photos of her seated
with her old friend, Rocky Graziano, or standing alone in straight
slit skirts, sexy little hats with veils, "in Jake La Motta's nightclub
in Miami."

"Hey, Colleen, did you hear 'bout me rapin' that gal the other
night?" asks Elbert, a fat, T-shirted photographer who has just arrived with some pals. He looks around the room to make sure we're
all listening. "She was one of them tourists. We were swimmin' in
the Days Inn pool where she was stayin'. Her friends went on inside, but she took off her suit, jumped in with us. We took 'er back
to 'er room, ev'ryone of us got into 'er!" "Well, I 'magine she got
what she was lookin' for," Colleen says in her whiskey voice.

"Hey, come on, we're all goin' over to the Dew Drop Inn,"
Bobby interjects. "Glenn's havin' a celebration party for winnin'
the Derby Friday night—he's settin' us *all* up. . . ." At the Dew
Drop, Glenn orders doubles all around. Across the bar, I see
Larry, the handsome GBI agent with whom I once slept. "Why
haven't you called me?" he says in a loud stage whisper, coming
around to my side, then motions toward the man with whom he has
been talking. "But don't say anythang to *him* 'bout who I am—I'm
settin' 'im up for a big bust!"

"Who's *that*?" Glenn asks as Larry turns back to his potential
bust. I suddenly realize he thinks he's my date and explain that
soon I must go home—that the man I live with will be waiting for

me—an excuse that, in the land of the double standard, doesn't cut much ice. "But I wanna have an affair wid you," he says petulantly, reverting to the Gullah accent common to Carolina men, while looking down the front of my blouse. "It'll jes' take five minutes!"

When I get home, Zane is sitting in the leather butterfly chair, drinking his sixth black Russian, listening to AC/DC on the stereo. He hasn't eaten all day, he says when I ask—a day of driving, jumping from planes. But then, it doesn't occur to the macho man to prepare food for himself when his mother-lover is due to arrive. And I've relearned enough of my role not to question its requirements; besides, there are too many other things to argue about. I go straight to the kitchen, make four sandwiches with white bread, sliced chicken, Miracle Whip, processed cheese.

"Cindy, your hair doesn't look so good this week—it looks sort of stringy," Bobby says to the woman sitting across from us when I run into him at the Office a couple of weeks later. He has just introduced the two of us and is now glancing lasciviously at her eighteen-year-old daughter, Patty, a Brooke Shields look-alike, who sips a Coke in the seat beside her.

"That Bobby Cox, tellin' me my hair looks stringy! Does *he* lose sleep nights, worryin' about payin' the rent?" she complains as he leaves the table for a beer. She has just told me wearily that she recently read *The Cinderella Complex*, how much the book had meant to her, how she, too, had always lived off men, how though she now has a job selling advertising on commission, the bills were piling up, and with Patty to support, 'n' Reaganomics 'n' all. . . .

I think of Bobby, sleeping late in his high rise, reading the latest hard-back novels; going to the beach in the afternoon with whatever young girl he can lure from her job or studies, then cruising the bars at night while Cindy, his paramour from years before, tosses and turns, wondering where she will get cash for next week's groceries.

"Hey, you'll call me, won't you?" Bobby is now asking the girl, stroking her blue-jeans-clad thighs. "We can jes' talk—why, I've known you since you were a baby—even changed your diapers!"

A sudden reckless anger fills me. "Bobby, you old lech," I lash out at him loudly. "All you *really* want is to stick your cock into some young flesh!" Cindy, Patty, the woman behind the bar, and those seated at it all look up, grinning appreciatively.

In a month, I run into Bobby in line in the supermarket across the street from Kim's Koner. Since I'm a housewife again, I have a basketful of food, he, two six-packs, a frozen pizza, an Earl Thompson novel in his pocket. We talk about the book for a few minutes, then he tells me ole Glenn has just remarried his fifth wife. "'N' this time, she's really got 'im on a tight leash!" he says admiringly. "'N' you should see this girl I'm goin' out with now. Darcy was too old for me, but this one's only seventeen. I think I'm really in love for the first time!"

The Fort Stewart Army hospital is a long wooden building on stilts that looks like a leftover from the First World War. Inside one of the endless wards, Zane lolls against the pillows of his bunk like a wounded lion, the official blue pajamas highlighting even in his pain his bright blue eyes.

I hug him gingerly—his spleen has been ruptured—and set the sack of Burger King double cheeseburgers, the Earl Thompson novels, the mail he has requested, on the table beside him. He presses his forehead against my breasts, mutely closes his eyes, showing how glad he is to see me.

For weeks, I have felt a growing rage, a desire to break this bond. Our seemingly basic value differences, our drunken fights, my resistance to being motherized, his unconscious coercion toward that end—not to speak of the beer cans, the overflowing ashtrays, the hard rock on the stereo—have begun to seem insurmountable obstacles. My experiment in living with a macho man rather than just sleeping with him now seems foolish. When Zane left for Fort Stewart for two weeks in the field, I secretly viewed the time apart as the perfect opportunity to fracture an increasingly uncomfortable arrangement.

But during the second week, Darcy, who was now dating an army medic, had rushed into my study. "Mother," she said, "Jon just called from Fort Stewart. Now don't get excited, but Zane's been in an accident." Without thought, I grabbed my car keys, rushed to the phone. As I held the receiver with a trembling hand, waiting for information, all my animal love for Zane rushed back through me, the thought of him writhing in pain, his beautiful body mutilated, plucked at my gut as though he were one of my children.

Now, as I wrap him in my arms, the tenderness is still there, the old problems on hold. We stroke hands, talk. Looking around, I see rows of other pitiable macho men in need of mother-lovers. Nearby, two young soldiers—one a patient—bend in deep concentration over an unfinished paint-by-number rendition of two Mack trucks. "Isn't that sweet," I say, "the way his friend has come to entertain him?" "Not quite," Zane says, trying not to jar his Percocet-induced haze by laughing. "The Pfc. who's the patient tried to go AWOL. When he didn't succeed in that, he tried to kill himself. They put him in here instead of the psych ward, 'n' the other private is his guard."

"Don't you think there's something especially touching about a strong man brought low?" I ask Darcy as her boyfriend Jon drives us in the '74 white Chrysler New Yorker I have recently bought from Colonel Cox back to Savannah. I had chosen Zane for visceral and emotional reasons, and apparently they still hold. Now that I know my lover will survive—indeed, that his recuperation will delay the separation I have anticipated—the day is pleasant again. Speeding down Highway 204, the three of us pass cans of Coors Light, a joint. A fine breeze blows through the automobile's big windows.

"Come on down, you girls! Bring your bathing suits next Saturday for the water-bed–baby-oil contest!" enthuses a deejay over the car radio. *"Come on down to Military TV, where even an E-Five can get a color set, no money down! And you Marines from Parris Island! Come on down and challenge the soldiers! . . ."*

CHALLENGING A SOLDIER, OR FINDING OUT MORE THAN I EVER WANTED TO KNOW ABOUT THE MILITARY.

When Zane and I first met, I assumed that everyone in the military either secretly or openly abhorred it, and was only waiting for the day when he could get out. My first husband had deliberately flunked out of Officer's Candidate School. A poet friend had been imprisoned for refusing the draft. To avoid induction, Robert John had declared his homosexuality in no uncertain terms ("What makes you think you're a homosexual?" "'Cause I like to suck men's penises 'n' fuck 'em in the ass."). My third husband, Ben, had feigned insanity during his physical. (His former friend and Columbia roommate, ex-Weatherman David Gilbert, was still, at thirty-eight, an enemy of the system. In September 1983, convicted of twenty-one counts arising from the $1.6 million Brink's armored car holdup two years before, he stated, along with two other defendants, "We are at war and have no respect for the laws, the verdict, or the sentence.")

Equally naïvely, I had assumed that, at heart, everyone was liberal—read "good"—and that all soldiers were reluctant victims. When I sat on a plane during the Vietnam conflict beside a uniformed child with startling blue eyes who argued all the way from Georgia to Texas the necessity of our military intervention, the need for the desensitization of soldiers through films of atrocities, mutilation, even torture, I had ascribed his views to brainwashing.

Even in Savannah, with its two military bases, the Army, for me, had been an abstraction. The three soldiers I had dated—Jay, Barry, Beau—had been, whatever else, officers and gentlemen who knew how, when it was useful, to gloss over any attraction to their calling.

But Zane—though as handsome as the sergeant in the TV serial "For Love and Honor"—was still a sergeant who looked like one. "Are you a *drill* sergeant?" a woman asked, despite his creamy shirt, navy blazer, at a cocktail party made up mostly of bankers and their wives. "My husband was just terrified of *his!*"

My first inkling that not everyone was interested in what I thought of as both sides of the story came soon after our meeting, when I offered Zane my copy of *Born on the Fourth of July*, Ron Kovic's story of his terrible maiming—paralysis from the chest down—in Vietnam, and his subsequent radicalization. It was a book that, like the film *The Deer Hunter*, had filled me with a deep and cathartic grief—one that I wanted to share with my new lover.

"Nope, I don't think I'd be interested in *that*," he had said definitely. "But why don't *you* read *this*? It'll help you understand about how I feel about being Airborne." When he handed me *Path for Our Valor* by Thomas Doulis, I flipped through the novel, puzzled. The story apparently had two threads that, braided, formed Zane's and the military proper's view of his role: the subscription to a cause higher than the preservation of one's own life and obedience to patriarchal authority, meaning those of higher rank, up unto the very Cowboy in the White House.

Nor did Zane want to read *Dispatches* by Michael Herr, *Going After Cacciato* by Tim O'Brien, or Peter Marin's article in *Psychology Today* on the guilt of the Vietnam vet. Even when—evoking the powers of what I considered the highest art form—I had read my favorite antiwar poems to him in bed, he had simply listened politely, skeptically. As I dramatized Wilfred Owens's piece on the horrors of gas warfare or Randall Jarrell's description of the ball turret gunner, "washed out of the turret with a hose," the only tears in our eyes were mine.

Indeed, the next morning he had jumped out of bed as usual at five a.m., cheerfully singing "I wanna go to Iran / I wanna kill an I-ran-ee-an!" as he pulled on his running shorts to drive out to the base and "smoke those mothers" in a fifteen-mile run. "You better watch out / parachutes gonna fill yore sky /oo-AH!" he would chant other days, grinning at me as he tied his running shoes. "We'll kill yore dawgs with our Bowie knives / wipe our ass with yore Mama's hair," he would intone till I felt like wiping mine with his. As he exuberantly concluded, "oo-AH! oo-AH! AIRBORNE ALL THE WAY!" I hid my head under my pillow to avoid the sight of his muscular legs, the way his pectorals bulged beneath his T-shirt. "Guess I'll go train some young maggots how to kill Commies," he would say breezily, ignoring my shudder of revulsion as he removed the barricade in order to kiss me a moist and lingering good-bye.

"I wish there was a huge brothel full of horny men for women like me!" my fiftyish friend Lily had once joked. "There are—Fort Stewart, Fort Benning, Fort Bragg," I replied, recalling the hundreds of physically perfect specimens—riding bicycles, jogging, playing tennis, or simply milling outside the barracks. The compound was a veritable anthill of military-induced male overdevelopment, reminding me of how, sometimes even sitting at home in the living room, listening to AC/DC on the stereo, Zane would shout out of nowhere, as though his very enthusiasm for the music provoked it, "*AIRBO-O-O-OR-N-NE!*" At other times, watching football on the black-and-white Sony, he would yell "*Booga! Booga!*" or, as if in sheer excess of male energy, bark "*Awf! Awf!*"

He had a military phrase for every situation—"No pain, no gain," "No brain, no pain," "No guts, no glory," and the compliment, "He's so right he doesn't even *have* a left wing!" Since Beowulf, Genghis Khan, King David, were his heroes, he liked to insert them in military metaphors: "Why, he had a two-oh-one [or personnel] file to equal the Bible," he declared of a soldier he admired. "'N' talk about David killin' Goliath—why that was nothin'! Least he didn't have to road-march fifty miles carryin' heavy metal —all *he* had to carry was a li'l ole slingshot!" Then there was the story of the soldier in the field who kept a tick under his arm for a pet, and the one who became so drunk that when he called a friend from a telephone booth to pick him up, he gave his address as "the corner of Telephone and Telephone."

"Read this," he instructed one afternoon, handing me a Xeroxed sheet printed with a story about a Ranger who stirred a campfire with his penis. "Pretty funny, isn't it?" he chuckled, sitting down on the stool in my study, still clad in the sexy camouflage he wore to the base each day. "One a the girls ran it off for us. 'N' oh, yeah, ole Humbert told me a really good one today—somethin' that happened last week. Seems there were these troopies—candidates for paratrooper school—sittin' in the bleachers to watch a jump demo. But one guy's chute didn't open 'n' he packed it in right in front of 'em. 'Bout half the whole goddamn stadium got up 'n' ran across the field hollerin' 'I'm not jumpin'! I'm not jumpin'!'" He hit his knee with his big hand, laughing till tears filled the corners of his azure eyes. "Those goddamn pussies! But I guess it's good to get 'em sorted out ahead a time! Damnit, it was funny—but I guess you wudda have to have heard the way ole Humbert told it," he added when he noticed I wasn't laughing at all. "I just don't see how someone being killed can be regarded as funny," I said sternly. "Wimmen! They ain't got a goddamn *bit* a humor about 'em!" he snorted as he left me torn between my disgust, and my desire for our regular passionate afternoon embrace on the couch beside my desk.

"He's *obsessed*," an artist friend in Atlanta said after meeting him. Like me, she had never known anyone voluntarily in the Army. Zane's attitude included complete subscription to the need to stem the Red Tide, the necessity of nuclear superiority, and right-wing politics in general. He had little tolerance for anyone critical of the military, or even working- and middle-class values; it would be some time before I realized the connection between the military and those values, or the repressed desires for enclosure, belonging, security, that army life satisfied. At the moment, I was learning primarily that good soldiers prided themselves on their toughness. "He's *hard-core*," was my lover's favorite description of a man he respected, and being hard-core meant never falling out of a road march, giving in, or quitting. "Two pussies in my basic tried to get out by committin' suicide," he grumbled as I cringed, recalling the eighteen-year-old who had recently died at Fort Benning after being left lying in the sun all afternoon after a road march, where he was kicked and tormented by other soldiers. "If a man can't do it, let 'im say it; if he's too pussy, let 'im get out!" he went on.

There were reasons for these attitudes, he explained to me, at first patiently, then less patiently as I persistently—"just like a woman or a pussy"—exhibited horror, shock. He was trained to see the enemy as Other: "You just can't afford to think of 'em any other way—and *some*body has to do it," he would answer logically, as though defense of one's life through the loss of someone else's was as natural as the azaleas blooming in spring. "It's people like *us*," Zane often protested in the middle of such discussions, "who make it possible for people like *you*—you idealists, artists—to live out your beliefs! Maybe if everybody was Mother Teresa, we *could* all be like that. But they aren't. So we can't."

At first, I had thought I would swiftly convert my new sex object to my views—after all, as a writer, I was verbal, articulate, logical, wasn't I? But the Army apparently provided a total belief system of a kind I had never come up against. Every time we argued about communism, we had to redefine the word: to Zane, it meant a menacing fanaticism, eventual fascism; to me, the term implied all those glorious goals of counterculture days—an enlightened socialism and freedom from want and oppression for all. And since he was far better read than I in areas like world politics, world and military history, I soon found myself faltering in my liberal or "feminine" arguments. "But what of Kant's Categorical Imperative?" I asked, drawing a weapon out of my limited arsenal. "What's that?" "The rule that states that what's okay for you to do has to be okay for everyone else, too." "But not for Commies," he stated adamantly. At best, he would concede that "Maybe you *are* morally right. But it's just not practical. . . ."

In any case, I now knew much about many things I had never wanted to know about at all, such as how to subdue a man with the Belgian Rear Takedown, which he demonstrated to me one night as I fried chicken ("You come up behind 'im like this," he said as he put his strong forearm around my throat, "then stab 'im in the back right here, 'n' jam your knees behind 'im as he falls—'n' if breakin' his neck doesn't kill 'im, the knife will!"); and the difference in maneuver ("Outmaneuver 'em so they retreat") and attrition warfare ("Kill as many of them as possible before they kill many of us"). "But that's obscene," I cried as he told me of boys forced to yell "*Kill!*" with every step as they ran into the mess hall. Zane could, and would, talk for fifteen minutes—ignoring my yawns, the polite glaze of my gaze—of the weapons, methods, and military reputation of German mercenaries during the sixteenth century.

At least he was a man who loved his work, I thought, hiding the T-shirts that read "Find 'Em, Fight 'Em, Finish 'Em," or the Green Beret motto, "Live by Chance, Love by Choice, Kill by Preference," at the back of his underwear drawer. When he promptly dug them out again, I took another tack, based on my theory that all aggression was repressed creativity. I was certain that Richard Speck would never have murdered those nine nurses had he become a painter *before* the crime, rather than waiting till he was in prison for it. And wouldn't Zane just love to move to New York, drive a taxi, go to acting school, become another Marlon Brando? Or even move with me to Key West or the Gulf of Mexico, where we would contemplate the sunset each evening over many margaritas? "Nope!" "But if you could do anything in the world you wanted—money or education no object—what would you do?" I pressed. I also believed implicitly in Buckminster Fuller's dictum that what everyone should do was go back to what they were doing before someone told them they had to make a living, and hoped to find beneath Zane's militarism a disappointed and promising dream. "Go to South Africa and be a mercenary," he said promptly, not even looking up from his book on *Airborne Warfare, 1918–1945*. "But what did you dream of doing when you were a little boy?" I persisted. "Joining the French Foreign Legion or driving a truck," he yawned, this time including the job he had held before joining the Army.

Was my lover's planned conversion just another of my relentlessly stubborn, yet hopeless, projects? Worse than my failed dominance was the fact that our differences did little to diminish my sexual response to him. How could I be sleeping, much less living, with a man so tenacious in these gruesome beliefs, I asked myself the next morning, waking from yet another night's orgasms through the auspices of his hard body. I couldn't believe I was the same woman who had published antiwar poems in counterculture papers during the seventies, who had been a semi-hippie with a shag hair-cut, even if a housewife and mother. "A trained killer," I murmured angrily as Zane came over to kiss me good-bye. "But *she's* a trained killer, 'n' you love *her*," he teased, referring to my cat, Darlene, purring on the pillow he had just vacated. "'N' neither one of you have any respect at all for dogs!" he added, unconsciously tapping into my chauvinistic association of dogs as male, thus morally inferior; cats as female, thus automatically superior.

That night, he followed the Falklands invasion on television with delight, I, with revulsion. Later, as I lay in bed reading first *A Flag for Sunrise*, Robert Stone's novel of Central American resistance, then Carolyn Forché's poems about the El Salvadorean guerrillas, I realized that were Zane and I there, we would probably be on opposite sides. Our fantasies were equally adventurous, but I—long attracted to martyrdom—imagined going to a war zone as a poet or journalist, he as a mercenary or U.S. adviser. As beside me he flipped through a motorcycle magazine, a woman rider dressed solely in chains, a black garter belt and stockings, and black boots on its cover, I felt a nausea compounded by my unsuspected pregnancy and the three Black Russians I had sipped earlier.

SLEEPING WITH SOLDIERS, AND
OTHER SCENES FROM SOUTHERN
FAMILY LIFE.

One morning soon after, as I lay reading in bed, Darcy came into my room. "Mother!" she exclaimed, staring at the cream lace top of my nightgown. "Your breasts are so big!" Neither of us had ever been top-heavy, but looking down, I suddenly saw she was right and understood the reason for the morning queasiness I had attributed to a tedious writing project. I had been helping my recently divorced friend Lily write her life story. Each day, as her barefoot black maid brought trays of coffee upstairs for me, I had requested crackers, cookies, anything to soak up what I thought was the acid of my tension. Then, finished with the stress of a morning's joint creation, we would look at ourselves in the huge mirrors of her Jacuzzi-centered bathroom, applying makeup for yet another lunch out, examining our figures—despite my forty-five, her fifty-five, years—as hysterically as teenagers. My current, water-filled plumpness, we both agreed, must be caused by the small yellow estrogen tablets a doctor had given me for what he was sure were the symptoms of premature menopause. The change of life was not a development I had wanted to discuss with my new, fifteen-years-younger lover. But now, fantasizing each of Zane's sperm propelling itself as energetically as Zane "out to smoke 'em" on an early-morning road march, I realized I was pregnant for the first time since I had given birth to the adult woman standing before me.

The night of the day of the positive lab report, Zane, Darcy, and I went with friends for drinks to the Mezzanine bar where we had first met, then dancing at a disco. As we twirled through purple-and-white strobe lights, I felt myself transported on waves of biological elation. The flickering unreality around me, the beat of the Sisters Sledge singing "We Are Family" mixed with whiskey-induced fantasies of the red-gold boy dancing near us as my and Zane's son or, less pleasantly—when my lover went over to speak to a younger woman friend—of myself seven months hence, lumbering into the disco with my womanizing, well-built mate.

My more euphoric fantasies continued for the next days—of a new extension into the future, of a child who looked just like Zane, most of all, of a new person to love. In my dreams—dreams in which all my and my young lover's differences had long since dissolved—I could already feel the infant's warm head pulsing heavily, comfortingly against my milk-filled breasts, just as his father's head, filled with his own new fantasies, now lay there during sleep.

Then, a week after I had discovered my pregnancy, Laura called, upset: she had just learned that in order to do the research for her Ph.D., she—who as a teenager had owned and loved black-and-white rats as pets—would be required to clip the heads from live mice with scissors, and cut the heads from rats with a special guillotine. Without hesitation, I advised her to harden her heart, her sensitivities, in order to achieve her ends.

And one morning soon after, I awoke with the knowledge that Zane and I barely knew one another—that our relationship had started only three months before as a sexual lark. That I now had, at least for a while, responsibility for Darcy, a child long since born. That I was forty-five years old, had little money, owned no property, wasn't sure I wanted to marry again. That I was—despite Zane's and my shared rent and expenses—basically dependent on myself for economic and emotional survival. That however much I might long for his wobbly neck bent trustingly against my breasts, I would—to ensure my own survival—abort this child before he was born.

With this knowledge, a new fury comes into my and Zane's battles.

I long to be held against his hard chest, comforted, but have just realized with horror that my quest for the exotic, the erotic, has a solid, malevolent underside—that Jack might have left me pregnant, alone; Sean could have led me into a permanent drug dream; that the man with whom I now live is trained to kill. Yet worse is my new awareness that, compared to mine, their potential for murderousness is minuscule—that my reaction against the military, against violence, is not merely ideological, a power struggle between my lover and me, but a rage against my own capacity for destruction.

Every day, despite Zane's efforts to soothe, pamper me, I incite fresh battles. "Well, if they *don't* keep up, somebody'll beat their ass," Zane says, stepping out of the shower where I have followed him. Tonight, the subject is road marches, the authority of officers. As he speaks, I reluctantly admire the heavy muscles, the apricot-colored body hair, the rosy flush of his flesh, the now soft yet still thick stalk of pink penis as he towels himself—a pink-and-gold tomcat, a creature made to be duplicated, I flash, but this time forcibly reject the thought.

"Oh, do they *beat* people to make them do things?"

"No, *they* don't beat 'em—the other guys do. It's peer pressure."

"Well, who created the peer pressure, makes them feel like they have to do it?" I suddenly recall Zane once yelling at me in anger, "Why don't you ever do what you're told to do?!"

"The patrol leaders, of course—they're in charge of the whole patrol. It looks bad for them, they get a bad march."

"Why do the others care, if it doesn't affect *them*—why can't the ones who don't like it just quit?"

"What if every time somebody said, 'Oh, Sarge, I can't go a *step* farther'"—Zane mimicked a falsetto voice—"we let 'em? What if we were on a road march in a battle area, tryin' to outrun the enemy? Would you want *your* son to just lie there 'n' die 'cause he was too pussy to march? Well, they have to learn it somewhere."

Violence is nauseous, I think, looking again at his naked body.

The next morning, the subject is ostensibly military haircuts:

"I *have* to keep it this way 'cause the Army says so."

"Why does the *Army*"—heavy sarcasm—"say so?"

"Because it's *tradition*—always has been." He looks at me with irritation.

"I couldn't stand someone telling me—some *authority*—how to cut *my* hair," I say furiously, "especially if the way they wanted it cut was within an inch of my scalp! Don't you feel castrated?"

"But if *I* don't follow authority, who'll follow mine? They called me maggot—now that I'm sergeant, I get to call *them* maggot."

"Well, I wouldn't want to call anybody maggot in the *first* place," I cry, revolted. "And there *are* other forms of authority, you know —the authority of achievement, knowledge. If I had someone in my writing class who didn't want to *write*, I sure wouldn't call them *maggot*—though I might ask them to leave."

"But you *can't* ask people to leave the Army. Besides, it's a leveling process—you take the rich, the poor, the middle class, the stupid, the intelligent—shave their heads in basic trainin', put 'em in the same clothes—they all look the same, everybody *is* the same—"

"*That's* the very idea that makes me shudder *most*!" I screech, my rebellious nature activated at the very notion. "And why do they shave their heads—make those poor boys feel so funny-looking when they go into town?!"

"Well, they only shave it *once*," Zane laughs. "The second time they say you *can* have it a little longer, don't *have* to have it shaved—but it'll go *easier* for you if you do."

"In other words, they *do* have to!" I say triumphantly.

One night, we debate long and horribly the proper responses of the pilots who had been assigned to bomb Hiroshima and Nagasaki. "Could *you* have done it?" I asked, wanting him to say no, yet suspecting what his answer will be. "If I was *ordered* to," he says predictably—and I yell that the only *sane* reaction, if one had done that, would be to go *crazy*, as I had read one of the pilots had done. He shouts back that men *have* to be tough to win wars, and what's better—going crazy or learning to live with it? That *more* American lives would have been lost in the long run—that it was bleeding-heart liberals like me, pussies who don't understand a goddamn thing about the history of the world, who'd caused us to give up in Nam.

"I get the feeling our relationship hinges on this conversation," he suddenly says quietly.

I'm thinking about the unwanted puppies he had told me his father had clubbed to death when he was a child. Doesn't he understand that those puppies, the North Vietnamese, this embryo, are all the same life? "I don't know whether I can live with a man who feels the way you do."

"Well, that can be arranged!"

"I just don't want to think about war and napalm and death!" I scream violently. "I want to think about art and beauty and truth and kindness," I stutter, bursting into tears.

And I want you to choose. Want you to change my own self-hate, guilt, the part of me that wants this abortion.

I want you, someone, anyone, to deliver me from it.

Despite our daytime dissension, Zane and I turned to each other when the lights were out with a desperate passion, as though the balm of flesh, the momentary oblivion of orgasm, could ease the pain of our choice.

Because of his early Insensitivity Training, Zane was even less articulate than I in expressing his distress. But he had his own means for punishing me for my part in our coming loss. The week before the abortion, he came in late from the Mezzanine, waking me to confess that while there he had been attracted to another woman—he named a plump girl I had seen drinking at the bar each time I had gone there with him—indeed, had wanted to go home with her, but because of me, had not. "Why are you telling me this?" I screamed instead of being pleased at his faithfulness, and saw from the sudden venom in his eyes that he was chalking up my puzzling response to that vast reservoir labeled *Female Bitchiness*.

Two afternoons before the operation—the next day, I was to go to the doctor's office, have the laminaria stick inserted into my cervix—I lay depressed in the four-poster bed as he came in from the base.

"Hey," he said cheerily, plopping down on the pillow beside me as though to cheer me up. "I heard a great joke today—it's about this Ranger who dismembers this frog, see—chops off his legs so he can't hop—"

"Zane! Stop!" I implore in disbelief. "Don't you know how that *sounds* to me?!"

"Wimmen! You can't say a damn thing to 'em!" he says grouchily from the kitchen, where I hear him popping the top of a Pabst.

"Why do you *always* go to these doctors who only treat the indigent?" Anne, twenty years a nurse, complained when I told her that I had chosen an Indian doctor who, because of Savannah's racism, served mostly blacks on Medicaid. I didn't explain that sitting in his shabby waiting room among other poor women somehow felt more comforting, more appropriate to what I was about to do, than being cosseted in the plush, Musak-fed office of some rich GYN. Yet because I wanted to be unconscious to commit murder, I had decided, at three times the cost, on a D and C under general anesthesia at a local day surgery.

On the day I went to the hospital for the preoperative blood tests and X rays, I asked for a metal apron to shield my abdomen in case I changed my mind at the last minute. As Zane and I sat in the surgery waiting room, I sat stunned, as though awaiting the guillotine. But when he began a story about a doctor who had dropped cigarette ashes on his former wife's pubis as she had lain spread-eagled on his examining table, I yanked my hand out of his angrily. When the nurse called my name, I was already distracted by another of our fights.

"It's all over!" I said euphorically to Darcy that night. I'm in love with my lover again, propped up in bed with a new novel, sipping the glass of Chablis Darcy has brought me, eating bad Chinese takeout Zane has brought in. Later, beside me, he tells me the stories of Ulysses, Beowulf, El Cid, again, then others of great military battles, and now they sound once more like harmless romances.

The next morning, he tells me that after I had gone to sleep, he had written a poem. "About the abortion?" I ask, touched. "Nope, about parachutin'—my first time jumpin'," he says. Will I forget that easily, I wonder with irritation. I don't realize yet that what a woman friend has told me—that I will suffer fresh grief each year at the time our child would have been born, will feel an involuntary wrench each time I see one who would have been his age, or who looks like Zane—will hold true far beyond the completion of this book and, perhaps, for the rest of my life.

In fact, I can't even predict how bad the next *week* will be. The following night, still relieved, my breasts already magically deflated, I put on my lavender cowboy boots, pink corduroy jeans, a pink cowboy hat, and insist that the three of us go out dancing. But as we sit in the Mezzanine bar, I have the eerie feeling—the *hope*—that I am still pregnant, that I still have time to marry the wealthy seventyish man, seated to my right, who always shows an interest in me whenever I see him, in order to bear the child of my young lover, played, of course, by Zane, Marlon Brando-ish in his black T-shirt to my left—a plot worthy of Tennessee Williams, I tease myself, trying to force away a fantasy that, for a few whiskey-distorted moments, had seemed genuinely possible.

On the third night, Darcy and I sit down at the kitchen table with a pint of Jose Cuervo, limes, and salt. Within an hour, I am in my daughter's arms, sobbing out my grief. But when I awake at two a.m., Zane is still not home, and I know instantly where he is. "Moth-ah!" Darcy cries, coming into my room when she hears me drunkenly pulling on my clothes, clattering into my boots. "Where are you *going*?" "To the Mezzanine to kill Zane!" I say, clutching my car keys and running down the stairs before she can stop me.

As I drive the dark streets to the bar, my fury at him fills my chest, making me feel as though I can hardly breathe. When I run up the steps into the dim, almost deserted barroom, I see that, yes, there he is, sitting beside the woman with whom he had wanted to sleep. "If I had a butcher knife, I would kill you!" I screech, coming up behind him. It's the first violent scene I have ever started in public, but I don't care. As we scream at one another to an audience of mildly curious Mezzanine habitués, we quickly get down to the real source of our destructiveness—our respective anger with the other's sex. It is as though all the pain that is my long-repressed love and rage for Daddy—the thrall I have been held in for a lifetime—is erupting for the first time.

As, during the next year, it will again and again and again.

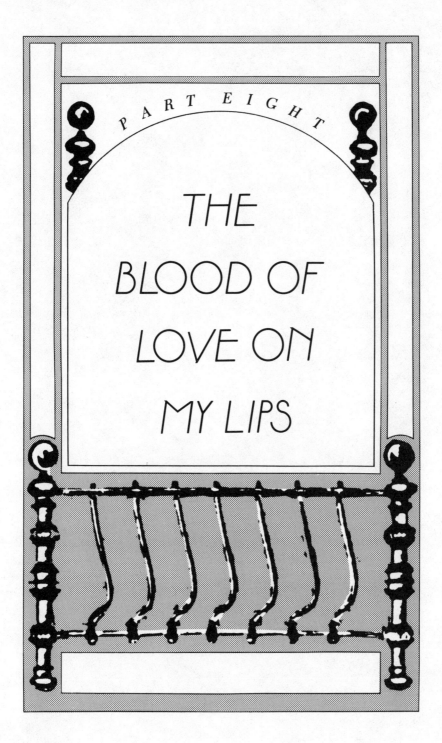

PART EIGHT

THE
BLOOD OF
LOVE ON
MY LIPS

SLEEPING WITH SOLDIERS, OR WHAT BECOMES OF OUR HERO AND HEROINE.

"All my life, I've wanted 'n' needed wimmen.

"When I was three 'n' four, Mama let me sleep with her, rub 'er nipples till they got hard. I could tell she liked it, but she never said anything. I nursed my mama till I was about two, so maybe she jes' thought it was a way to get me to sleep. But ever since, I've always liked to rub wimmen's titties that way.

"Then, when I crawled around on the floor, I would try to look up my aunts' 'n' mama's friends' dresses to see if I could see their pussies. Wimmen still wore stockin's 'n' garter belts then—as far as I'm concerned, panty hose are a Commie plot!

"Then in school, there was this girl who sat near me. She'd get up in 'er desk, lean over, showin' her ass. I thought I'd go crazy. I think I was about eight. I always liked girls even when you weren't s'posed to. 'N' of course, in high school it was worse—the girls in my classes still wore stockin's 'n' garter belts. 'N' then, there were the teachers. Just like when Rosemary's daughter, Darcy, was here, 'n' they were both sittin' on the couch with their legs up, talkin' 'n' not payin' any attention to me at all. Then I felt like I'd go crazy, too. 'N' I've always liked my porn hard-core. Books like *Nurse's Sex Treatments*, 'n' things like that.

"But I have one aunt, Mama's sister—she was always a little diff'rent, readin' books, keepin' up with things—who I always felt really understood me. Once, right after her husband's funeral—he had died of cancer, 'n' then her daughter did, too—she laid 'er hand on my arm 'n' said, 'Zane, you're too hard on yourself.' She was in her fifties, I think I was about nineteen, but a thrill went through me, a sexy thrill.

"The wimmen in my family—my aunts, grandmothers—didn't talk much. Then, Mama was deaf. When I was three 'n' four, 'n' Daddy was on the night shift, she let me sleep with her 'n' we would talk in bed. I could tell what she was sayin' from the vibrations in her chest; she could read my lips by puttin' 'er fingers over

·

my mouth. When my two brothers were born, she put their cribs near her bed so she could feel the vibrations when they cried.

"So that always made our family diff'rent. But not in a bad way. It jes' made us work harder to talk to each other. 'N' then, we had home sign—not the regular sign language, but what people make up at home for themselves. 'N' sometimes it was funny—like when the whole family would go to Burger King, 'n' Mama would always order a 'Whooper'—she jes' couldn't say 'Whopper.' 'N' once Mama was out on the porch callin' me, 'n' what voice she has is strange. A boy visitin' our neighborhood asked, 'Who is that?' 'n' a buddy a mine said, 'Oh, that's Zane's mama, she's from Czechoslovakia'—so I was the only guy around with a mother from Czechoslovakia!

"Our family was always very physical. Daddy would let me sit on his lap—he had a huge chest, arms, even bigger than now—'n' he would read me stories. Once he read me a whole story out of *Argosy* magazine, jes' because I wanted to know what it said, 'n' I couldn't read yet. 'N' the smell of cigarettes—I always associated that with Daddy. Even now, if I go into his 'n' Mama's room, smell that smell, I feel safe.

"Daddy 'n' Mama were both from the mountains up in North Car'lina, they both had been poor, dirt poor—outdoor bathrooms, no runnin' water. But then Daddy got this job—the one he's had for the last twenty years—as an air traffic controller, 'n' he 'n' Mama have been able to have most ev'rything they want—color televisions, a microwave, all kinds of furniture. I never wanted for anything, or my brothers—that's one thing Rosemary says she doesn't understand—what I'm afraid of, when I never went without. But I know where my folks came from, 'n' it hasn't been that long. So I understand when Daddy didn't want to strike. Mama's brother—he was an air traffic controller, too—did, 'n' now his wife left 'im, 'n' he's drivin' a truck again.

"Ev'rybody in our family has always had a bad temper. When I failed readin' in first grade, Daddy called me dummy, 'n' made me start over in my readin' book, back to the very first word, even if it took till three in the mornin', when I made one little mistake. I've felt like a dummy ever since—'n' didn't like readin' for a long time. But the only real mistake my father ever made was not lettin' me start skydivin' when I was sixteen, instead a waitin' till later. I cudda had three thousand jumps by now!

"Oh, he ust to beat our ass. 'N' do things like kill the extra puppies when our dog had babies. But later, after he had cancer, he said he didn't see how he had ever done that 'n' that he didn't see how anybody could kill a deer. Oh, he had lots of guns jes' like all his buddies—onc't he even came in drunk 'n' said he was goin' to kill Mama with one—but it seemed like he jes' went huntin' to get out in the woods. He never wudda made me kill a deer, slit its belly, then smear the blood all over my face 'n' chest like somma my friends' fathers did. But then, as I always say, he only beat us when we needed it. 'N' his daddy had beat him a lot worse.

"Well, when I got back to likin' readin' again, I liked to read stories about heroes like El Cid 'n' Beowulf, to hear about King David 'n' how he killed the enemy, Goliath, with that sling shot, 'n' to dream of goin' into the French Foreign Legion. Just before I went into the Army, I wrote off for an application blank. I've still got it. So goin' into the Army, bein' a hero, was one thang I wanted to do.

"The other thing was drive a truck. When I was three or four, I ust to see trucks with 'RABBIT' on the side of 'em, 'n' a picture a one. I thought that's what I want to do someday, drive the big trucks—prob'ly 'cause I liked rabbits! I didn't know then about runnin' three days on three hours' sleep, what it was like to unload nine hundred and sixty-five cartons of Clorox all by myself in Mississippi in July when you're already so tired you're about to pass out. I didn't know it till I was a driver myself, 'n' started lookin' around me at how young men turned old from truckin'. Right now, I've already got those deep lines in my face—that's why people don't know sometimes that Rosemary's fifteen years older 'n me.

"Of course, by the time I found all that out, I had a wife. I was twenty-one when I got married 'n' didn't have much choice. I had to keep food in the house, the rent paid, no matter how hard it was. I was a man, wasn't I? 'N' drivin' a truck was the only thing I knew how to do.

"We had had a big weddin', all our folks there. I thought she was so pretty, was in love with 'er body. The first time we had gone to bed, I had gone over to this apartment she was sharin' with another girl I was datin'. But the other girl wasn't home, 'n' she was there baby-sittin' with the girl's baby, 'n' had on these little baby-doll pajamas. When she bent over in those pajamas to pick up a toy, I knew we were gonna fuck.

"But after we'd been married jes' a few months, I realized somethin' was wrong. I didn't know she was what one of the doctors I fin'lly took 'er to called a 'borderline personality.' All I knew was the drugs 'n' her cuttin' 'er wrists. It got where takin' 'er to the emergency room was as regular as takin' out the garbage. Then I had to worry about 'er runnin' 'round with other men while I was on the road 'n' spendin' all the money I left 'er for groc'ries for dope. 'N' I only hit 'er onc't durin' that time. Then there were her medical bills. She had a hysterectomy, things like that. Then she would cry all the time 'cause she couldn't have a baby. So I bought 'er a horse. She liked it for a while.

"I finally lucked out when she met a man she wanted to live with in the last mental hospital I committed 'er to. The guy before that had cried when he had to take 'er to the emergency room for the first time after she O.D.'d on 'im. I told 'im, 'Don't worry, it won't bother you after a while.' Well, after we got divorced, I owed more than three thousand dollars on her back medical bills, 'n' fifty-five thousand dollars to the mental hospital—the Army paid that one, but I never would be able to pay the others. So one day I got drunk 'n' just threw the whole file a bills in the garbage can. So now I don't have any credit 'n' prob'ly won't be able to get any for a few years. As the woman I lived with before Rosemary ust to say, 'With my luck, if I had a duck it would drown!'

"By then, I was in the Army because I needed a more stable job so I wasn't out on the road all the time, wonderin' what she was doin' at home. 'N' I jes' wanted to do somethin' *I* wanted to do for a change. I was twenty-seven when I went through basic. 'N' I *was* in Airborne 'n' got to jump. But the first time I was in Ranger school, I had to leave. They called me outta the field 'cause she had been put in jail for writin' a bad check up in Charleston where we were still livin', 'n' I had to go up, move ev'rything 'n' put it in storage, bring 'er back to Savannah with me, 'n' buy ev'rything new. I moved 'er into a furnished apartment, then we went to K-Mart, where we bought a TV set—that was one thing she *had* to have, so she could watch the soap operas. But the new place was right above the Office, so she was back to doin' her ole stuff in jus' a few weeks. 'N' when I tried to get back into Ranger school, they said no, that I might be too anxious with all those problems with my wife to be jumpin' 'n' all—that, 'n' I didn't pass the swimmin' test, swimmin' across a river with a full pack on. I've never been afraid of any physical thing but water. But I could have practiced, done it. So she cost me Ranger school, too.

"One of the things I've always resented is the way men need wimmin—need the pussy, have to have it, 'n' how they have to limit themselves, not do what they want to do to get it. Why do men go to war? I've often thought it was because women are watchin'—you want to impress 'em. It all boils down to a sexual thing—you've got to have that poontang! For that, a man will tie himself down far beyond what he wants to. 'N' that's one of the things I hate most—that emotional 'n' sexual need of 'em—it makes you more dependent on 'em than you would like to be. I feel like wimmen have shit on me all my life, 'n' I guess that's why I do some things. Like goin' to a bar without callin' home. It's the same way I did with Mama when I was little—I went as far away from the house as I could, 'n' stayed as long as I could get away with it. Even back then, I had to feel like a man.

"In high school—things were innocent back in those days, we didn't have any drugs at my school—my main concern was jes' gettin' laid. I thought I was ugly, a dummy, even though I made my grades, 'n' was the football star all four years—the bes' line-backer that school ever had! Later, I found out the girls thought I was stuck-up. But I didn't know that then. Anyway, there was this chick who looked like she was jes' made to be fucked, if you know what I mean. I wanted to fuck that chick so bad that if somebody had told me, 'Lay your li'l finger out on this table 'n' let me chop it off with this meat cleaver 'n' you can fuck 'er,' I wudda stuck it right out there! Well, one day her 'n' her brother were standin' behind me in the lunchroom line 'n' he said, 'What duh yuh think'll happen with the game Friday night?' 'N' she said, real bored-like, 'Oh, you play football?' 'N' there I was, the captain of the team! A helluva lot of good *that* did me! It was as though all those years playin' hadn't meant anything!

"Then I started goin' with June. Her Daddy was a Navy doctor, she wore those li'l Lady Bug shirts 'n' skirts, had that long straight hair parted down the middle—I still have a thing for that preppy stuff. We'd fuck in the car—she'd have to be drunk so it wouldn't hurt so much. She'd put her feet on the roof 'n' keep her socks on so 'er feet wouldn't get cold. 'N' onc't, after, we tried to do sixty nine, I went to take a piss 'n' felt somethin sticky on my balls—it turned out she'd been chewin bubble gum. But I guess I thought we'd get married someday. That's all I ever wanted—to get married 'n' have a regular life like my father had.

"In the meantime, we'd go out to Art's Seaside, get drunk. Or to a beach house on Myrtle Beach during the school holidays. We'd go there with other kids, 'n' sometimes I'd go by myself with these two guys I knew, Eddie 'n' Charlie. They were big football players, but they were already outta school. We'd get drunk, talk about, oh, who was the best football player, who had the best car, who had the best-lookin' girl friend, who had the best-lookin' mama—stuff like that. I'll never forget ole Eddie, sittin' out on the porch wearin' 'is football helmet with the deer antlers off the livin' room wall stuck through it, eatin' Cheese Bugles 'n' Tums, 'n' drinkin' Pabst. 'N' onc't Charlie got so drunk—it was one a the times the girls were there—that he opened a kitchen drawer, dropped 'is pants, 'n' shit in it like it was the toilet 'n' is girlfriend had to clean it up.

"Maybe it was thinkin' I'd marry June was one of the things that influenced me to go to this little college on a football scholarship instead a doin' what I really wanted to do, which was joinin' the Army and goin' to Vietnam. But I was afraid of makin' a four-year mistake. 'N' ev'ry time I get afraid of makin' a mistake I usually make one! Well, after about a year, I was sick of school, of playin' football, 'n' dropped out. All durin' high school, I had had jobs— the summer before, as a dump-truck driver—'n' I got that job back again.

"Then one day I went to meet June at the Medical College of Charleston, where she was takin' a technician's course. We had been talkin' about gettin' married. But she was out by the pool talkin' to this medical student, 'n' when she saw how dirty I was from drivin' the dump truck—I hadn't had time to change yet— she said, 'Don't you ever come here like that again!' 'N' then she told me she thought we should just break up, that she wanted to marry a man who would make good money. I guess with her daddy bein' a doctor 'n' all, I had set my sights too high.

"But one thing good about my daddy was that he always understood about things like that—he didn't think it was silly to cry over a girl.

"After that, I skydived 'n' drove a truck—had an apartment with a guy, we had furniture 'n' ev'rything. I didn't go into the Army, 'cause I had car and furniture payments by then. Once, I tried to get a job as a dispatcher, but they thought I was too young. A couple of times, I lost jobs—when I saw the movie *The Exorcist*, I got anxious, couldn't sleep, 'n' kept goin' in late. Another time, I saved up some money, 'n' took a couple of months off, jes' stayin' home watchin' soap operas with Mama. Findin' girls to go out with wasn't that easy, especially when I was drivin' a truck.

"There was a girl out in North Dakota who I met drivin'. She was kinda fat, but I thought she was real cute. She was divorced from a submarine sailor, said she didn't like it that he was away all the time. I thought we were in love, that we had a real thing goin'. Then one night I called 'er 'n' she had a guy there. She was gigglin' 'n' laughin' 'n' didn't wanna see me. I felt like a fool. 'Specially when she married 'im 'n' he was another submarine sailor! That hurt even more than June.

"Then I met my wife 'n' married 'er 'n' quit skydivin' 'n' tried to be what a man should be. I had this idea that I should do all the things Daddy did—have a certain kind a wife, a house in the suburbs, 'n' kids. Even now, I have fantasies sometimes of havin' a house trailer out 'n' the country, with maybe a blue tick hound or a beagle, or a house with a tin roof with a porch all around it—I've seen some pretty ones up in Pennsylvania. I always drive the back roads when I can.

"But maybe it was all just a desire for security. I remember readin' in the newspaper durin' my teens about an ole man. He was starvin' 'n' didn't have anything to eat but the cardboard off a cereal box. He was so hungry he was eatin' that before he died. 'N' that stuck in my mind, 'n' I've always been afraid of endin' up like that ole man.

"Because I feel like I tried to fit into the middle class 'n' failed, tried to do all the conventional thangs 'n' couldn't do 'em. I always felt like other men knew somethin' I didn't know, even my father— that maybe I never can be the man my father is. There's an ole sayin' 'round where I'm from, 'A man's not a man till his father tells 'im he is.'

"What Rosemary didn't understand when I said I didn't like to go to country-western bars was that I felt like I had tried to be like those good country people, 'n' had failed. That at those cocktail parties she takes me to, I don't feel good enough. 'N' yuh know, I could tell Daddy felt the same way around some men, men who had better jobs, or more education and money, than he did, even if he *was* an air traffic controller 'n' ev'rybody in the neighborhood called 'im 'mister' because they respected 'im so much.

"But on the other hand, maybe I didn't even want that life. Maybe that's why I picked that crazy wife, so I wouldn't have to have it. Sometimes when I'm drivin', I fantasize bein' an actor, or comedian. Movies 'n' plays are my favorite thing besides world 'n' military history. When me 'n' Rosemary went to New York, we saw four plays in one week 'n' I picked 'em all out. So when I ride along, I make up plays or a comedy routine in my head. Or sometimes poems. For a while, I wrote 'em down—prob'ly because Rosemary liked 'em, but then I stopped. I was always drunk when I wrote 'em. Rosemary said maybe we should go to New York, I could drive a cab, go to actin' school part-time. But I said no— nobody like me becomes an actor 'r writer 'r any of those thangs.

"When I got in the Army, I loved it. I felt like I was just where I wanted to be. Even with the road marches, it was easier than drivin' a truck 'n' a helluva lot better than baggin' groceries 'r workin' at the paper mill! 'N' I had a sense of commitment, like I was doin' somethin'. 'Cause of what I made on my enlistment tests, they wanted me to go into intelligence. But I didn't want to. I wanted to go into the infantry, be in the *real* Army. In the Army, ev'rybody's the same—regardless of where they came from, or what race they are, or what kind of job they had before. I felt like I had a place, that I belonged. Like I was doin' somethin', somethin' I believed in, was good at. It makes me sick when people are prejudiced against the Army. Some people jes' don't understand the meanin' of the word *patriotism*. Some people don't know what it means to be willin' to die for a cause.

"Besides, I felt guilty because I didn't get to Vietnam. Like I shoulda gone right after high school insteada worryin' about marryin' June 'n' bein' the first person in my fam'ly to graduate college.

"But now I'm out, drivin' a truck again. I'm thirty-two, 'n' beginnin' to wonder if I'll ever do any of those great things that I really wanted to do. Last week, when some guys from my base got sent to Grenada, some people from my old unit to Lebanon, I felt really down, wonderin' what I'm doin', what I'm doin' here. Jes' like Vietnam again. 'N' all because of a woman again.

"So I've got to have sleaze. I tend to drink to forget, to get a buzz on'. Like the song says, 'I'd rather have a bottle in front of me than have a frontal lobotomy.' When Rosemary 'n' me met, I'd been on leave for a month 'n' had been drunk all thirty days. I guess that's why she thought I was such a wild 'n' *craz*-ee guy!

"When she walked into the Mezzanine that night with my gay drinkin' buddy, Robert John, I thought *she* was a schoolteacher—about twenty-five—with that long hair, that sorta elegant way a dressin'. I wouldn't've believed a woman like that would look at me. But she smiled at me 'n' I was thankin', I wanna *get* me somma that. Then Robert John called me over to their table to introduce us, 'n' the next thing I know, we're sittin' there talkin'. We talked about skydivin', my divorce, psychotherapy, a lotta things—'n' she's puttin' my hand on 'er thigh inside the slit of that slinky skirt she's wearin'. But even when I asked 'er to go by my place with me so I could change, take 'er somewhere nice, I didn't realize it would be so easy. When we got there, she just lay back on my roommate's water bed, 'n' I started kissin' 'er 'n' takin' off my clothes as fast as I could.

"'N' there're jes' two things today that it'd take to make me happy. To be married to Rosemary 'n' be a good man—take care of my responsibilities 'n' my woman, to work hard, don't lie or cheat. 'N' to be a soldier again."

. . .

"Let Joanne Woodward be a macho man!" Zane exclaimed, exasperated at my designation of him.

Indeed, instead of a bad guy, I had inadvertently picked a good one; instead of a mere sex object, a complex human being.

I had read about a painter who had painted the same scene, viewed through her window, over and over until it gradually took on new, revealing nuances. That was what I now wanted to do with one man—to concentrate so intently that surface fell away, helping me break through into new feeling, understanding.

That Zane was so beautifully transparent made my mission easier. When my children had been toddlers, I had wondered what it would be like to meet an adult with the same degree of spontaneity, and now I had. "Theatrical," Darcy called him—that's why we both thought he should follow his interest in acting. ("But you'll need to put moisturizer on your face," she would tell him critically

as she stood in the bathroom door, watching him shave.) He expressed his feelings more freely than any man I had known, and
when I met his family, I saw that this openness came partly from
his mother's deafness. Like sunlight on water, childlike delight or
dismay fluttered across her sweet, round face, such emotion emphasized by exaggerated gestures. And Zane's countenance, too,
could move momentarily from a carefree smile to a quivering lower
lip to red-faced rage.

I had chosen Zane for emotional and sexual, rather than prag-
matic or intellectual, reasons, and those were the two ways we were
alike. We were both stubborn, tempestuous, ruled by our sexuality
and our emotions (and, it would turn out, our rage). We each had a
mania for dominance and control. And like British punk rockers,
we both needed sleaze.

THE CAT THEORY OF LOVE.

Based on my desire to continue seeing men as pleasurable, nonde-
manding companions, I had developed the cat theory of love. That
is, I have had many cats, but have always preferred an affectionate
alley cat to a neurasthenic Siamese or Burmese, and have never
expected one to make a certain amount of money, come from a
certain social class, or stimulate me intellectually. On television, I
had seen a news segment in which, as part of a new way of treating
the old and bedridden, people were given pets as a part of their
therapy. "He's made me the happiest woman alive!" exclaimed an
old, white-haired woman with a kitten on her lap. I, too, had had
cats simply to pet and enjoy them—and that was the way I wanted
to enjoy Zane.

"Zane is like a flower, and having him is like having a bunch of
flowers every day," I wrote in my journal during the first months of
our relationship. For flowers had become the motif for our love. He
gave me flowers, and I bought them, too. We had an apartment full
of carnations and roses, tall red gladiolas at Christmas, pots of red
tulips on Valentine's day. To add to this aura of romance, I wore all
the things he especially liked—slit skirts, strappy garter belts,
satin mules, and the long lacy nightgowns, the satin wrappers I
already preferred. "You were made for love," I whispered to him in
bed. But I didn't pay enough attention when he immediately an-

swered, "No, I'm not—I'm made to work till I drop dead!" Or when he didn't like me to call him "my pet."

What I hadn't reckoned on was the Top Sergeant in his head, the strength of his drive—typical of every macho man once on what he considers his own turf—to motherize the woman he has eroticized and to dominate the environment that surrounds him. "When my children were two-year-olds, their heads seemed a lot bigger than they really were," Anne said, referring to the way they had cannibalized her consciousness, her life. That was the way I felt about my lover as well. Totally ignoring the years I had lived alone, Zane now warned me against walking in the lanes (alleys between the major streets in Savannah) or wearing my French-maid costume at Halloween. "I want you to be sweet and quiet, so other men won't look at you," he said. In fact, the way I had gotten him to begin calling to let me know his plans was by stating that if he didn't, I would simply make plans of my own, maybe even go out to a bar alone. "But I don't want *you* to do that!" he said. When we did go out to his favorite hangouts together, he sometimes seemed slightly uncomfortable: "I wouldn't like it if some guy talked rough around you," he said protectively, assigning me a delicacy that no longer existed, if it ever had. But when he was angry, his futile demands for dominance were less tactful: "Why don't you *ever* just do what I tell you to do?" he would cry in frustration. Nor was excessive assertiveness well received. "If you would just keep your mouth shut!" he would say. Or if I made plans for the two of us about which he wasn't enthusiastic—perhaps an afternoon at an art opening or a movie that didn't involve the military, science fiction, or medieval adventure—he wouldn't actively object, but would put up obstacles at the last moment—like his drunkenness and/or the immovability of his body from the couch. On the other hand, he rarely made plans for us himself. "I wonder what we would do this weekend if I didn't make any plans," I mused to a woman friend. "You know damn well what you'd do!" she snorted. "Stay inside, cook, 'n' watch him watch football!" Though I knew that one of the reasons Zane adored for me to wear sheer stockings, lacy garter belts, was that as a small child he had crawled around the floor, looking up the dresses of his aunts and mother, I also knew it was because he liked me *in harness.*

What he didn't realize yet—poor deluded thing!—was that if a Good Woman is chaste, cloistered, submissive, dependent, I was an obvious failure. And while I might enjoy sleeping with a man, my children had all grown up, and I had no intention of being a mother again except when he put his mouth on my breast in bed.

To Zane, there was little logic in my aversion to his cigarette smoke wreathing my face, rock music or television blaring at all hours, or an alarm that regularly shrilled me awake at five a.m. Yet that sound mediated against the night life that had been our first mutual interest besides sex and against my previous life-style as well. Alone, I had followed my natural inclinations—sleeping late, reading and writing in my journal over coffee in bed, then working from eleven or twelve till early evening, after which I did as I pleased. But now the cocktail hour had become the time of day when I worried about what I would cook for dinner that night, and, if he stopped off at a bar without calling or inviting me, fumed like any traditional housewife.

With a force more inexorable than my own considerable will, my early imprints, long dead, I had thought, now leaped alive. I felt compelled to mother my lover, to cook special meals for him, and to empty his ashtrays, whether I smoked or not—the only apparent alternative to becoming that worst of all female creatures, a nag. The cooking skills I had been pulling out only for special occasions, the concerns with bathroom fixtures, scouring powders, I had imagined banished forever, emerged as though they had only been briefly in hiding. "But you're so *good* at it!" he enthused of my cooking, shopping, cleaning, reminding me of Lisa's story of the one meal—macaroni-and-cheese from a box—her husband had cooked for her during five years of marriage. Despite myself, I began rushing to the cleaner's with his uniforms and the extra towels, or, at the supermarket, wondering whether he was eating enough green things and picking up a few extra cakes of his favorite deodorant soap. In short, a wife again.

Yet if I was satisfying, at least for a while, his need for a caring mother, Zane was filling mine for a tender, attentive father. When I visited his parents, I thrilled to the sexily exaggerated movements of his sensuous mouth as he talked to his angel-faced mother, the gentle way he kissed the top of her white hair as she sat at the formica kitchen table. Since we weren't married, I was to sleep in the guest room. Yet as I lay beneath the covers alone, the rumble of male voices—Zane's, his father's, his two brothers'—speaking only, aside from an occasional feminine squeak from his mother, of male things, gave me a strange feeling of safety. As I drifted off to sleep to the satisfying bass tones, I thought of Carrie Ten Boom, survivor of World War Two, whose father had gone into her room each night when she had been a child, momentarily placing his large hand over her face, then dreamed of Zane, coming into the room, leaning over the bed, kissing me. When he did so at that very moment, I felt dream and reality merge—and a rush of the warmth, the security, I had always wanted, but had never had, with Daddy. It was only later that I would think of the low ceilings of that room—of the low ceilings Zane had placed on his life.

At that time, I still viewed him as the super-romantic lover, the perfect sex object, the caricature of what I wanted him to be. At first, I gloried in his physical strength, disassociating it from his politics, his occasional insensitivity. To me, he was my sweetheart, my red-haired pet, my harmless attack cat. When we went by Darcy's old apartment in New York to get her things, he carried over his shoulder a duffel bag full of her belongings so heavy that I couldn't lift it from the floor. When a friend was mugged on the sidewalk in front of our Savannah apartment, he ran straight downstairs to his defense, barely hesitating, despite my and Darcy's hysteria, at the sounds of gunshots.

Yet when he threw an obnoxious guest down the apartment stairs, tossing his backpack behind him, I was shocked. "Zane!" I cried as he chuckled, pleased with himself. "You could have broken his neck, gone to prison!" While I visited Anne in Atlanta, he called. "I just didn't want you to hear about this from anybody else," he said sheepishly, "but I got into a fight in a bar last night—it was pretty bad." He had seen a man hit a woman, had gone to her defense, and in the process, had beaten the man so relentlessly that the police had been called. "He was really bloody when he came home," Darcy reported.

But the worst was yet to come. When he went with me to cocktail parties populated by artists and other, often well-off, liberals, I assumed he was having as much fun as I was, till the night he grabbed me around the neck as we went out to the Fiat, banged me up against the side of the automobile, then threw his drink—carried in a plastic cup—into my face. His handsome face contorted by a primeval rage, an opaque alcoholic glaze coating his unfocused gaze, he sarcastically snarled, in response to the casual comment I had made before his attack, the very same words I had heard Daddy drunkenly snarl time after time to Mother: "Yap! Yap! Yap!"

I had twice been battered by the men in my life: First by my father, whose abuse had ranged from the sexual to the verbal to the murderous, then by the brutal and obsessively jealous young first husband who had threatened on our Florida honeymoon to drown me, and, later, had bruised me and teasingly held pillows over my face till I couldn't breathe. But that had all been twenty-five years ago, was long forgotten, I thought. Even then, I had gotten out quickly—in fact, had married the husband to escape the father, then had married the second husband to escape the first, and in the interim had become—I imagined—a woman who understood, and knew how to handle, men.

Yet now, like the women interviewed by Lenore Walker for her book, *The Battered Woman*, my first response was surprise. Even as Zane beat my head against the inside of the car door, then, once home, banged it against the foyer wall, pulling out hunks of my hair with his big fists, I couldn't believe it was happening.

As he passed out on the bed beside me, I winced at the aches surfacing in my body, the dent in the wall above the headboard where he had hit it with his knuckles, and looked at him in shock, thinking how he would have to leave the next morning. But when light finally came through the lace curtains, I saw his quivering lower lip, heard him cry that it would never happen again—and, like countless women before me, rolled over on top of him to kiss away his pain, impale myself on the rose-colored penis.

COLLUSION, COMPLICITY, CULPABILITY. AND THE BLOOD OF LOVE ON MY LIPS.

Brutalized by Daddy—and by my first husband, as well—my response had been a sullen passivity, secret plans to escape, and a feeling of moral superiority. My rage at that mistreatment had never been fully expressed—indeed, had simmered like Mount St. Helens for a lifetime, keeping me, however dependent socially and sexually on the men in my life, from full empathy for them. It was that unresolved anger inside me that I had feared that day as I walked beneath the dam—my own aggression hanging over my head, keeping me emotionally on hold, my energy used in resentment, lowered expectations, rather than true understanding or love.

But in Zane, I had at last found—through the marvelous serendipity of the unconscious—a man held in an equal thrall. And as though something had broken inside me, all my fury at Daddy—at every man who had hurt me, held me back—boiled forth. In the grip of a lifelong grudge, I no longer cared that Zane weighed a hundred pounds more than I, that he could easily, accidentally, kill me. I, who had never been physically aggressive toward anyone in my life, responded, after the shock of the initial incidents, in kind.

For the next months, we fought in bars, restaurants, other people's houses, the car, at home. And while Zane instigated our fights, I stayed to slug it out, matching him blow for blow, snarl for snarl. "Don't fight back, Mother," Darcy would plead, worried for my life, but I was in the grip of something stronger than the desire for mere survival. Even the police, called by an alarmed neighbor, didn't stop us. Zane ripped off my skirt, smashed a hamburger in my face, banged my head against the floor, choking my neck. I stabbed him with my car keys, beat him with my high heels, overhanded perfume bottles across the room at his head. Soon I had a small scar on my forehead, a nearly dislocated jaw, a black eye. He had a back and neck gashed by my nails, a mark on his face where I had burned him with his own cigarette. Walls had been dented, stained by thrown drinks, the door pulled off the refrigerator, the handles off drawers, the gearshift stripped from my car.

What happened during our battles didn't hurt—that came the next morning. Instead, I was like Tex Cobb in the ring with Larry Holmes—outclassed, but unable to leave the ring without losing face, protected, for the time being, by a temporary anesthesia, an excitement almost like sex. In the grip of our mutual rage, I was mesmerized. The main thing was the adrenaline rush of the fight. If Norman Mailer thinks, as he has said, that a little violence is good for a man's soul, then maybe it is for a woman's, too. (In fact, I wondered whether spouse abuse would exist if women were equal to men in strength, and, more important, in touch with their own potential for aggression.)

When Laura was a teenager, she had a pet King snake; I once watched as she fed him a live white mouse. Instead of trying to flee when placed in the cage with the reptile, the mouse had immediately become quiescent, as though submissive to its fate. Though at times I now felt like the mouse in the cage with Laura's snake, I knew this was different. I was freely permitting Zane to stay—not for economic or social reasons, but for psychosexual ones. If I was paralyzed by anything, it was my own need for resolution—and he had become the vehicle for that process.

On CNN Radio, call-in talk therapist Dr. Susan Forward mentioned several characteristics—including excessive drinking, poor impulse control—a woman should look for in assessing men to avoid; my new lover had had them all. But if chickens can recognize one another from photographs, as claimed in *Omni* magazine, I had certainly been able to recognize in Zane, during the first moment I saw him, his potential for providing me with just the right set of difficulties for my task. Naturally, a man like Daddy, who, unknown to me or him, would reenact with me the primal scene, would help me resolve my attraction to the macho man.

Occasionally, I did try to put an end to it. One fine Saturday, Zane drove off in my Fiat, saying he would get the door fixed, and be back in an hour or so. When twelve o'clock had passed and he hadn't returned, I called him at the Office. "What're you callin' me *here* for?" he snarled drunkenly, but reluctantly acceded when I angrily insisted he bring my car back. As he stumbled up the stairs a few minutes later, I began yelling from the landing—a long diatribe of his sins, ending with a demand for his house keys—which he threw at my feet, staggering back down the stairs to slam the door, take off in his own vehicle. "It's all over," I said to Darcy with sad relief. We sat on the couch for a while, her arm comfortingly around my shoulder, then decided to go out for a drink to, if not celebrate, at least cheer up. As I watched the dancers in Who's Who, tears came into my eyes at the ending of months of strain, and grief for my lost love, my homeless pet. But as Darcy would say the next day, "A man like that is like a tomcat—no matter how long you let them out, they always come back." I hadn't reckoned on what it meant to be, as Zane had sometimes described himself, "a butt-fuckin' space pirate" or the fact that to a former Ranger who shimmied up walls, rappeled up cliffs, jumped from planes, a locked door would mean little. When I got home, Zane snored contentedly, my two-hundred-pound baby again, in my bed. He had simply scaled the side of the house and climbed through the second-floor window.

It wasn't to end that simply, I realized confusedly. One night, I dreamed of a lion—an untamable one this time—prowling the room where I slept. On another evening, as we lay reading in bed, Zane took something metal—his nail clippers—from the drawer beside him, and I flashed that he was pulling out a knife. "Haven't you ever had fantasies in which *you* were the violent one!" asked the therapist to whom I had recently run, when I repeated my vision. Later, covering Ginny Foat's murder trial for *Mother Jones* magazine, hearing the prosecutor say, "This passive woman you have seen on the witness stand is not the real Ginny Foat," I would inwardly nod in agreement. But now, still the eternal pacifist, I shook my head. Despite my taste for risk-taking, my outspoken writings, the fistfights I had had with peers as a child, I had always considered myself, as an adult, to be gentle, soft-spoken, the possessor—despite an occasional flash of Southern-belle hysteria during my conventional early marriages—of a genuinely sunny disposition. Yet now I had to admit that violence, turbulence, rage, and fear were suddenly dominating my life. "I hope *you're* not attracted to drunken, abusive men," the psychologist whom I was interviewing on Post-Traumatic Stress Syndrome said to me pointedly as Zane sat across the room, smoking. When I visited Anne in Atlanta, driving alone on the multilane freeway for the first time in months, I was gripped by a sudden terror, my legs trembling so badly that I pulled over to the shoulder, trying to regain control of myself as semis and automobiles whizzed by inches away at seventy miles an hour. Yet when I went to an Atlanta pub with Anne that night, I twisted the forearm of a man who enraged me by saying Alice Walker had only won the Pulitzer Prize because she was female and black. "I see why you and Zane like each other," my sister said, shocked, dragging me from the scene of my embarrassing crime. "You both love to fight."

Luckily, before either of our deaths, our rage was spent.

On Easter morning, as Darcy, Zane, and I sat eating croissants and strawberry jam, a pot of red tulips on the kitchen table, my forehead bloomed with blue bruises. On the night of the Fourth of July, as we watched red, white, and blue fireworks sparkle above our heads over the Savannah River, my own blue-black eye was barely concealed by makeup.

A few nights before, Zane had broken my antique mirror with his fist and, blood pouring from every knuckle, had burst into tears. Now, as I looked at a woman standing near me in the crowd, holding a red-haired baby who would have been the same age as ours, I did, too.

It was all over. I would never, I felt, be that angry again with anyone for the rest of my life.

It was the drinking that had to stop first, I realized. The worst thing that had ever happened to me while inebriated had been falling into bed with some unattractive—or even frightening—stranger. (Would I now be living with Zane had I not been drinking the night we met, I wondered?) But now, the pleasant buzzes, even the drunken evenings, I had enjoyed as a single woman just didn't work anymore. Zane's traditional macho habits of medicating any pain he felt with alcohol and/or expressing it physically, rather than dealing with it through introspection, the slow process of understanding, then real changes in life-style—skills perhaps more available to women because other means are less available to them—made our drinking together dangerous for both of us.

Once, during our madness, Zane had gone, at my request, to an Army counselor. "He just said I didn't seem to agree with the idea that violence is no way to handle things," he said that evening, grinning with self-satisfied relief. "If I want to stop, all I have to do is think up some good reason—like my girl friend doesn't like it!"

To date, I had been doing at forty-five exactly what I had been taught at fifteen—repressing my own feelings and needs in favor of the relationship, and assuming more than half the blame for the results. (Though, to Zane's credit, he—doing exactly what he had been taught—probably thought he had been upholding his end via the flowers, lingerie, dinners out, and extravagant compliments with which one placated a demanding woman.) If he acted badly, it was undoubtedly my fault for not—like a good mother—setting enough limits. For, despite my worldliness, I was still as much a woman in search of the perfect romance as the readers of Janet Dailey, but had confused—understandably, since they so often go hand in hand—"emotional and passionate" with "macho and fucked up." But now, if we were to remain together at all, Zane would have to begin to take responsibility for his part in things. From now on, I told him, there would have to be therapy not just for one—me—but for two.

AND CONCILIATION.

While in New Orleans for the Ginny Foat trial, I talked with Michael Groetsch, a municipal probation officer who had started and supervised a five-year model program for men arrested in the city for spouse abuse. "The thing that drives a man with problems with alcohol and aggression craziest is an independent woman!" he told me. "I need to feel like a *man*," Zane had told me over and over during our quarrels. Now I saw that what I needed to maintain my own autonomy often denied him—according to the rigid standards by which he judged himself—what he needed to "feel like a man"—dominance in his home and over the woman in his life. I realized why Zane was able to accept patriarchal authority as exemplified by the Army. He still identified with the patriarchal father of whom he had had a positive experience, and had not yet been able to acknowledge his rage at the limitations that role placed upon him.

And I understood for the first time the genuine "hidden injuries of class." Before Zane, many of my friends had been the kind of people who laugh about the folks who live in mobile homes, surround themselves with the kind of objects sold in K-Marts, and choose Shoney's over Szechuan restaurants. When he and I met, Zane had a "muscle car," a long red '71 Dodge Charger "Super Bee," with a shiny bumblebee on its hood, many stripes, and fancy mag wheels.

"You have to get rid of either the car or the tattoo," Darcy and I would tease him, "and, especially, don't go out in it wearing your Claxton Rattlesnake Roundup cap!"

I may have been angered by Albert Goldman's supercilious account of *Elvis*, what I considered his total misunderstanding of a boy from Mississippi farm country, and resented writers like Paul

Fussell, author of *Class: A Guide through the American Status System*, who refer to "proles" and otherwise make fun of blue-collar workers. But now, like a civil-rights worker who finds racism in her heart, I learned that in Zane's eyes I was as snobbish as they were.

One afternoon, as he came up the stairs drunk, I saw that he held out a peace offering: a single rose, unnaturally red-orange, in a small glass vase. As he came nearer, I realized the flower was a fake, and began laughing—and laughed even harder as he enthused that "It's made of wood shavin's—I bought it from a guy sellin' 'em at a traffic light." Then, seeing the look on my face, asked, "What's the matter—don't you like it?"

"It's just that I don't like artificial flowers," I explained.

"Well, I'm gonna burn it up, 'n' throw the ashes away, 'n' throw this vase out the window, too," he exploded, offended, pulling out his cigarette lighter, then reaching for the window sash.

"Oh, don't be silly," I said, pulling his arm down. "Just calm down," I added, still laughing, for his enthusiasm for the rose struck me as funny. I chuckled on my way out to the supermarket, thinking that when I got back, we'd sit down, joke about it together. But instead, when I climbed the stairs, I saw a neat pile of ashes on the kitchen table, the glass vase broken in half, and a note that read, "fuck you & your classist attitudes!" And by the time he came back a half-dozen hours later, he was in no condition to discuss the issue further.

Zane was far from the man I had seen in a DeBeer's Diamond ad—hard-hatted, denim-clad, yet proud of his expensive ring. It wasn't just that such a man could rarely afford such a piece of jewelry; it was that if he felt like Zane, he could never have permitted himself such an extravagance. (On the other hand, Zane surmised, the ad was probably an attempt "to make pussies feel better about wearing a diamond ring.") For like a monk choosing asceticism, my lover deliberately set limits on his ambitions, preferring, as he said, being an infantry sergeant to going into intelligence or on to Officer Candidate School, staying *within* the working class. To do otherwise would cause worse anxiety than the familiar limitations of blue-collar life. It was as though the low ceilings of his parents' pleasant ranch house, the security of the small rooms in which he had grown up, had become metaphors for what he could permit himself.

I had long understood the pain of women—the way they were

held back by their social roles, the standards to which they held themselves. But, in bondage to my own oppression, I had never been able to allow myself to see the comparable frustration in the men I had known. Now, for the first time, I began to understand the demanding scales on which men, particularly macho and/or traditional men, weigh themselves.

"I guess I'm just a wimp, a pussy," Zane would cry out against himself at a legitimate day spent in bed with the flu. The luxuries through which women keep their psyches intact—introspection, intimate chats with friends, frivolous shopping trips, even psychotherapy and exercise classes—all ring suspiciously feminine to the Man who would be Real.

"But I couldn't do that—my peers would think I was just complaining about doing what a man *should* do," a male writer and single parent with a brain-damaged child said when I suggested he write about the difficulties of his situation. "Just liked baseball, I guess," Southern poet David Bottoms said, explaining why his father, a funeral-home director, had spent hour after hour throwing balls to David when he came home from work each day; yet Bottoms concludes a poem entitled "Sign for My Father, Who Stressed the Bunt" with the line, "I'm getting a grip on the sacrifice"; and in another, "The Christmas Rifle," says that "Just behind me, my father is walking on needles; the weight of his hand comes down on my shoulder." In his work as well as that of novelist Harry Crews, whose male protagonists destroy themselves in various ways including drink, the burden of being traditionally male is made clear—without quest for, or hope of, resolution or change. In that way, they were far behind women authors; but I now had a new understanding, if no more liking for, the frequently ugly self-destructiveness of the male writers I knew.

SEXUAL HEALING.

As the façade of Zane's personality fell away, I began to see and feel the real person. With my rage no longer blocking it, all my repressed love and pain for Daddy began at last to surface as well; and if its images were fuzzy—proving, as Freud would have predicted, that Mother was still my major imprint—at least they were positive. Like new pictures developed from old, forgotten negatives, I began to recall the good things: Daddy, cozily sandwiching me between him and Mother in a movie theater, till he stands up, as is his ritual, at the beginning of the cartoon to tease, "Well, I guess it's time to go now!" Daddy, solicitously wiping the remnants of a chocolate sundae from the corners of my mouth, with a saliva-dampened handkerchief as, at five, dressed in cap and muff, fitted coat, white high-topped shoes, I perch beside him on a Woolworth's lunch counter stool. Daddy, refusing to call my cats anything but "Mouser," whatever their names. His holiday gifts, at gatherings of our puritanical clan, of magic tricks and rolls of toilet paper with a joke printed on every sheet. His fondness for pickled eggs, guava jelly, Camembert cheese—all exotica in the Bible Belt world in which we lived.

Like Daddy, Zane smelled of cigarette smoke and Old Spice. Indeed, it may have been his scent that gave me the first unconscious clue of what he might mean in my life. One night, my lover and I lay in bed in the dark, listening to the tape of an old radio show. As the segment began with the sound of a squeaking door, I was suddenly suffused by a warm memory: Daddy and me lying in bed in the dark, listening to *Suspense* or *The Inner Sanctum*—me, so terrified at the scary program that I got up time after time during the thirty minutes to run to the bathroom, yet, at the same time, comforted by my father's presence. And now, in the same setting, hearing the same sounds, with Zane's comforting bulk and smell— so like Daddy's—nearby, it was as though I was miraculously reliving that scene, the feelings of a long-fractured love and trust flooding through me again. Time after time in the future, I would sit on my lover's lap, put my arms around his neck—and, re-creating that moment, feel like a little girl again. When I went to the gynecologist's office for a painful endometrial biopsy, it was him I wanted with me. When I burst into tears at a sad book or movie, I now called out inside for my baby doll, my Zane, rather than the Mother who had once dominated my consciousness.

Along with these memories, I also began to recall tender feelings—long repressed—toward other men in my life. The picture I had liked best of my first husband, T.J., had been taken when he was nine. He had just ridden his bicycle into a clothesline, yet grinned broadly into the camera, unfazed by the dark mark across his throat. Our son, David, with whom my relationship was still at times distressingly discordant, had once cried to own swans and horses, and had lived for the tadpole eggs, the new frogs, that filled the creek each spring. My second husband, Paul, had once been a painfully shy boy who existed through his toy soldiers, his drawing pencils. And the photo I had treasured most of my third husband, Ben, was of him at three, dressed in cap and pants, standing beside his seated father, his baby brother, in their backyard in Brookline, Massachusetts. He looks expectantly, hopefully into the camera, already the boy who, at eight, will dream of becoming an angel who will sacrifice himself for the world. All my life, I had liked to imagine the men I loved as babies, children, thus defusing them of the overlay of an often harshly developed masculinity. It was their crushed hopes, their human potential I had loved, not necessarily what they had become. And now I could afford to remember, to love, again. As in the title of the song by Marvin Gaye, "Sexual Healing" had taken place.

THE CAMOUFLEUR.

Sometimes, lying in bed beside Zane in Savannah, I would briefly recall, like some distant life, sleeping alone in my pristine apartment, the only sound throughout the four rooms my cat Darlene's toenails clicking across the hardwood floor, the faint rustle of the lace curtains as they were blown by a light breeze.

One night, I dreamed of sitting at a kitchen table with a red-haired woman who messily ate spaghetti from a chipped plate, poured herself glass after glass of jug wine. "No, thank you," I answered primly when she offered me a glass. When she opened a cabinet door to throw her leftovers into a greasy brown paper bag, I saw the roaches crawling beneath it, just as at my old apartment. "It's a good thing you're not too compulsive," I teased. As she answered the phone, discussing with a boyfriend what she would wear when they went out that night—a feather boa? the French-maid costume?—I realized who she was: the old, free me.

Now, for better or worse, things were different. My new life required new controls, but there had been gains for both Zane and me. Though he still admired the military—indeed, was considering reenlisting—and liked "getting a buzz on," he had also bought a sewing machine and taken a sail-making course. He was in therapy, attending community theater, beginning his own stories and plays, and even reading good novels as often as adventure stories. And while my own political views had not changed, my perceptions of myself had. I could no longer delude myself that being feminine automatically meant being passive, nonviolent. The dictionary definition of "camoufleur" is "one who conceals military objects by camouflage," and I had long concealed my more masculine impulses behind my feminine façade. But now newly in touch with my own potential for aggression, adventure, I had begun exercising at a gym frequented by women weight lifters. And instead of making Zane—or any man—metaphor for that risk-loving part of myself, and even thinking of learning to fly. When I saw the handsome wild-animal tamer Gunther Gebel-Williams on the cover of *Psychology Today*—as I thrilled to the photo of him inside, his arm affectionately around a huge beast—I knew it was not him I wanted, but to *be* him.

Aware as never before of the stresses of living male, I would never again be able to look at a handsome young truck driver or construction worker and see him as merely a sex object. And now Zane and I could joke about the differences between us. "Why don't you just say you have a gorilla for a lover because he can carry more luggage," he laughed. Even his working-class macho habit of calling every woman in his path "hon" or "honey" now amused, rather than irritated, me. I laughed when he asked the waitress in the truck stop from which he had phoned me to "Bring me another cuppa coffee, hon," then concluded *our* conversation by saying, "Bye, hon."

It was hard to see the future. Walking down the street in Savannah, lulled into daydream by the soft beauty of the city around me, I envisioned travel, more writing, but relationships were fuzzy. Jack had called to say he was going to federal prison at Eglin Air Force Base for a while, "but I think I'll learn Spanish while I'm down there—it'll help me in my business!" he told me, laughing. Darcy had moved to Atlanta to pursue a career in television; Laura was finishing work on her Ph.D.; and while my son, David, and I were still not as close as I wished, at least I no longer viewed him through the veil of my distorted relationship with Daddy. Then, at home, there was Zane, whom I had grown to love despite—because of?—our differences. "The lion is a family animal, and a big lover as well," Gebel-Williams said, describing the character of the creature. In that case, Zane was definitely a lion, and through him, I had—at least in the area of the heart—tamed the wild beast at last.

.   .   .

June. Four in a sultry afternoon.
As I sit at my desk in the study of my Savannah apartment, Hank Williams, Jr., sings over the radio of how he likes to "ride my horses and shoot my gun . . . to have wimmen I've never had. . . ." The disc jockey recommends that if I'm "thinkin' 'bout buyin' a hand gun, git yoreself over to Joe's Gun and Tackle Shop. . . ."

Will I soon crave a man who prefers Nabokov to guns and ammo? Who chooses a Mercedes sedan over a Ranger pickup? Who, when he says he's going out to wash the car, does just that, rather than coming back a dozen hours later, cut up from a bar-room brawl? Who, tattoo-free and dressed by Brooks Brothers, carries a briefcase—or even a pocketbook—just like mine?

A book on women and modern poetry open on my lap, I languidly watch, through my lace curtains, my second-floor window, a muscular telephone lineman climb the pole across the street. He grips the pole with his thighs, twists my way, flexes a biceps. . . .